HARDPRESS.NET
HOME OF HARD-TO-FIND BOOKS

Life in the Open Air
by Theodore Winthrop

Address:
HardPress
8345 NW 66TH ST #2561
MIAMI FL 33166-2626
USA
Email: info@hardpress.net

LIFE IN THE OPEN AIR,

AND OTHER PAPERS.

BY

THEODORE WINTHROP,

AUTHOR OF "CECIL DREEME," "JOHN BRENT," ETC., ETC.

Let me not waste in skirmishes my power,
In petty struggles.   Rather in the hour
Of deadly conflict may I nobly die, —
In my first battle perish gloriously.
From an unpublished Poem by THEODORE WINTHROP.

BOSTON:
TICKNOR AND FIELDS.
1863.

UNIVERSITY PRESS:
WELCH, BIGELOW, AND COMPANY,
CAMBRIDGE.

NOTE.

THIS is the last volume of Theodore Winthrop's works. The reader will be interested to know that, with a very few slight omissions, they are published precisely as he left them. Beside these, which he had himself prepared for the press, there remains manuscript enough for more than another volume, comprising poems, lectures, sketches, the beginning of another novel, and a completed earlier tale; but not in fit form for publication. A man who wrote so much and so well was not of course indifferent to the publication of his works, for the desire of an audience is part of the author's instinct; and that they are first printed after his death is not owing to any want of effort upon his part, but to circumstances which no author can control. He can but do his work. It is for others to receive or decline it.

At the close of a lecture upon the Fine Arts in America, which he wrote in 1856, Winthrop said:

"This composite people may, in its wide realm, attain to the most varied splendor of success in all pursuits that can make its future rich, refined, noble, and happy. But let us not forget that our march must be sustained by a hearty devotion to the true principles of freedom. If we fail of public or private duty, — if we cleave to any national wrong, — this great experiment of mankind will fail, and our life corrupt away, through slow decaying, to dishonorable death."

In that faith Theodore Winthrop wrote and fought, — he lived and died.

G. W. C.

STATEN ISLAND, February, 1863.

———

THE portrait in this volume is engraved from Mr. Rowse's crayon likeness of the author, drawn from life a few years since. The wood-cut of Katahdin is copied from an original sketch in oil by Mr. Church.

CONTENTS.

LIFE IN THE OPEN AIR.

KATAHDIN AND THE PENOBSCOT.

1

LIFE IN THE OPEN AIR.

CHAPTER I.

OFF.

At five P. M. we found ourselves — Iglesias, a party of friends, and myself — on board the Isaac Newton, a great, ugly, three-tiered box that walks the North River, like a laboratory of greasy odors.

In this stately cinder-mill were American citizens. Not to discuss spitting, which is for spittoons, not literature, our fellow-travellers on the deck of the "floating palace" were passably endurable people in looks, style, and language. I dodge discrimination, and characterize them *en masse* by negations. The passengers of the Isaac Newton, on a certain evening of July, 18—, were not so intrusively green and so gasping as Britons, not so ill-dressed and pretentious as Gauls, not so ardently futile and so lubberly as Germans. Such were the negative virtues of our fellow-citizen travellers ; and base would it be to exhibit their positive vices.

And so no more of passengers or passage. I will not describe our evening on the river. Alas for the duty of straightforwardness and dramatic

unity ! Episodes seem so often sweeter than plots !
The wayside joys are better than the final successes ; the flowers along the vista, brighter than
the victor-wreaths at its close. I may not dally
on my way, turning to the right and the left for
beauty and caricature. I will balance on the strict
edge of my narrative, as a seventh-heavenward Ma-
hometan, with wine-forbidden steadiness of poise,
treads Al Seràt, his bridge of a sword-blade.

Next morning, at Albany, divergent trains cleft
our party into a better and a worser half. The
beautiful girls, our better half, fled westward to
ripen their pallid roses with richer summer-hues in
mosquitoless inland dells. Iglesias and I were still
northward bound.

At the Saratoga station we sipped a dreary, faded
reminiscence of former joys and sparkling brilliancy
long dead, in cups of Congress-water, brought by
unattractive Ganymedes and sold in the train, —
draughts flat, flabby, and utterly bubbleless, luke-
warm heel-taps with a flavor of savorless salt.

Still northward journeying, and feeling the sea-
side moisture evaporate from our blood under inland suns and sultry inland breezes, we came to
Lake Champlain.

As before banquets, to excite appetite, one takes
the gentle oyster, so we, before the serious pleasure
of our journey, tasted the Adirondack region, paradise of Cockney sportsmen. There, through the
forest, the stag of ten trots, coquetting with green-
horns. He likes the excitement of being shot at

and missed. He enjoys the smell of powder in a battle where he is always safe. He hears Greenhorn blundering through the woods, stopping to growl at briers, stopping to revive his courage with the Dutch supplement. The stag of ten awaits his foe in a glade. The foe arrives, sees the antlered monarch, and is panic-struck. He watches him prance and strike the ground with his hoofs. He slowly recovers heart, takes a pull at his flask, rests his gun upon a log, and begins to study his mark. The stag will not stand still. Greenhorn is baffled. At last his target turns and carefully exposes that region of his body where Greenhorn has read lies the heart. Just about to fire, he catches the eye of the stag winking futility into his elaborate aim. His blunderbuss jerks upward. A shower of cut leaves floats through the smoke, from a tree thirty feet overhead. Then, with a mild-eyed melancholy look of reproachful contempt, the stag turns away, and wanders off to sleep in quiet coverts far within the wood. He has fled, while for Greenhorn no trophy remains. Antlers have nodded to the sportsman; a short tail has disappeared before his eyes; — he has seen something, but has nothing to show. Whereupon he buys a couple of pairs of ancient weather-bleached horns from some colonist, and, nailing them up at impossible angles on the wall of his city den, humbugs brother-Cockneys with tales of *vénerie*, and has for life his special legend, " How I shot my first deer in the Adirondacks."

The Adirondacks provide a compact, convenient, accessible little wilderness, — an excellent field for the experiments of tyros.   When the tyro, whether shot, fisherman, or forester, has proved himself fully there, let him dislodge into some vaster wilderness, away from guides by the day and superintending hunters, away from the incursions of the Cockney tribe, and let out the caged savage within him for a tough struggle with Nature.   It needs a struggle tough and resolute to force that Protean lady to observe at all her challenger.

It is well to go to the Adirondacks.   They are shaggy, and shagginess is a valuable trait.   The lakes are very well, — very well indeed.   The objection to the region is not the mountains, which are reasonably shaggy, — not the lakes and rivers, which are water, a capital element.   The real difficulty is the society : not the autochthonous society, — they are worthy people, and it is hardly to be mentioned as a fault that they are not a discriminating race, and will asseverate that all fish are trout, and the most arrant mutton is venison, — but the immigrant, colonizing society.   Cockneys are to be found at every turn, flaunting their banners of the awkward squad, proclaiming to the world with protuberant pride that they are the veritable backwoodsmen, — rather doing it, rather astonishing the natives, they think.   And so they are.   One squad of such neophytes might be entertaining ; but when every square mile echoes with their hails, lost, poor babes, within a furlong of their camps, and when the woods become dim and the air civic with their cooking-smokes, and the subtile odor of fried pork overpowers methylic fragrance among the trees, then he who loves forests for their solitude leaves these brethren to their clumsy joys, and wanders elsewhere deeper into sylvan scenes.

Our visit to the Adirondacks was episodic; and as I have forsworn episodes, I turn away from them with this mild slander, and strike again our Maine track. With lips impurpled by the earliest huckleberries, we came out again upon Champlain. We crossed that water-logged valley in a steamboat, and hastened on, through a pleasant interlude of our rough journey, across Vermont and New Hampshire, two States not without interest to their residents, but of none to this narrative.

By coach and wagon, by highway and by-way, by horse-power and steam-power, we proceeded, until it chanced, one August afternoon, that we left railways and their regions at a wayside station, and let our lingering feet march us along the valley of the Upper Connecticut. This lovely river, baptizer of Iglesias's childhood, was here shallow and musical, half river, half brook; it had passed the tinkling period, and plashed and rumbled voicefully over rock and shallow.

It was a fair and verdant valley where we walked, overlooked by hills of pleasant pastoral slope. All the land was gay and ripe with yellow harvest. Strolling along, as if the business of travel were forgotten, we placidly identified ourselves with the placid scenery. We became Arcadians both. Such is Arcadia, if I have read aright : a realm where sunshine never scorches, and yet shade is sweet ; where simple pleasures please ; where the blue sky and the bright water and the green fields satisfy forever.

We were in lightest marching-trim. Iglesias bore an umbrella, our armor against what heaven could do with assault of sun or shower. I was weaponed with a staff, should brute or biped uncourteous dispute our way. We had no impediments of "great trunk, little trunk, bandbox, and bundle." A thoughtful man hardly feels honest in his life except as a pedestrian traveller. "*La propriété c'est le vol*," — which the West more briefly expresses by calling baggage "plunder." What little plunder our indifferent honesty had packed for this journey we had left with a certain stage-coachman, perhaps to follow us, perhaps to become his plunder. We were thus disconnected from any depressing influence ; we had no character to sustain ; we were heroes in disguise, and could make our observations on life and manners without being invited to a public hand-shaking, or to exhibit feats in jugglery, for either of which a traveller with plenteous portmanteaus, hair or leather, must be prepared in villages thereabouts. Totally unembarrassed, we lounged along or leaped along, light-hearted. When the river neared us, or winsome brooklet from the hill-side thwarted

our path, we stooped and lapped from their pools
of coolness, or tasted that most ethereal tipple,
the mingled air and water of electric bubbles, as
they slid brightly toward our lips.

The angle of the sun's rays grew less and less,
the wheat-fields were tinged more golden by the
clinging beams, our shadows lengthened, as if
exercise of an afternoon were stimulating to such
unreal essences. Finally the blue dells and gorges
of a wooded mountain, for two hours our landmark,
rose between us and the sun. But the sun's Par-
thian arrows gave him a splendid triumph, more
signal for its evanescence. A storm was inevitable,
and sunset prepared a reconciling pageant.

Now, as may be supposed, Iglesias has an eye
for a sunset. That summer's crop had been very
short, and he had been some time on starvation-
allowance of cloudy magnificence. We therefore
halted by the road-side, and while I committed the
glory to memory, Iglesias intrusted his distincter
memorial to a sketch-book.

We were both busy, he repeating forms, noting
shades and tints, and I studying without pictorial
intent, when we heard a hail in the road below our
bank. It was New Hampshire, near the Maine
line, and near the spot where nasal organs are fab-
ricated that twang the roughest.

"Say!" shrieked up to us a freckled native,
holding fast to the tail of a calf, the last of a gam-
bolling family he was driving, — "Say! whodger
doon up thurr? Layn aoot taoonshup lains naoou,

1 *

aancher? Cauds ur suvvares raoond. Spekkle-
ayshn goan on, ur guess.''

We allowed this unmelodious vocalist to respect
us by permitting him to believe us surveyors in
another sense than as we were.   One would not be
despised as an unpractical citizen, a mere looker
at Nature with no immediate view to profit, even
by a freckled calf-driver of the Upper Connecticut.
While we parleyed, the sketch was done, and the
pageant had faded quick before the storm.

Splendor had departed ; the world in our neighborhood had fallen into the unillumined dumps.
An ominous mournfulness, far sadder than the pen-
siveness of twilight, drew over the sky.   Clouds,
that donned brilliancy for the fond parting of moun-
tain-tops and the sun, now grew cheerless and
gray ; their gay robes were taken from them, and
with bended heads they fled away from the sorrowful wind.   In western glooms beyond the world
a dreary gale had been born, and now came wailing
like one that for all his weariness may not rest, but
must go on harmful journeys and bear evil tidings.
With the vanguard gusts came volleys of rain, ma-
licious assaults, giving themselves the trouble to
tell us in an offensive way what we could discover
for ourselves, that a wetting impended and umbrellas would soon be naught.

While the storm was thus nibbling before it bit,
we lengthened our strides to escape.   Water, concentrated in flow of stream or pause of lake, is
charming ; not so to the shelterless is water diffused

in dash of deluge. Water, when we choose our method of contact, is a friend ; when it masters us, it is a foe ; when it drowns us or ducks us, a very exasperating foe. Proud pedestrians become very humble personages, when thoroughly vanquished by a ducking deluge. A wetting takes out the starch not only from garments, but the wearers of them. Iglesias and I did not wish to stand all the evening steaming before a kitchen-fire, inspecting meanwhile culinary details : Phillis in the kitchen is not always as fresh as Phillis in the field. We therefore shook ourselves into full speed, and bolted into our inn at Colebrook ; and the rain, like a portcullis, dropped solid behind us.

In town, the landlord is utterly merged in his hotel. He is a sovereign rarely apparent. In the country, the landlord is a personality. He is greater than the house he keeps. Men arriving inspect the master of the inn narrowly. If his first glance is at the pocket, cheer will be bad ; if at the eyes or the lips, you need not take a cigar before supper to keep down your appetite.

Our landlord was of the latter type. He surged out of the little box where he was dispensing not too fragrant rummers to a circle of village-politicians, and congratulated us on our arrival before the storm. He was a discriminating person. He detected us at once, saw we were not tramps or footpads, and led us to the parlor, a room attractively furnished with a map of the United States and an oblong music-book open at " Old Hundred."

Our host further felicitated us that we had not stopped, at a certain tavern below, where, as he said, —

"They cut a chunk er beef and drop 't into a pot to bile, and bile her three days, and then don't have noth'n' else for three weeks."

He put his head out of the door and called, —

"George, go aoot and split up that 'ere wood as fine as chaowder : these men 'll want their supper right off."

Drawing in his head, he continued to us confidentially, —

"That 'ere George is jes' like a bird : he goes off at one snappin'."

Our host then rolled out toward the bar-room, to discuss with his cronies who we might be. From the window we perceived the birdlike George fly and alight near the specified wood, which he proceeded to bechowder. He brought in the result of his handiwork, as smiling as a basket of chips. Neat-handed Phillis at the door received the chowder, and by its aid excited a sound and a smell, both prophetic of supper. And we, willing to repose after a sixteen-mile afternoon-walk, lounged upon sofa or tilted in rocking-chair, taking the available mental food, namely, "Godey's Lady's Book" and the Almanac.

CHAPTER II.

GORMING AND GETTING ON.

NEXT morning it poured. The cinders before the blacksmith's shop opposite had yielded their black dye to the dismal puddles. The village cocks were sadly draggled and discouraged, and cowered under any shelter, shivering within their drowned plumage. Who on such a morn would stir? Who but the Patriot? Hardly had we breakfasted, when he, the Patriot, waited upon us. It was a Presidential campaign. They were starving in his village for stump-speeches. Would the talking man of our *duo* go over and feed their ears with a fiery harangue? Patriot was determined to be first with us; others were coming with similar invitations; he was the early bird. Ah, those portmanteaus! they had arrived, and betrayed us.

We would not be snapped up. We would wriggle away. We were very sorry, but we must start at once to pursue our journey.

" But it pours," said Patriot.

" Patriot," replied our talking member, " man is flesh; and flesh, however sweet or savory it may be, does not melt in water."

Thus fairly committed to start, we immediately opened negotiations for a carriage. " No go," was the first response of the coachman. Our willy was met by his nilly. But we pointed out to him that we could not stay there all a dismal day, — that we must, would, could, should go. At last we got within coachee's outworks. His nilly broke down into shilly-shally. He began to state his objections ; then we knew he was ready to yield. We combated him, clinking the supposed gold of coppers in our pockets, or carelessly chucking a tempting half-dollar at some fly on the ceiling. So presently we prevailed, and he retired to make ready.

By and by a degraded family-carriage came to the door. It came by some feeble inertia left latent in it by some former motive-power, rather than was dragged up by its more degraded nags. A very unwholesome coach. No doubt a successful quack-doctor had used it in his prosperous days for his wife and progeny ; no doubt it had subsequently become the property of a second-class undertaker, and had conveyed many a quartette of cheap clergymen to the funerals of poor relations whose leaking sands of life left no gold-dust behind. Such was our carriage for a rainy day.

The nags were of the huckleberry or flea-bitten variety, — a freckled white. Perhaps the quack had fed them with his refuse pills. These knobby-legged unfortunates we of course named Xanthus and Balius, not of podargous or swift-footed, but podagrous or gouty race. Xanthus, like his Achillean namesake, (*vide* Pope's Homer,)

" Seemed sensible of woe, and dropped his head, —
Trembling he stood before the (seedy) wain."

Balius was in equally deplorable mood. Both seemed more sensible to "Whoä" than to "Hadaap." Podagrous beasts, yet not stiffened to immobility. Gayer steeds would have sundered the shackling drag. These would never, by any gamesome caracoling, endanger the coherency of pole with body, of axle with wheel. From end to end the equipage was congruous. Every part of the machine was its weakest part, and that fact gave promise of strength: an invalid never dies. Moreover, the coach suited the day: the rusty was in harmony with the dismal. It suited the damp, unpainted houses, and the tumble-down blacksmith's-shop. We contented ourselves with this artistic propriety. We entered, treading cautiously. The machine, with gentle spasms, got itself in motion, and steered due east for Lake Umbagog. The smiling landlord, the disappointed Patriot, and the birdlike George waved us farewell.

Coachee was in the sulks. The rain beat upon him, and we by purse-power had compelled him to encounter discomfort. His self-respect must be restored by superiority over somebody. He had been beaten and must beat. He did so. His horses took the lash until he felt at peace with himself. Then half turning toward us, he made his first remark.

" Them two hosses is gorming."

" Yes," we replied, " they do seem rather so."

This was of course profound hypocrisy ; but " gorming " meant some bad quality, and any

might be safely predicated of our huckleberry pair.
Who will admit that he does not know all that is to
be known in horse-matters? We therefore asked
no questions, but waited patiently for information.

Delay pays demurrage to the wisely patient.
Coachee relapsed into the sulks. The driving rain
resolved itself into a dim chaos of mist. Xanthus
and Balius plodded on, but often paused and gasped,
or, turning their heads as if they missed something, strayed from the track and drew us against
the dripping bushes. After one such excursion,
which had nearly been the ruin of us, and which
by calling out coachee's scourging powers had put
him thoroughly in good humor, he turned to us and
said, superlatively, —

"Them's the gormingest hosses I ever see.
When I drew 'em in the four-hoss coach for
wheelers, they could keep a straight tail. Now
they act like they was drunk. They's gorming,
— *they won't do nothin' without a leader.*"

To gorm, then, is to err when there is no leader.
Alas, how mankind gorms!

By sunless noon we were well among the mountains. We came to the last New Hampshire
house, miles from its neighbors. But it was a self-
sufficing house, an epitome of humanity. Grand-
mamma, bald under her cap, was seated by the
stove dandling grandchild, bald under its cap.
Each was highly entertained with the other. Grand-
papa was sandy with grandboy's gingerbread-
crumbs. The intervening ages were well repre-

sented by wiry men and shrill women. The house, also, without being tavern or shop, was an amateur bazaar of *vivers* and goods. Anything one was likely to want could be had there, — even a melodeon and those inevitable Patent-Office Reports. Here we descended, lunched, and providently bought a general assortment, namely, a large plain cake, five pounds of cheese, a ball of twine, and two pairs of brown ribbed woollen socks, native manufacture. My pair of these indestructibles will outlast my last legs and go as an heirloom after me.

The weather now, as we drove on, seemed to think that Iglesias deserved better of it. Rain-globes strung upon branches, each globe the possible home of a sparkle, had waited long enough unillumined. Sunlight suddenly discovered this desponding patience and rewarded it. Every drop selected its own ray from the liberal bundle, and, crowding itself full of radiance, became a mirror of sky and cloud and forest. Also, by the searching sunbeams' store of regal purple, ripe raspberries were betrayed. On these, magnified by their convex lenses of water, we pounced. Showers shook playfully upon us from the vines, while we revelled in fruitiness. We ran before our gormers, they gormed by us while we plucked, we ran by, plucked again, and again were gormingly overtaken and overtook. Thus we ate our way luxuriously through the Dixville Notch, a capital cleft in a northern spur of the White Mountains.

B

Picturesque is a curiously convenient, undiscriminating epithet. I use it here. The Dixville Notch is, briefly, picturesque, — a fine gorge between a crumbling conical crag and a scarped precipice, — a pass easily defensible, except at the season when raspberries would distract sentinels.

Now we came upon our proper field of action. We entered the State of Maine at Township Letter B. A sharper harshness of articulation in stray passengers told us that we were approaching the vocal influence of the name Androscoggin. People talked as if, instead of ivory ring or coral rattle to develop their infantile teeth, they had bitten upon pine knots. Voices were resinous and astringent. An opera, with a chorus drummed up in those regions, could dispense with violins.

Toward evening we struck the river, and found it rasping and crackling over rocks as an Androscoggin should. We passed the last hamlet, then the last house but one, and finally drew up at the last and northernmost house, near the lumbermen's dam below Lake Umbagog. The damster, a stalwart brown chieftain of the backwoodsman race, received us with hearty hospitality. Xanthus and Balius stumbled away on their homeward journey. And after them the crazy coach went moaning : it was not strong enough to creak or rattle.

Next day was rainy. It had, however, misty intervals. In these we threw a fly for trout and caught a chub in Androscoggin. Or, crouched on the bank of a frog-pond, we tickled frogs with straws. Yes, and fun of the freshest we found it. Certain animals, and especially frogs, were created, shaped, and educated to do the grotesque, that men might study them, laugh, and grow fat. It was a droll moment with Nature, when she entertained herself and prepared entertainment for us by devising the frog, that burlesque of bird, beast, and man, and taught him how to move and how to speak and sing. Iglesias and I did not disdain batrachian studies, and set no limit to our merriment at their quaint, solemn, half-human pranks. One question still is unresolved, — Why do frogs stay and be tickled ? They snap snappishly at the titillating straw ; they snatch at it with their weird little hands ; they parry it skilfully. They hardly can enjoy being tickled, and yet they endure, paying a dear price for the society of their betters. Frogs the frisky, frogs the spotted, were our comedy that day. Whenever the rain ceased, we rushed forth and tickled them, and thus vicariously tickled ourselves into more than patience, into jollity. So the day passed quickly.

CHAPTER III.

THE PINE-TREE.

WHILE we were not tickling frogs, we were talking lumber with the Umbagog damster. I had
already coasted Maine, piloted by Iglesias, and
knew the fisherman-life ; now, under the same experienced guidance, I was to study inland scenes,
and take lumbermen for my heroes.

Maine has two classes of warriors among its sons,
— fighters of forest and fighters of sea. Braves
must join one or the other army. The two are
close allies. Only by the aid of the woodmen can
the watermen build their engines of victory. The
seamen in return purvey the needful luxuries for
lumber-camps. Foresters float down timber that
seamen may build ships and go to the saccharine
islands of the South for molasses : for without
molasses no lumberman could be happy in the un-
sweetened wilderness. Pork lubricates his joints ;
molasses gives tenacity to his muscles.

Lumbering develops such men as Pindar saw
when he pictured Jason, his forest hero. Life is a
hearty and vigorous movement to them, not a
drooping slouch. Summer is their season of preparation ; winter, of the campaign ; spring, of victory. All over the north of the State, whatever is
not lake or river is forest. In summer, the Viewer,
like a military engineer, marks out the region, and

the spots of future attack. He views the woods; and wherever a monarch tree crowns the leafy level, he finds his way, and blazes a path. Not all trees are worthy of the axe. Miles of lesser timber remain untouched. A Maine forest after a lumber-campaign is like France after a *coup d'état:* the *bourgeoisie* are prosperous as ever, but the great men are all gone.

While the viewer views, his followers are on commissariat and quartermaster's service. They are bringing up their provisions and fortifying their camp. They build their log-station, pile up barrels of pork, beans, and molasses, like mortars and Paixhans in an arsenal, and are ready for a winter of stout toil and solid jollity.

Stout is the toil, and the life seemingly dreary, to those who cower by ingle-nooks or stand over registers. But there is stirring excitement in this bloodless war, and around plenteous camp-fires vigor of merriment and hearty comradry. Men who wield axes and breathe hard have lungs. Blood aerated by the air that sings through the pine-woods tingles in every fibre. Tingling blood makes life joyous. Joy can hardly look without a smile or speak without a laugh. And merry is the evergreen-wood in electric winter.

Snows fall level in the sheltered, still forest. Road-making is practicable. The region is already channelled with watery ways. An imperial pine, with its myriads of feet of future lumber, is worth another path cut through the bush to the frozen

river-side. Down goes his Majesty Pinus I., three
half-centuries old, having reigned fifty years high
above all his race. A little fellow with a little
weapon has dethroned the quiet old king. Pinus I.
was very strong at bottom, but the little revolu-
tionist was stronger at top. Brains without much
trouble had their will of stolid matter. The tree
fallen, its branches are lopped, its purple trunk is
shortened into lengths. The teamster arrives with
oxen in full steam, and rimy with frozen breath
about their indignant nostrils. As he comes and
goes, he talks to his team for company ; his conversation is monotonous as the talk of lovers, but
it has a cheerful ring through the solitude. The
logs are chained and dragged creaking along over
the snow to the river-side. There the subdivisions
of Pinus the Great become a basis for a mighty
snow-mound. But the mild March winds blow
from seaward. Spring bourgeons. One day the
ice has gone. The river flows visible ; and now
that its days of higher beauty and grace have come,
it climbs high up its banks to show that it is ready
for new usefulness. It would be dreary for the
great logs to see new verdure springing all around
them, while they lay idly rotting or sprouting with
uncouth funguses, not unsuspect of poison. But
they will not be wasted. Lumbermen, foes to idle-
ness and inutility, swarm again about their winter's
trophies. They imprint certain cabalistic tokens of
ownership on the logs, — crosses, xs, stars, crescents, alphabetical letters, — marks respected all

along the rivers and lakes down to the boom where the sticks are garnered for market. The marked logs are tumbled into the brimming stream, and so ends their forest-life.

Now comes "the great spring drive." Maine waters in spring flow under an illimitable raft. Every camp contributes its myriads of brown cylinders to the millions that go bobbing down rivers with jaw-breaking names. And when the river broadens to a lake, where these impetuous voyagers might be stranded or miss their way and linger, they are herded into vast rafts, and towed down by boats, or by steam-tugs, if the lake is large as Moosehead. At the lake-foot the rafts break up and the logs travel again dispersedly down stream, or through the " thoro'fare " connecting the members of a chain of lakes. The hero of this epoch is the Head-Driver. The head-driver of a timber-drive leads a disorderly army, that will not obey the word of command. Every log acts as an individual, according to certain imperious laws of matter, and every log is therefore at loggerheads with every other log. The marshal must be in the thick of the fight, keeping his forces well in hand, hurrying stragglers, thrusting off the stranded, leading his phalanxes wisely round curves and angles, lest they be jammed and fill the river with a solid mass. As the great sticks come dashing along, turning porpoise-like somersets or leaping up twice their length in the air, he must be everywhere, livelier than a monkey in a mimosa, a wonder of acrobatic agility in biggest boots. *He* made the proverb, "As easy as falling off a log."

Hardly less important is the Damster. To him it falls to conserve the waters at a proper level. At his dam, generally below a lake, the logs collect and lie crowded. The river, with its obstacles of rock and rapid, would anticipate wreck for these timbers of future ships. Therefore, when the spring drive is ready, and the head-driver is armed with his jack-boots and his iron-pointed sceptre, the damster opens his sluices and lets another river flow through atop of the rock-shattered river below. The logs of each proprietor, detected by their marks, pay toll as they pass the gates and rush bumptiously down the flood.

Far down, at some water-power nearest the reach of tide, a boom checks the march of this formidable body. The owners step forward and claim their sticks. Dowse takes all marked with three crosses and a dash. Sowse selects whatever bears two crescents and a star. Rowse pokes about for his stock, inscribed clip, dash, star, dash, clip. Nobody has counterfeited these hieroglyphs. The tale is complete. The logs go to the saw-mill. Sawdust floats seaward. The lumbermen junket. So ends the log-book.

"Maine," said our host, the Damster of Umbagog, "was made for lumbering-work. We never could have got the trees out, without these lakes and dams."

CHAPTER IV.

UMBAGOG.

RAIN ends, as even Noah and the Arkites discovered. The new sensation of tickling frogs
could entertain us for one day ; bounteous Nature
provided other novelties for the next. We were
at the Umbagog chain of lakes, and while it rained
the damster had purveyed us a boat and crew. At
sunrise he despatched us on our voyage. We
launched upon the Androscoggin, in a *bateau* of
the old Canadian type. Such light, clincher-built,
high-nosed, flat-bottomed boats are in use wherever
the fur-traders are or have been. Just such boats
navigate the Saskatchawan of the North, or Fra-
zer's River of the Northwest ; and in a larger
counterpart of our Androscoggin bark I had three
years before floated down the magnificent Columbia
to Vancouver, bedded on bales of beaver-skins.

As soon as sunrise wrote itself in shadows over
the sparkling water, as soon as through the river-
side belt of gnarled arbor-vitæ sunbeams flickered,
we pushed off, rowed up-stream by a pair of stout
lumbermen. The river was a beautiful way, admitting us into the *penetralia* of virgin forests. It
was not a rude wilderness : all that Northern
woods have of foliage, verdurous, slender, delicate,
tremulous, overhung our shadowy path, dense as
the vines that drape a tropic stream. Every giant

2

tree, every one of the Pinus oligarchy, had been lumbered away : refined sylvan beauty remained. The dam checked the river's turbulence, making it slow and mirror-like. It merited a more melodious name than harsh Androscoggin.

Five miles of such enchanting voyage brought us to Lake Umbagog. Whiffs of mist had met us in the outlet. Presently we opened chaos, and chaos shut in upon us. There was no Umbagog to be seen, — nothing but a few yards of gray water and a world of gray vapor. Therefore I cannot criticise, nor insult, nor compliment Umbagog. Let us deem it beautiful. The sun tried at the fog, to lift it with leverage of his early level beams. Failing in this attempt to stir and heave away the mass, he climbed, and began to use his beams as wedges, driving them down more perpendicularly. Whenever this industrious craftsman made a successful split, the fog gaped, and we could see for a moment, indefinitely, an expanse of water, hedged with gloomy forest, and owning for its dominant height a wild mountain, Aziscohos, or, briefer, Esquihos.

But the fog was still too dense to be riven by slanting sunbeams. It closed again in solider phalanx. Our gray cell shut close about us. Esquihos and the distance became nowhere. In fact, ourselves would have been nowhere, except that a sluggish damp wind puffed sometimes, and, steering into this, we could guide our way within a few points of our course.

Any traveller knows that it is no very crushing disappointment not to see what he came to see. Outside sights give something, but inside joys are independent. We enjoyed our dim damp voyage heartily, on that wide loneliness. Nor were our shouts and laughter the only sounds. Loons would sometimes wail to us, as they dived, black dots in the mist. Then we would wait for their bulbous reappearance, and let fly the futile shot with its muffled report, — missing, of course.

No being has ever shot a loon, though several have legends of some one who has. Sound has no power to express a profounder emotion of utter loneliness than the loon's cry. Standing in piny darkness on the lake's bank, or floating in dimness of mist or glimmer of twilight on its surface, you hear this wailing note, and all possibility of human tenancy by the shore or human voyaging is annihilated. You can fancy no response to this signal of solitude disturbed, and again it comes sadly over the water, the despairing plaint of some companionless and incomplete existence, exiled from happiness it has never known, and conscious only of blank and utter want. Loon-skins have a commercial value; so it is reported. The Barabinzians of Siberia, a nation "up beyond the River Ob," tan them into water-proof *paletots* or *aquascutums*. How they catch their loon, before they skin their loon, is one of the mysteries of that unknown realm.

Og, Gog, Magog, Memphremagog, all agog,

Umbagog, — certainly the American Indians were the Lost Tribes, and conserved the old familiar syllables in their new home.

Rowing into the damp breeze, we by and by traversed the lake. We had gained nothing but a fact of distance. But here was to be an interlude of interest. The "thoro'fare" linking Umbagog to its next neighbor is no thoro'fare for a *bateau*, since a *bateau* cannot climb through breakers over boulders. We must make a "carry," an actual portage, such as in all chronicles of pioneer voyages strike like the excitement of rapids into the monotonous course of easy descent. Another boat was ready on the next lake, but our chattels must go three miles through the woods. Yes, we now were to achieve a portage. Consider it, *blasé* friend, — was not this sensation alone worth the trip ?

The worthy lumbermen, and our supernumerary, the damster's son, staggered along slowly with our traps. Iglesias and I, having nothing to carry, enjoyed the carry. We lounged along through the glades, now sunny for the moment, and dallied with raspberries and blueberries, finer than any ever seen. The latter henceforth began to impurple our blood. Maine is lusciously carpeted with them.

As we oozed along the overgrown trail, dripping still with last night's rain, drops would alight upon our necks and trickle down our backs. A wet spine excites hunger, — if a pedestrian on a portage, after voyaging from sunrise, needs any appetizer when his shadow marks noon. We halted, fired up, and lunched vigorously on toasted pork and trimmings. As pork must be the Omega in forest-fare, it is well to make it the Alpha. Fate thus becomes choice. Citizens uneducated to forest-life with much pains transport into the woods sealed cans of what they deem will dainties be, and scoff at woodsmen frizzling slices of pork on a pointed stick. But Experience does not disdain a Cockney. She broods over him, and will by and by hatch him into a full-fledged forester. After such incubation, he will recognize his natural food, and compactest fuel for the lamp of life. He will take to his pork like mother's milk.

Our dessert of raspberries grew all along the path, and lured us on to a log-station by the water, where we found another *bateau* ready to transport us over Lakes Weelocksebacook, Allegundabagog, and Mollychunkamug. Doubters may smile and smile at these names, but they are geography.

We do not commit ourselves to further judgment upon the first, than that it is doubtless worthy of its name. My own opinion is, that the scenery felt that it was dullish, and was ashamed to "exhibit" to Iglesias; if he pronounced a condemnation, Umbagog and its sisters feared that they would be degraded to fish-ponds merely. Therefore they veiled themselves. Mists hung low over the leaden waters, and blacker clouds crushed the pine-dark hills.

A fair curve of sandy beach separates Weelock-

sebacook from its neighbor.   There is buried one
Melattach, an Indian chief.   Of course there has
been found in Maine some one irreverent enough to
trot a lame Pegasus over this grave, and accuse the
frowzy old red-skin of Christian virtues and delicate
romance.

There were no portages this afternoon.   We took
the three lakes at easy speed, persuading ourselves
that scenes fog would not let us see were unscenic.
It is well that a man should think what he cannot
get unworthy of his getting.   As evening came,
the sun made another effort, with the aid of west
winds, at the mist.   The sun cleft, the breeze
drove.   Suddenly the battle was done, victory
easily gained.   We were cheered by a gush of
level sunlight.   Even the dull, gray vapor became
a transfigured and beautiful essence.   Dull and
uniform it had hung over the land ; now the plastic
winds quarried it, and shaped the whole mass into
individuals, each with its character.   To the cloud-
forms modelled out of formlessness the winds gave
life of motion, sunshine gave life of light, and they
hastened through the lower atmosphere, or sailed
lingering across the blue breadths of mid-heaven,
or dwelt peacefully aloft in the region of the *cirri* ;
and whether trailing gauzy robes in flight, or
moving stately, or dwelling on high where scope
of vision makes travel needless, they were still the
brightest, the gracefullest, the purest beings that
Earth creates for man's most delicate pleasure.

When it cleared, — when it purveyed us a broad-

ening zone of blue sky and a heavenful of brilliant
cloud-creatures, we were sailing over Lake Mollychunkamug. Fair Mollychunkamug had not smiled
for us until now ; — now a sunny grin spread over
her smooth cheeks. She was all smiling, and presently, as the breeze dimpled her, all a " snicker "
up into the roots of her hair, up among her forest-
tresses. Mollychunkamug ! Who could be aught
but gay, gay even to the farcical, when on such a
name ? Is it Indian ? Bewildered Indian we deem
it, — transmogrified somewhat from aboriginal sound
by the fond imagination of some lumberman, finding in it a sweet memorial of his Mary far away in
the kitchens of the Kennebec, his Mary so rotund
of blooming cheek, his Molly of the chunky mug.
To him who truly loves, all Nature is filled with
Amaryllidian echoes. Every sight and every sound
recalls her who need not be recalled, to a heart that
has never dislodged her.

We lingered over our interview with Mollychunkamug. She may not be numbered among
the great beauties of the world ; nevertheless, she
is an attractive squaw, — a very honest bit of flat-
faced prettiness in the wilderness.

Above Mollychunkamug is Moosetocmaguntic
Lake. Another innavigable thoro'fare unites them.
A dam of Titanic crib-work, fifteen hundred feet
long, confines the upper waters. Near this we
disembarked. We balanced ourselves along the
timbers of the dam, and reached a huge log-cabin
at its farther end.

Mr. Killgrove, the damster, came forth and offered us the freedom of his settlement in a tobacco-box. Tobacco is hospitality in the compactest form. Civilization has determined that tobacco, especially in the shape of smoke, is essential as food, water, or air. The pipe is everywhere the pipe of peace. Peace, then, and anodyne-repose, after a day of travel, were offered us by the friendly damster.

A squad of lumbermen were our new fellow-citizens. These soldiers of the outermost outpost were in the regulation-uniform, — red-flannel shirts impurpled by wetting, big boots, and old felt-hats. Blood-red is the true soldierly color. All the residents of Damville dwelt in a great log-barrack, the Hôtel-de-Ville. Its architecture was of the early American style, and possessed the high art of simplicity. It was solid, not gingerbreadesque. Primeval American art has a rude dignity, far better than the sham splendors of our mediæval and transition period.

Our new friends, luxurious fellows, had been favored by Fate with a French-Canadian cook, himself a Three of Frères Provinciaux. Such was his reputation. We saw by the eye of him, and by his nose, formed for comprehending fragrances, and by the lines of refined taste converging from his whole face toward his mouth, that he was one to detect and sniff gastronomic possibilities in the humblest materials. Joseph Bourgogne looked the cook. His phiz gave us faith in him : eyes small and discriminating ; nose upturned, nostrils expanded and receptive ; mouth saucy in the literal sense. His voice, moreover, was a cook's, — thick in articulation, dulcet in tone. He spoke as if he deemed that a throat was created for better uses than laboriously manufacturing words, — as if the object of a mouth were to receive tribute, not to give commands, — as if that pink stalactite, his palate, were more used by delicacies entering, than by rough words or sorry sighs going out of the inner caverns.

When we find the right man in the right place, our minds are at ease. The future becomes satisfactory as the past. Anticipation is glad certainty, not anxious doubt. Trusting our gastronomic welfare fully to this great artist, we tried for fish below the dam. Only petty fishlings, weighing ounces, took the bit between their teeth. We therefore doffed the fisherman and donned the artist and poet, and chased our own fancies down the dark whirlpooling river, along its dell of evergreens, now lurid with the last glows of twilight. Iglesias and I continued dreamily gazing down the thoro'fare. toward Mollychunkamug only a certain length of time. Man keeps up to his highest elations hardly longer than a *danseuse* can poise in a *pose*. To be conscious of the highest beauty demands an involuntary intentness of observation so fanatically eager that presently we are prostrated and need stimulants. And just as we sensitively felt this exhaustion and this need, we heard

2* c

a suggestive voice calling us from the front-door of the mansion-house of Damville, and "Supper" was the cry.

A call to the table may quell and may awaken romance. When, in some abode of poetized luxury, the "silver knell" sounds musically six, and a door opens toward a glitter that is not pewter and Wedgewood, and, with a being fair and changeful as a sunset cloud upon my arm, I move under the archway of blue curtains toward the asphodel and the nectar, then, O Reader! O Friend! romance crowds into my heart, as color and fragrance crowd into a rose-bud. Joseph Bourgogne, cook at Damville on Moosetocmaguntic, could not offer us such substitute for æsthetic emotions. But his voice of an artist created a winning picture half veiled with mists, evanescent and affectionate, such as linger fondly over Pork-and-Beans.

Fancied joy soon to become fact. We entered the barrack. Beneath its smoky roof-tree was a pervading aroma; near the centre of that aroma, a table dim with wefts of incense; at the innermost centre of that aroma and that incense, and whence those visible and viewless fountains streamed, was their source, — a Dish of Pork-and-Beans.

Topmostly this. There were lesser viands, buttresses to this towering triumph. Minor smokes from minor censers. A circle of little craterlings about the great crater, — of little fiery cones about that great volcanic dome in the midst, unopened, but bursting with bounty. We sat down, and one of the red-shirted boldly crushed the smoking dome. The brave fellow plunged in with a spoon and heaped our plates.

A priori we had deduced Joseph Bourgogne's results from inspection of Joseph. Now we could reason back from one *experimentum crucis* cooked by him. Effect and cause were worthy of each other.

The average world must be revenged upon Genius. Greatness must be punished by itself or another. Joseph Bourgogne was no exception to the laws of the misery of Genius. He had a distressing trait, whose exhibition tickled the *dura ilia* of the reapers of the forest. Joseph, poet-cook, was sensitive to new ideas. This sensitiveness to the peremptory thought made him the slave of the wags of Damville. Whenever he had anything in his hands, at a stern, quick command he would drop it nervously. Did he approach the table with a second dish of pork-and-beans, a yellow dish of beans, browned delicately as a Sèvres vase, then would some full-fed rogue, waiting until Joseph was bending over some devoted head, say sharply, " Drop that, Joseph ! " — whereupon down went dish and contents, emporridging the poll and person of the luckless wight beneath. Always, were his burden pitcher of water, armful of wood, axe dangerous to toes, mirror, or pudding, still followed the same result. And when the poet-cook had done the mischief, he would stand shuddering at his work of ruin, and sigh, and curse his too sensitive nature.

In honor of us, the damster kept order. Joseph disturbed the banquet only by entering with new triumphs of Art. Last came a climax-pie, — contents unknown. And when that dish, fit to set before a king, was opened, the poem of our supper was complete. J. B. sailed to the Parnassus where Ude and Vattel feast, forever cooking immortal banquets in star-lighted spheres.

Then we sat in the picturesque dimness of the lofty cabin, under the void where the roof shut off the stars, and talked of the pine-woods, of logging, measuring, and spring-drives, and of moose-hunting on snow-shoes, until our mouths had a wild flavor more spicy than if we had chewed spruce-gum by the hour. Spruce-gum is the aboriginal quid of these regions. Foresters chew this tenacious morsel as tars nibble at a bit of oakum, grooms at a straw, Southerns at tobacco, or school-girls at a slate-pencil.

The barrack was fitted up with bunks. Iglesias rolled into one of these. I mummied myself in my blankets and did penance upon a bench. Pine-knots in my pallet sought out my tenderest spots. The softer wood was worn away about these projections. Hillocky was the surface, so that I beat about uneasily and awoke often, ready to envy Iglesias. But from him, also, I heard sounds of struggling.

CHAPTER V.

UP THE LAKES.

MR. KILLGROVE, slayer of forests, became the pilot of our voyage up Lake Moosetocmaguntic. We shoved off in a *bateau*, while Joseph Bourgogne, sad at losing us, stood among the stumps, waving adieux with a dish-clout. We had solaced his soul with meed of praise. And now, alas! we left him to the rude jokes and half-sympathies of the lumbermen. The artist-cook saw his appreciators vanish away, and his proud dish-clout drooped like a defeated banner.

" A fine lake," remarked Iglesias, instituting the matutinal conversation in a safe and general way.

" Yes," returned Mr. Killgrove, " when you come to get seven or eight feet more of water atop of this in spring, it *is* considerable of a puddle."

Our weather seemed to be now bettering with more resolution. Many days had passed since Aurora had shown herself, — many days since the rising sun and the world had seen each other. But yesterday this sulky estrangement ended, and, after the beautiful reconciliation at sunset, the faint mists of doubt in their brief parting for a night had now no power against the ardors of anticipated meeting. As we shot out upon the steaming water, the sun was just looking over the lower ridges of a mountain opposite. Air, blue and quivering, hung under

shelter of the mountain-front, as if a film from the
dim purple of night were hiding there to see what
beauty day had, better than its own. The gray fog,
so dreary for three mornings, was utterly vanquished; all was vanished, save where "swimming
vapors sloped athwart the glen," and "crept from
pine to pine." These had dallied, like spies of a
flying army, to watch for chances of its return;
but they, too, carried away by the enthusiasms of
a world liberated and illumined, changed their alle-
giance, joined the party of hope and progress, and
added the grace of their presence to the fair pageant of a better day.

Lake Moosetocmaguntic is good, — above the
average. If its name had but two syllables, and
the thing named were near Somewhere, poetry and
rhetoric would celebrate it, and the world would
be prouder of itself for another " gem." Now nobody sees it, and those who do have had their an-
ticipations lengthened leagues by every syllable
of its sesquipedalian title. One expects, perhaps,
something more than what he finds. He finds a
good average sheet of water, set in a circlet of
dark forest, — forests sloping up to wooded hills,
and these to wooded mountains. Very good and
satisfactory elements, and worth notice, — especially when the artistic eye is also a fisherman's eye,
and he detects fishy spots. As to wilderness, there
can be none more complete. At the upper end of
the lake is a trace of humanity in a deserted cabin
on a small clearing. There a hermit pair once

lived, — man and wife, utterly alone for fifteen years, — once or twice a year, perhaps, visited by lumbermen. Fifteen years alone with a wife! a trial, certainly, — not necessarily in the desponding sense of the word ; not as Yankees have it, making trial a misfortune, but a test.

Mr. Killgrove entertained us with resinous-flavored talk. The voyage was unexcitingly pleasant. We passed an archipelago of scrubby islands, and, turning away from a blue vista of hills northward, entered a lovely curve of river richly overhung with arbor-vitæ, a shadowy quiet reach of clear water, crowded below its beautiful surface with reflected forest and reflected sky.

"Iglesias," said I, "we divined how Molly-chunkamug had its name ; now, as to Moosetocmaguntic, — whence that elongated appellative ? "

"It was named," replied Iglesias, "from the adventure of a certain hunter in these regions. He was moose-hunting here in days gone by. His tale runs thus : — 'I had been four days without game, and naturally without anything to eat except pine-cones and green chestnuts. There was no game in the forest. The trout would not bite, for I had no tackle and no hook. I was starving. I sat me down, and rested my trusty but futile rifle against a fallen tree. Suddenly I heard a tread, turned my head, saw a Moose, — took — my — gun, — tick ! he was dead. I was saved. I feasted, and in gratitude named the lake Moosetookmyguntick.' Geography has modified it, but the name cannot be misunderstood."

We glided up the fair river, and presently came to the hut of Mr. Smith, fisherman and misogynist. And there is little more to be said about Mr. Smith. He appears in this chronicle because he owned a boat which became our vehicle on Lake Oquossok, Aquessok, Lakewocket, or Rangeley. Mr. Smith guided us across the carry to the next of the chain of lakes, and embarked us in a crazy skiff. It was blowing fresh, and, not to be wrecked, we coasted close to the gnarled arbor-vitæ thickets. Smith sogered along, drawling dull legends of trout-fishing.

"Drefful notional critturs traout be," he said, — "olluz bitin' at whodger haänt got. Orful contrairy critturs, — jess like fimmls. Yer can cotch a fimml with a feather, ef she's ter be cotched; ef she haänt ter be cotched, yer may scoop ther bul world dry an' yer haänt got her. Jess so traout."

The misogynist bored us with his dull philosophy. The buffetings of inland waves were not only insulting, but dangerous, to our leaky punt. At any moment, Iglesias and I might find ourselves floundering together in thin fresh water. Joyfully, therefore, at last, did we discern clearings, culture, and habitations at the lake-head. There was no tavernous village of Rangeley; that would have been too great a contrast, after the forest and the lakes, where loons are the only disturbers of silence, — incongruity enough to overpower utterly the ringing of woodland music in our hearts. Rangeley was a townless township, as the outermost township should be. We had, however, learnt from Killgrove, feller of forests, that there was a certain farmer on the lake, one of the chieftains of that realm, who would hospitably entertain us. Smith, wheedler of trout, landed us in quite an ambitious foamy surf at the foot of a declivity below our future host's farm.

We had now traversed Lakes Umbagog, Weelocksebacook, Allegundabagog, Mollychunkamug, Moosetocmaguntic, and Oquossok.

We had been compelled to pronounce these names constantly. Of course our vocal organs were distorted. Of course our vocal nervous systems were shattered, and we had a chronic lameness of the jaws. We therefore recognized a peculiar appropriateness in the name of our host.

Toothaker was his name. He dwelt upon the lawn-like bank, a hundred feet above the lake. Mr. Toothaker himself was absent, but his wife received us hospitably, disposed us in her guest-chamber, and gratified us with a supper.

This was Rangeley Township, the outer settlement on the west side of Maine. A "squire" from England gave it his name. He bought the tract, named it, inhabited several years, a popular squire-arch, and then returned from the wild to the tame, from pine woods and stumpy fields to the elm-planted hedge-rows and shaven lawns of placid England. The local gossip did not reveal any cause for Mr. Rangeley's fondness for contrasts and exile.

Mr. Toothaker has been a careful dentist to the stumps of his farm. It is beautifully stumpless, and slopes verdantly, or varied with yellow harvest, down to the lake and up to the forest primeval. He has preserved a pretty grove of birch and maple as shelter, ornament, partridge-cover, and perpendicular wood-pile. Below his house and barns is the lovely oval of the lake, seen across the fair fields, bright with wheat, or green with pasture. A road, hedged with briskly-aspiring young spruces, runs for a mile northward, making a faint show at attacking the wilderness. A mile's loneliness is enough for this unsupported pioneer; he runs up a tree, sees nothing but dark woods, thinks of Labrador and the North Pole, and stops.

Next morning, Mr. Toothaker returned from a political meeting below among the towns. It was the Presidential campaign, — stirring days from pines to prairies, stirring days from codfish to cocoa-nuts. Tonguey men were talking from every stump all over the land. Blatant patriots were heard, wherever a flock of compatriots could be persuaded to listen. The man with one speech containing two stories was making the tour of all the villages. The man with two speeches, each with three stories, one of them very broad indeed, was in request for the towns. The oratorical Stentorian man, with inexhaustible rivers of speech and rafts of stories, was in full torrent at mass-meetings. There was no neighborhood that might not see and hear an M. C. But Rangeley had been the *minus* town, and by all the speech-makers really neglected ; there was danger that its voters must deposit their ballots according to their own judgment, without any advice from strangers. This, of course, would never do. Mr. Toothaker found that we fraternized in politics. He called upon us, as patriots, to become the orators of the day. Why not? Except that these seldom houses do not promise an exhilarating crowd. We promised, however, that, if he would supply hearers, we between us would find a speaker.

Mr. Toothaker called a nephew, and charged him to boot and saddle, and flame it through the country-side that two "Men from New York" were there, and would give a "Lecture on Politics," at the Red School-house, at five that evening.

And to the Red School-house, at five, crowded the men, ay, and the women and children, of Rangeley and thereabout. They came as the winds and waves come when forests and navies are rended and stranded. Horse, foot, and charioteers, they thronged toward the rubicund fountain of education. From houses that lurked invisible in clearings suddenly burst forth a population, an audience ardent with patriotism, eager for politics even from a Cockney interpreter, and numerous enough to stir electricity in a speaker's mind. Some of the matrons brought bundles of swaddled infants, to be early instructed in good citizenship ; but too often these young patriots were found to have but crude notions on the subject of applause, and they were ignominiously removed, fighting violently for their privilege of free speech, doubling their unterrified fists, and getting as red in the face as the school-house.

Mr. Toothaker, in a neat speech, introduced the orator, who took his stand in the schoolmaster's pulpit, and surveyed his stalwart and gentle hearers, filling the sloping benches and overflowing out-of-doors. Gaffer and gammer, man and maiden, were distributed, the ladies to the right of the aisle, the gentlemen to the left. They must not be in contact, — perhaps because gaffer will gossip with gammer, and youth and maid will toy. Dignity demanded that they should be distinct as the conservative Right and radical Left of a French Assembly. Convenient, this, for the orator ; since thus his things of beauty, joys forever, he could waft, in dulcet tones, over to the ladies' side, and his things of logic, tough morsels for life-long digestion, he could jerk, like bolts from an arbalist, over at the open mouths of gray gaffer and robust man.

I am not about to report the orator's speech. Stealing another's thunder is an offence punishable condignly ever since the days of Salmoneus. Perhaps, too, he may wish to use the same eloquent bits in the present Olympiad ; for American life is measured by Olympiads, signalized by nobler contests than the petty states of Greece ever knew.

The people of Rangeley disappeared as mysteriously as they had emerged from the woods, having had their share of the good or bad talk of that year of freedom. If political harangues educate, the educated class was largely recruited that summer.

Next day, again, was stormy. We stayed quietly under shelter, preparing for our real journey after so much prelude. The Isaac Newton's steam-whistle had sent up the curtain; the overture had followed with strains Der-Freischutzy in the Adirondacks, pastoral in the valleys of Vermont and New Hampshire, funebral and andante in the fogs of Mollychunkamug; now it was to end in an allegretto gallopade, and the drama would open.

At last the sun shone bright upon the silky ripples of the lake. Mr. Toothaker provided two buggies, — one for himself and our traps, one for Iglesias and me. We rattled away across county and county. And so at full speed we drove all day, and, with a few hours' halt, all night, — all a fresh, starry night, — until gay sunrise brought us to Skowhegan, on the road to Moosehead Lake.

As we had travelled all night, breakfast must be our substitute for slumber. Repletion, instead of repose, must restore us. Two files of red-shirted lumbermen, brandishing knives at each other across a long table, only excited us to livelier gymnastics; and when we had thus hastily crammed what they call in Maine beefsteak, and what they infuse down

East for coffee, we climbed to the top of a coach of the bounding-billow motion, and went pitching northward.

Two facts we learned from our coachman : one, that we were passing that day through a "pretty sassy country"; also, that the same region was "only meant to hold the world together." Personal "sassiness" is a trait of which every Yankee is proud; Iglesias and I both venture to hope that we appreciate the value of that quality, and have properly cultivated it. Topographical "sassiness," unmodified by culture and control, is a rude, rugged, and unattractive trait; and New England is, on the whole, "sassier" than I could wish. Let the dullish day's drive, then, be passed over dumbly. In the evening we dismounted at Greenville, at the foot of Moosehead Lake.

CHAPTER VI.

THE BIRCH.

THE rivers of Maine, as a native observed to me, "olluz spread 'mselves inter bulges." Mollychunkamug and her fellows are the bulges of the Androscoggin ; Moosehead, of the Kennebec. Sluggish streams do not need such pauses. Peace is thrown away upon stolidity. The torrents of

Maine are hasty young heroes, galloping so hard when they gallop, and charging with such rash enthusiasm when they charge, hurrying with such Achillean ardor toward their eternity of ocean, that they would never know the influence, in their heart of hearts, of blue cloudlessness, or the glory of noonday, or the pageantries of sunset, — they would only tear and rive and shatter carelessly. Nature, therefore, provides valleys for the streams to bulge in, and entertain celestial reflections.

Nature, arranging lake-spots as educational episodes for the Maine rivers, disposes them also with a view to utility. Mr. Killgrove and his fellow-lumbermen treat lakes as log-puddles and raft-depots. Moosehead is the most important of these, and keeps a steamboat for tugging rafts and transporting raftsmen.

Moosehead also provides vessels far dearer to the heart of the adventurous than anything driven by steam. Here, mayhap, will an untravelled traveller make his first acquaintance with the birch-bark canoe, and learn to call it by the affectionate diminutive, "Birch." Earlier in life there was no love lost between him and whatever bore that name. Even now, if the untravelled one's first acquaintance be not distinguished by an unlovely ducking, so much the worse. The ducking must come. Caution must be learnt by catastrophe. No one can ever know how unstable a thing is a birch canoe, unless he has felt it slide away from under his misplaced feet. Novices should take nude practice in empty birches, lest they spill themselves and the load of full ones, — a wondrous easy thing to do.

A birch canoe is the right thing in the right place. Maine's rivers are violently impulsive and spasmodic in their running. Sometimes you have a foamy rapid, sometimes a broad shoal, sometimes a barricade of boulders with gleams of white water springing through or leaping over its rocks. Your boat for voyaging here must be stout enough to buffet the rapid, light enough to skim the shallow, agile enough to vault over, or lithe enough to slip through, the barricade. Besides, sometimes the barricade becomes a compact wall, — a baffler, unless boat and boatmen can circumvent it, — unless the nautical carriage can itself be carried about the obstacle, — can be picked up, shouldered, and made off with.

A birch meets all these demands. It lies, light as a leaf, on whirlpooling surfaces. A tip of the paddle can turn it into the eddy beside the breaker. A check of the setting-pole can hold it steadfast on the brink of wreck. Where there is water enough to varnish the pebbles, there it will glide. A birch thirty feet long, big enough for a trio and their traps, weighs only seventy-five pounds. When the rapid passes into a cataract, when the wall of rock across the stream is impregnable in front, it can be taken in the flank by an amphibious birch. The navigator lifts his canoe out of water and bonnets himself with it. He wears it on head and shoulders, around the impassable spot. Below the rough water, he gets into his elongated chapeau and floats away. Without such vessel, agile, elastic, imponderable, and transmutable, Androscoggin, Kennebec, and Penobscot would be no thoro'fares for human beings. Musquash might dabble, chips might drift, logs might turn somersets along their lonely currents; but never voyager, gentle or bold, could speed through brilliant perils, gladdening the wilderness with shout and song.

Maine's rivers must have birch canoes; Maine's woods, of course, therefore, provide birches. The white-birch, paper-birch, canoe-birch, grows large in moist spots near the stream where it is needed. Seen by the flicker of a camp-fire at night, they surround the intrusive traveller like ghosts of giant sentinels. Once, Indian tribes with names that "nobody can speak and nobody can spell" roamed these forests. A stouter second growth of humanity has ousted them, save a few seedy ones who gad about the land, and centre at Oldtown, their village near Bangor. These aborigines are the birch-builders. They detect by the river-side the tree barked with material for canoes. They strip it, and fashion an artistic vessel, which civilization cannot better. Launched in the fairy lightness of this, and speeding over foamy waters between forest-solitudes, one discovers, as if he were the first to know it, the truest poetry of pioneer-life.

3   D

Such poetry Iglesias had sung to me, until my life seemed incomplete while I did not know the sentiment by touch : description, even from the most impassioned witness, addressed to the most imaginative hearer, is feeble.   We both wanted to be in a birch : Iglesias, because he knew the fresh, inspiring vivacity of such a voyage ; I, because I divined it.   We both needed to be somewhere near the heart of New England's wildest wilderness.   We needed to see Katahdin, — the distinctest mountain to be found on this side of the continent.   Katahdin was known to Iglesias.   He had scuffled up its eastern land-slides with a squad of lumbermen.   He had birched it down to Lake Chesuncook in bygone summers, to see Katahdin distant.   Now, in a birch we would slide down the Penobscot, along its line of lakes, camp at Katahdin, climb it, and speed down the river to tidewater.

That was the great object of all our voyage, with its educating preludes, — Katahdin and a breathless dash down the Penobscot.   And while we flashed along the gleam of the river, Iglesias fancied he might see the visible, and hear the musical, and be stirred by the beautiful.   These, truly, are not far from the daily life of any seer, listener, and perceiver ; but there, perhaps, up in the strong wilderness, we might be recreated to a more sensitive vitality.   The Antæan treatment is needful for terrestrials, unless they would dwindle.   The diviner the power in any artist-soul, the more distinctly is he commanded to get near the divine without him. Fancies pale, that are not fed on facts. It is very easy for any man to be a plagiarist from himself, and present his own reminiscences half disguised, instead of new discoveries. Now up by Katahdin there were new discoveries to be made; and that mountain would sternly eye us, to know whether Iglesias were a copyist, or I a Cockney.

Katahdin was always in its place up in the woods. The Penobscot was always buzzing along toward the calm reaches, where it takes the shadow of the mountain. All we needed was the birch.

The birch thrust itself under our noses as we drove into Greenville. It was mounted upon a coach that preceded us, and wabbled oddly along, like a vast hat upon a dwarf. We talked with its owner, as he dismounted it. He proved our very man. He and his amphibious canoe had just made the trip we proposed, with a flotilla. Certain Bostonians had essayed it,—vague Northmen, preceding our Columbus voyage.

Enter now upon the scene a new and important character, Cancut the canoe-man. Mr. Cancut, owner and steerer of a birch, who now became our "guide, philosopher, and friend," is as American as a birch, as the Penobscot, or as Katahdin's self. Cancut was a jolly fatling,—almost too fat, if he will pardon me, for sitting in the stern of the imponderable canoe. Cancut, though for this summer boatman or bircher, had other strings to his bow. He was taking variety now, after employment more

monotonous.   Last summer, his services had been
in request throughout inhabited Maine, to "peddle
gravestones and collect bills."   The Gravestone-
Peddler is an institution of New England.   His
wares are wanted, or will be wanted, by every one.
Without discriminating the bereaved households, he
presents himself at any door, with attractive drawings of his wares, and seduces people into paying
the late tribute to their great-grandfather, or laying
up a monument for themselves against the inevitable day of demand.   His customers select from his
samples a tasteful "set of stones"; and next summer he drives up and unloads the marble, with the
names well spelt, and the cherub's head artistically
chiselled by the best workmen of Boston.   Cancut
told us, as an instance of judicious economy, how,
when he called once upon a recent widow to ask
what he could do in his line for her deceased husband's tomb, she chose from his patterns neat head-
and foot-stones for the dear defunct, and then bar-
gained with him to throw in a small pair for her boy
Johnny, — a poor, sick crittur, that would be wanting his monument long before next summer.

This lugubrious business had failed to infect Mr.
Cancut with corresponding deportment.   Undertak-
ers are always sombre in dreary mockery of woe.
Sextons are solemncholy, if not solemn.   I fear
Cancut was too cheerful for his trade, and therefore
had abandoned it.

Such was our guide, the captain, steersman, and
ballaster of our vessel.   We struck our bargain

with him at once, and at once proceeded to make preparations. Chiefly we prepared by stripping ourselves bare of everything except "must-haves." A birch, besides three men, will carry only the simplest baggage of a trio. Passengers who are constantly to make portages will not encumber themselves with what-nots. Man must have clothes for day and night, and must have provisions to keep his clothes properly filled out. These two articles we took in compact form, regretting even the necessity of guarding against a ducking by a change of clothes. Our provision, that unrefined pork and hard-tack, presently to be converted into artist and friend, was packed with a few delicacies in a firkin, — a commodious case, as we found.

A little steamer plies upon the lake, doing lumber-jobs, and not disdaining the traveller's dollars. Upon this, one August morning, we embarked ourselves and our frail birch, for our voyage to the upper end of Moosehead. Iglesias, in a red shirt, became a bit of color in the scene. I, in a red shirt, repeated the flame. Cancut, outweighing us both together, in a broader red shirt, outglared us both. When we three met, and our scarlet reflections commingled, there was one spot in the world gorgeous as a conclave of cardinals, as a squad of British grenadiers, as a Vermont maple-wood in autumn.

CHAPTER VII.

MOOSEHEAD.

MOOSEHEAD LAKE is a little bigger than the Lago
di Guarda, and therefore, according to our American standard, rather more important. It is not
very grand, not very picturesque, but considerably
better than no lake, — a meritorious mean ; not
pretty and shadowy, like a thousand lakelets all
over the land, nor tame, broad, and sham-oceanic,
like the tanks of Niagara. On the west, near its
southern end, is a well-intended blackness and
roughness called Squaw Mountain. The rest on
that side is undistinguished pine woods.

Mount Kinneo is midway up the lake, on the east.
It is the show-piece of the region, — the best they
can do for a precipice, and really admirably done.
Kinneo is a solid mass of purple flint rising seven
hundred feet upright from the water. By the side
of this block could some Archimedes appear, armed
with a suitable *"pou stô"* and a mallet heavy
enough, he might strike fire to the world. Since
percussion-guns and friction cigar-lighters came in,
flint has somewhat lost its value ; and Kinneo is
of no practical use at present. We cannot allow
inutilities in this world. Where is the Archimedes? He could make a handsome thing of it by
flashing us off with a spark into a new system of
things.

Below this dangerous cliff on the lake-bank is the Kinneo House, where fishermen and sportsmen may dwell, and kill or catch, as skill or fortune favors. The historical success of all catchers and killers is well balanced, since men who cannot master facts are always men of imagination, and it is as easy for them to invent as for the other class to do. Boston men haunt Kinneo. For a hero who has not skill enough or imagination enough to kill a moose stands rather in Nowhere with Boston fashion. The tameness of that pleasant little capital makes its belles ardent for tales of wild adventure. New York women are less exacting ; a few of them, indeed, like a dash of the adventurous in their lover ; but most of them are business-women, fighting their way out of vulgarity into style, and romance is an interruption.

Kinneo was an old station of Iglesias's, in those days when he was probing New England for the picturesque. When the steamer landed, he acted as cicerone, and pointed out to me the main object of interest thereabouts, — the dinner-table. We dined with lumbermen and moose-hunters, scufflingly.

The moose is the lion of these regions. Near Greenville, a gigantic pair of moose-horns marks a fork in the road. Thenceforth moose-facts and moose-legends become the staple of conversation. Moose-meat, combining the flavor of beefsteak and the white of turtle, appears on the table. Moose-horns with full explanations, so that the buyer can play the part of hunter, are for sale. Tame moose-lings are exhibited. Sportsmen at Kinneo can choose a *matinée* with the trout or a *soirée* with the moose.

The chief fact of a moose's person is that pair of strange excrescences, his horns. Like fronds of tree-fern, like great corals or sea-fans, these great palmated plates of bone lift themselves from his head, grand, useless, clumsy. A pair of moose-horns overlooks me as I write; they weigh twenty pounds, are nearly five feet in spread, on the right horn are nine developed and two undeveloped antlers, the plates are sixteen inches broad, — a doughty head-piece.

Every year the great, slow-witted animal must renew his head-gear. He must lose the deformity, his pride, and cultivate another. In spring, when the first anemone trembles to the vernal breeze, the moose nods welcome to the wind, and as he nods feels something rattle on his skull. He nods again, as Homer sometimes did. Lo! something drops. A horn has dropped, and he stands a bewildered unicorn. For a few days he steers wild; in this ill-balanced course his lone horn strikes every tree on this side as he dodges from that side. The un-happy creature is staggered, body and mind. In what Jericho of the forest can he hide his dimin-ished head? He flies frantic. He runs amuck through the woods. Days pass by in gloom, and then comes despair; another horn falls, and he becomes defenceless; and not till autumn does his brow bear again its full honors.

I make no apology for giving a few lines to the great event of a moose's life. He is the hero of those evergreen-woods, — a hero too little recognized, except by stealthy assassins, meeting him by midnight for massacre. No one seems to have viewed him in his dramatic character, as a forest-monarch enacting every year the tragicomedy of decoronation and recoronation.

The Kinneo House is head-quarters for moose-hunters. This summer the waters of Maine were diluvial, the feeding-grounds were swamped. Of this we took little note : we were in chase of something certain not to be drowned ; and the higher the deluge, the easier we could float to Katahdin. After dinner we took the steamboat again for the upper end of the lake.

It was a day of days for sunny summer sailing. Purple haziness curtained the dark front of Kinneo, — a delicate haze purpled by this black promontory, but melting blue like a cloud-fall of cloudless sky upon loftier distant summits. The lake rippled pleasantly, flashing at every ripple.

Suddenly, " Katahdin ! " said Iglesias.

Yes, there was a dim point, the object of our pilgrimage.

Katahdin, — the more I saw of it, the more grateful I was to the three powers who enabled me to see it : to Nature for building it, to Iglesias for guiding me to it, to myself for going.

We sat upon the deck and let Katahdin grow, —

3 *

and sitting, talked of mountains, somewhat to this effect : —

Mountains are the best things to be seen. Within the keen outline of a great peak is packed more of distance, of detail, of light and shade, of color, of all the qualities of space, than vision can get in any other way. No one who has not seen mountains knows how far the eye can reach. Level horizons are within cannon-shot. Mountain horizons not only may be a hundred miles away, but they lift up a hundred miles at length, to be seen at a look. Mountains make a background against which blue sky can be seen ; between them and the eye are so many miles of visible atmosphere, domesticated, brought down to the regions of earth, not resting overhead, a vagueness and a void. Air, blue in full daylight, rose and violet at sunset, gray like powdered starlight by night, is collected and isolated by a mountain, so that the eye can comprehend it in nearer acquaintance. There is nothing so refined as the outline of a distant mountain : even a rose-leaf is stiff-edged and harsh in comparison. Nothing else has that definite indefiniteness, that melting permanence, that evanescing changelessness. Clouds in vain strive to imitate it ; they are made of slighter stuff ; they can be blunt or ragged, but they cannot have that solid positiveness.

Mountains, too, are very stationary, — always at their post. They are characters of dignity, not without noble changes of mood ; but these changes are not bewildering, capricious shifts. A mountain can be studied like a picture ; its majesty, its grace, can be got by heart. Purple precipice, blue pyramid, cone or dome of snow, it is a simple image and a positive thought. It is a delicate fact, first, of beauty, — then, as you approach, a strong fact of majesty and power. But even in its cloudy, distant fairness there is a concise, emphatic reality altogether uncloudlike.

Manly men need the wilderness and the mountain. Katahdin is the best mountain in the wildest wild to be had on this side the continent. He looked at us encouragingly over the hills. I saw that he was all that Iglesias, connoisseur of mountains, had promised, and was content to wait for the day of meeting.

The steamboat dumped us and our canoe on a wharf at the lake-head about four o'clock. A wharf promised a settlement, which, however, did not exist. There was population, — one man and one great ox. Following the inland-pointing nose of the ox, we saw, penetrating the forest, a wooden railroad. Ox-locomotive, and no other, befitted such rails. The train was one great go-cart. We packed our traps upon it, roofed them with our birch, and, without much ceremony of whistling, moved on. As we started, so did the steamboat. The link between us and the inhabited world grew more and more attenuated. Finally it snapped, and we were in the actual wilderness.

I am sorry to chronicle that Iglesias hereupon turned to the ox, and said impatiently, —

"Now, then, bullgine!"

Why a railroad, even a wooden one, here? For this: the Penobscot at this point approaches within two and a half miles of Moosehead Lake, and over this portage supplies are taken conveniently for the lumbermen of an extensive lumbering country above, along the river.

Corduroy railroad, ox-locomotive, and go-cart train up in the pine woods were a novelty and a privilege. Our cloven-hoofed engine did not whirr turbulently along, like a thing of wheels. Slow and sure must the knock-kneed chewer of cuds step from log to log. Creakingly the wain followed him, pausing and starting and pausing again with groans of inertia. A very fat ox was this, protesting every moment against his employment, where speed, his duty, and sloth, his nature, kept him bewildered by their rival injunctions. Whenever the engine-driver stopped to pick a huckleberry, the train, self-braking, stopped also, and the engine took in fuel from the tall grass that grew between the sleepers. It was the sensation of sloth at its uttermost.

Iglesias and I, meanwhile, marched along and shot the game of the country, namely, one *Tetrao Canadensis*, one spruce-partridge, making in all one bird, quite too pretty to shoot with its red and black plumage. The spruce-partridge is rather rare in inhabited Maine, and is malignantly accused of being bitter in flesh, and of feeding on spruce-buds to make itself distasteful. Our bird we found sweetly berry-fed. The bitterness, if any, was that we had not a brace.

So, at last, in an hour, after shooting one bird and swallowing six million berries, for the railroad was a shaft into a mine of them, we came to the terminus. The chewer of cuds was disconnected, and plodded off to his stable. The go-cart slid down an inclined plane to the river, the Penobscot.

We paid quite freely for our brief monopoly of the railroad to the superintendent, engineer, stoker, poker, switch-tender, brakeman, baggage-master, and every other official in one. But who would grudge his tribute to the enterprise that opened this narrow vista through toward the Hyperbore-ans, and planted these once not crumbling sleepers and once not rickety rails, to save the passenger a portage? Here, at Bullgineville, the pluralist rail-road-manager had his cabin and clearing, ox-engine house and warehouse.

To balance these symbols of advance, we found a station of the rear-guard of another army. An Indian party of two was encamped on the bank. The fusty sagamore of this pair was lying wound-ed; his fusty squaw tended him tenderly, minding, meanwhile, a very witch-like caldron of savory fume. No skirmish, with actual war-whoop and sheen of real scalping-knife, had put this prostrate chieftain here *hors du combat*. He had shot him-self cruelly by accident. So he informed us feebly,

in a muddy, guttural *patois* of Canadian French.
This aboriginal meeting was of great value ; it
helped to eliminate the railroad.

CHAPTER VIII.

PENOBSCOT.

It was now five o'clock of an August evening.
Our work-day was properly done. But we were
to camp somewhere, "anywhere out of the world"
of railroads. The Penobscot glimmered winningly.
Our birch looked wistful for its own element. Why
not marry shallop to stream ? Why not yield to
the enticement of this current, fleet and clear, and
gain a few beautiful miles before nightfall ? All
the world was before us where to choose our bivouac. We dismounted our birch from the truck,
and laid its lightness upon the stream. Then we
became stevedores, stowing cargo. Sheets of
birch-bark served for dunnage. Cancut, in flamboyant shirt, ballasted the after-part of the craft.
For the present, I, in flamboyant shirt, paddled in
the bow, while Iglesias, similarly glowing, sat *à la
Turque* midships among the traps. Then, with a
longing sniff at the caldron of Soggysampcook, we
launched upon the Penobscot.

Upon no sweeter stream was voyager ever

launched than this of our summer-evening sail.
There was no worse haste in its more speed; it
went fleetly lingering along its leafy dell. Its current, unripplingly smooth, but dimpled ever, and
wrinkled with the whirls that mark an underflow
deep and shady, bore on our bark. The banks
were low and gently wooded. No Northern forest, rude and gloomy with pines, stood stiffly and
unsympathizingly watching the graceful water, but
cheerful groves and delicate coppices opened in
vistas where level sunlight streamed, and barred
the river with light, between belts of lightsome
shadow. We felt no breeze, but knew of one,
keeping pace with us, by a tremor in the birches
as it shook them. On we drifted, mile after mile,
languidly over sweet calms. One would seize his
paddle, and make our canoe quiver for a few spasmodic moments. But it seemed needless and impertinent to toil, when noiselessly and without any
show of energy the water was bearing us on, over
rich reflections of illumined cloud and blue sky,
and shadows of feathery birches, bearing us on so
quietly that our passage did not shatter any fair
image, but only drew it out upon the tremors of
the water.

So, placid and beautiful as an interview of first
love, went on our first meeting with this Northern
river. But water, the feminine element, is so mobile and impressible that it must protect itself by
much that seems caprice and fickleness. We
might be sure that the Penobscot would not al-

ways flow so gently, nor all the way from forests
to the sea conduct our bark without one shiver of
panic, where rapids broke noisy and foaming over
rocks that showed their grinding teeth at us.

Sunset now streamed after us down the river.
The arbor-vitæ along the banks marked tracery
more delicate than any ever wrought by deftest
craftsman in western window of an antique fane.
Brighter and richer than any tints that ever poured
through painted oriel flowed the glories of sunset.
Dear, pensive glooms of nightfall drooped from the
zenith slowly down, narrowing twilight to a belt
of dying flame. We were aware of the ever fresh
surprise of starlight: the young stars were born
again.

Sweet is the charm of starlit sailing where no
danger is. And in days when the Munki Manna-
kens were foes of the pale-face, one might dash
down rapids by night in the hurry of escape. Now
the danger was before, not pursuing. We must
camp before we were hurried into the first "rips"
of the stream, and before night made bush-ranging
and camp-duties difficult.

But these beautiful thickets of birch and alder
along the bank, how to get through them? We
must spy out an entrance. Spots lovely and damp,
circles of ferny grass beneath elms offered themselves. At last, as to patience always, appeared
the place of wisest choice. A little stream, the
Ragmuff, entered the Penobscot. "Why Ragmuff?" thought we, insulted. Just below its

mouth two spruces were *propylœa* to a little glade, our very spot. We landed. Some hunters had once been there. A skeleton lodge and frame of poles for drying moose-hides remained.

Like skilful campaigners, we at once distributed ourselves over our work. Cancut wielded the axe; I the match-box; Iglesias the *batterie de cuisine.* Ragmuff drifted one troutling and sundry chubby chub down to nip our hooks. We re-roofed our camp with its old covering of hemlock-bark, spreading over a light tent-cover we had provided. The last glow of twilight dulled away; monitory mists hid the stars.

Iglesias, as *chef*, with his two *marmitons*, had, meanwhile, been preparing supper. It was dark when he, the colorist, saw that fire with delicate touches of its fine brushes had painted all our viands to perfection. Then, with the same fire stirred to illumination, and dashing masterly glows upon landscape and figures, the trio partook of the supper and named it sublime.

Here follows the *carte* of the Restaurant Ragmuff, — woodland fare, a banquet simple, but elegant : —

Poisson.

Truite.   Meunier.

Entrées.

Porc frit au naturel.
Côtelettes d'Élan.

Rôti.

Tetrao Canadensis.

E

DESSERT.

Hard-Tack. Fromage.

VINS.

Ragmuff blanc. Penobscot mousseux.
Thé. Chocolat de Bogotá.
Petit verre de Cognac.

At that time I had a temporary quarrel with the frantic nineteenth century's best friend, tobacco, — and Iglesias, being totally at peace with himself and the world, never needs anodynes. Cancut, therefore, was the only cloud-blower.

We two solaced ourselves with scorning civilization from our vantage-ground. We were beyond fences, away from the clash of town-clocks, the clink of town-dollars, the hiss of town-scandals. As soon as one is fairly in camp and has begun to eat with his fingers, he is free. He and truth are at the bottom of a well, — a hollow, fire-lighted cylinder of forest. While the manly man of the woods is breathing Nature like an Amreeta draught, is it anything less than the *summum bonum* ?

"Yet some call American life dull."

"Ay, to dullards ! " ejaculated Iglesias.

Moose were said to haunt these regions. Toward midnight our would-be moose-hunter paddled about up and down, seeking them and finding not. The waters were too high. Lily-pads were drowned. There were no moose looming duskily in the shallows, to be done to death at their banquet. They were up in the pathless woods, browsing on leaves and deappetizing with bitter bark. Starlight paddling over reflected stars was enchanting, but somniferous. We gave up our vain quest and glided softly home, — already we called it home, — toward the faint embers of our fire. Then all slept, as only woodmen sleep, save when for moments Cancut's trumpet-tones sounded alarums, and we others awoke to punch and batter the snorer into silence.

In due time, bird and cricket whistled and chirped the reveille. We sprang from our lair. We dipped in the river and let its gentle friction polish us more luxuriously than ever did any hair-gloved polisher of an Oriental bath. Our joints crackled for themselves as we beat the current. From bath like this comes no unmanly kief, no sensuous, slumberous, dreamy indifference, but a nervous, intent, keen, joyous activity. A day of deeds is before us, and we would be doing.

When we issue from the Penobscot, from our baptism into a new life, we need no valet for elaborate toilet. Attire is simple, when the woods are the tiring-room.

When we had taken off the water and put on our clothes, we simultaneously thought of breakfast. Like a circle of wolves around the bones of a banquet, the embers of our fire were watching each other over the ashes ; we had but to knock their heads together and fiery fighting began. The skirmish of the brands boiled our coffee and fried our pork, and we embarked and shoved off. A thin blue smoke, floating upward, for an hour or two,

marked our bivouac ; soon this had gone out, and
the banks and braes of Ragmuff were lonely as if
never a biped had trodden them. Nature drops
back to solitude as easily as man to peace ; — how
little this fair globe would miss mankind !

The Penobscot was all asteam with morning
mist. It was blinding the sun with a matinal obla-
tion of incense. A crew of the profane should not
interfere with such act of worship. Sacrilege is
perilous, whoever be the God. We were instantly
punished for irreverence. The first " rips " came
up-stream under cover of the mist, and took us by
surprise. As we were paddling along gently, we
suddenly found ourselves in the midst of a boiling
rapid. Gnashing rocks, with cruel foam upon their
lips, sprang out of the obscure, eager to tear us.
Great jaws of ugly blackness snapped about us, as
if we were introduced into a coterie of crocodiles.
Symplegades clanged together behind ; mighty
gulfs, below seducing bends of smooth water,
awaited us before. We were in for it. We spun,
whizzed, dashed, leaped, " cavorted " ; we did
whatever a birch running the gantlet of whirl-
pools and breakers may do, except the fatal finality
of a somerset. That we escaped, and only escaped.
We had been only reckless, not audacious ; and
therefore peril, not punishment, befell us. The
rocks smote our frail shallop ; they did not crush
it. Foam and spray dashed in our faces ; solid
fluid below the crest did not overwhelm us. There
we were, presently, in water tumultuous, but not

frantic. There we were, three men floating in a birch, not floundering in a maelstrom, — on the water, not under it, — sprinkled, not drowned, — and in a wild wonder how we got into it and how we got out of it.

Cancut's paddle guided us through. Unwieldy he may have been in person, but he could wield his weapon well. And so, by luck and skill, we were not drowned in the magnificent uproar of the rapid. Success, that strange stirabout of Providence, accident, and courage, were ours. But when we came to the next cascading bit, though the mist had now lifted, we lightened the canoe by two men's avoirdupois, that it might dance, and not blunder heavily, might seek the safe shallows, away from the dangerous bursts of mid-current, and choose passages where Cancut, with the setting-pole, could let it gently down. So Iglesias and I plunged through the labyrinthine woods, the stream along.

Not long after our little episode of buffeting, we shot out again upon smooth water, and soon, for it is never smooth but it is smoothest, upon a lake, Chesuncook.

CHAPTER IX.

CHESUNCOOK.

CHESUNCOOK is a "bulge" of the Penobscot : so much for its topography. It is deep in the woods, except that some miles from its opening there is a lumbering-station, with house and barns. In the wilderness, man makes for man by a necessity of human instinct. We made for the log-houses. We found there an ex-barkeeper of a certain well-known New York cockney coffee-house, promoted into a frontiersman, but mindful still of flesh-pots. Poor fellow, he was still prouder that he had once tossed the foaming cocktail than that he could now fell the forest-monarch. Mixed drinks were dearer to him than pure air. When we entered the long, low log-cabin, he was boiling doughnuts, as was to be expected. In certain regions of America every cook who is not baking pork and beans is boiling doughnuts, just as in certain other gastronomic quarters *frijoles* alternate with *tortillas*.

Doughnuts, like peaches, must be eaten with the dew upon them. Caught as they come bobbing up in the bubbling pot, I will not say that they are despicable. Woodsmen and canoemen, competent to pork and beans, can master also the alternative. The ex-barkeeper was generous with these brown and glistening langrage-shot, and aimed volley after volley at our mouths. Nor was he content with giving us our personal fill; into every crevice of our firkin he packed a pellet of future indigestion. Besides this result of foraging, we took the hint from a visible cow that milk might be had. Of this also the ex-barkeeper served us out galore, sighing that it was not the punch of his metropolitan days. We put our milk in our tea-pot, and thus, with all the ravages of the past made good, we launched again upon Chesuncook.

Chesuncook, according to its quality of lake, had no aid to give us with current. Paddling all a hot August midday over slothful water would be tame, day-laborer's work. But there was a breeze. Good! Come, kind Zephyr, fill our red blanket-sail! Cancut's blanket in the bow became a sub-stitute for Cancut's paddle in the stern. We swept along before the wind, unsteadily, over Lake Che-suncook, at sea in a bowl, — "rolled to starboard, rolled to larboard," in our keelless craft. Zephyr only followed us, mild as he was strong, and strong as he was mild. Had he been puffy, it would have been all over with us. But the breeze only sang about our way, and shook the water out of sunny calm. Katahdin to the north, a fair blue pyramid, lifted higher and stooped forward more imminent, yet still so many leagues away that his features were undefined, and the gray of his scalp undistin-guishable from the green of his beard of forest. Every mile, however, as we slid drowsily over the hot lake, proved more and more that we were not befooled, — Iglesias by memory, and I by anticipation.   Katahdin lost nothing by approach, as some of the grandees do : as it grew bigger, it grew better.

Twenty miles, or so, of Chesuncook, of sun-cooked Chesuncook, we traversed by the aid of our blanket-sail, pleasantly wafted by the unboisterous breeze. Undrowned, unducked, as safe from the perils of the broad lake as we had come out of the defiles of the rapids, we landed at the carry below the dam at the lake's outlet.

The skin of many a slaughtered varmint was nailed on its shingle, and the landing-place was carpeted with the fur.   Doughnuts, ex-barkeepers, and civilization at one end of the lake, and here were muskrat-skins, trappers, and the primeval. Two hunters of moose, in default of their fern-horned, blubber-lipped game, had condescended to muskrat, and were making the lower end of Chesuncook fragrant with muskiness.

It is surprising how hospitable and comrade a creature is man.   The trappers of muskrats were charmingly brotherly.   They guided us across the carry ; they would not hear of our being porters. "Pluck the superabundant huckleberry," said they, "while we, suspending your firkin and your traps upon the setting-pole, tote them, as the spies of Joshua toted the grape-clusters of the Promised Land."

Cancut, for his share, carried the canoe.   He wore it upon his head and shoulders.   Tough work he found it, toiling through the underwood, and poking his way like an elongated and mobile mushroom through the thick shrubbery. Ever and anon, as Iglesias and I paused, we would be aware of the canoe thrusting itself above our heads in the covert, and a voice would come from an unseen head under its shell, — "It's soul-breaking, carrying is ! "

The portage was short. We emerged from the birchen grove upon the river, below a brilliant cascading rapid. The water came flashing gloriously forward, a far other element than the tame, flat stuff we had drifted slowly over all the dullish hours. Water on the go is nobler than water on the stand ; recklessness may be as fatal as stagnation, but it is more heroic.

Presently, over the edge, where the foam and spray were springing up into sunshine, our canoe suddenly appeared, and had hardly appeared, when, as if by one leap, it had passed the rapid, and was gliding in the stiller current at our feet. One of the muskrateers had relieved Cancut of his headpiece, and shot the lower rush of water. We again embarked, and, guided by the trappers in their own canoe, paddled out upon Lake Pepogenus.

4

CHAPTER X.

RIPOGENUS.

RIPOGENUS is a tarn, a lovely oval tarn, within a rim of forest and hill; and there behold, *O gioja!* at its eastern end, stooping forward and filling the sphere, was Katahdin, large and alone.

But we must hasten, for day wanes, and we must see and sketch this cloudless summit from *terra firma*. A mile and half-way down the lake, we landed at the foot of a grassy hill-side, where once had been a lumberman's station and hay-farm. It was abandoned now, and lonely in that deeper sense in which widowhood is lonelier than celibacy, a home deserted lonelier than a desert. Tumble-down was the never-painted house; ditto its three barns. But, besides a camp, there were two things to be had here, — one certain, one possible, probable even. The view, that was an inevitable certainty; Iglesias would bag that as his share of the plunder of Ripogenus. For my bagging, bears, perchance, awaited. The trappers had seen a bear near the barns. Cancut, in his previous visit, had seen a disappearance of bear. No sooner had the birch's bow touched lightly upon the shore than we seized our respective weapons, — Iglesias his peaceful and creative sketch-book, I my warlike and destructive gun, — and dashed up the hill-side.

I made for the barns to catch Bruin napping or

lolling in the old hay. I entertain a *vendetta* toward the ursine family. I had a *duello*, pistol against claw, with one of them in the mountains of Oregon, and have nothing to show to point the moral and adorn the tale. My antagonist of that hand-to-hand fight received two shots, and then dodged into cover and was lost in the twilight. Soon or late in my life, I hoped that I should avenge this evasion. Ripogenus would, perhaps, give what the Nachchese Pass had taken away.

Vain hope! I was not to be an ursicide. I begin to fear that I shall slay no other than my proper personal bearishness. I did my duty for another result at Ripogenus. I bolted audaciously into every barn. I made incursions into the woods around. I found the mark of the beast, not the beast. He had not long ago decamped, and was now, perhaps, sucking the meditative paw hard-by in an arbor of his bear-garden.

After a vain hunt, I gave up Beast and turned to Beauty. I looked about me, seeing much.

Foremost I saw a fellow-man, my comrade, fondled by breeze and brightness, and whispered to-by all sweet sounds. I saw Iglesias below me, on the slope, sketching. He was preserving the scene at its *bel momento*. I repented more bitterly of my momentary falseness to Beauty while I saw him so constant.

Furthermore, I saw a landscape of vigorous simplicity, easy to comprehend. By mellow sunset the grass slope of the old farm seemed no longer tanned and rusty, but ripened. The oval lake was blue and calm, and that is already much to say; shadows of the western hills were growing over it, but flight after flight of illumined cloud soared above, to console the sky and the water for the coming of night. Northward, a forest darkled, whose glades of brightness I could not see. Eastward, the bank mounted abruptly to a bare fire-swept table-land, whereon a few dead trees stood, parched and ghostly skeletons draped with rags of moss.

Furthermost and topmost, I saw Katahdin twenty miles away, a giant undwarfed by any rival. The remainder landscape was only minor and judiciously accessory. The hills were low before it, the lake lowly, and upright above lake and hill lifted the mountain pyramid. Isolate greatness tells. There were no underling mounts about this mountain-in-chief. And now on its shoulders and crest sunset shone, glowing. Warm violet followed the glow, soothing away the harshness of granite lines. Luminous violet dwelt upon the peak, while below the clinging forests were purple in sheltered gorges, where they could climb nearer the summit, loved of light, and lower down gloomed green and sombre in the shadow.

Meanwhile, as I looked, the quivering violet rose higher and higher, and at last floated away like a disengaged flame. A smouldering blue dwelt upon the peak. Ashy-gray overcame the blue. As dusk thickened and stars trembled into sight, the gray grew luminous. Katahdin's mighty presence seemed to absorb such dreamy glimmers as float in limpid night-airs : a faint glory, a twilight of its own, clothed it. King of the daylit-world, it became queen of the dimmer realms of night, and like a woman-queen it did not disdain to stoop and study its loveliness in the polished lake, and stooping thus it overhung the earth, a shadowy creature of gleam and gloom, an eternized cloud.

I sat staring and straying in sweet reverie, until the scene before me was dim as metaphysics. Suddenly a flame flashed up in the void. It grew and steadied, and dark objects became visible about it. In the loneliness — for Iglesias had disappeared — I allowed myself a moment's luxury of superstition. Were these the Cyclops of Katahdin? Possibly. Were they Trolls forging diabolic enginery, or Gypsies of Yankeedom? I will see, — and went tumbling down the hill-side.

As I entered the circle about the cooking-fire of drift-wood by the lake, Iglesias said, —

"The beef-steak and the mutton-chops will do for breakfast ; now, then, with your bear ! "

" Haw, haw ! " guffawed Cancut ; and the sound, taking the lake at a stride, found echoes everywhere, till he grew silent and peered suspiciously into the dark.

" There 's more bears raound 'n yer kin shake a stick at," said one of the muskrateers. " I would n't ricommend yer to stir 'em up naow, haowlin' like that."

" I meant it for laffin'," said Cancut, humbly.

" Ef yer call that 'ere larfin', could n't yer cry a
little to kind er slick daown the bears ? " said the
trapper.

Iglesias now invited us to *chocolat à la crème*,
made with the boon of the ex-barkeeper. I suppose I may say, without flattery, that this tipple
was marvellous. What a pity Nature spoiled a
cook by making the muddler of that chocolate a
painter of grandeurs! When Fine Art is in a
man's nature, it must exude, as pitch leaks from
a pine-tree. Our muskrat-hunters partook injudi-
ciously of this unaccustomed dainty, and were
visited with indescribable Nemesis. They had
never been acclimated to chocolate, as had Iglesias
and I, by sipping it under the shade of the mimosa
and the palm.

Up to a certain point, an unlucky hunter is more
likely to hunt than a lucky. Satiety follows more
speedily upon success than despair upon failure.
Let us thank Heaven for that, brethren dear! I
had bagged not a bear, and must needs satisfy my
assassin instincts upon something with hoofs and
horns. The younger trapper of muskrat, being
young, was ardent, — being young, was hopeful,
— being young, believed in exceptions to general
rules, — and being young, believed that, given a
good fellow with a gun, Nature would provide
a victim. Therefore he proposed that we should
canoe it along the shallows in this sweetest and
stillest of all the nights. The senior shook his

head incredulously-; Iglesias shook his head nod-
dingly.

"Since you have massacred all the bears," said
Iglesias, "I will go lay me down in their lair in
the barn. If you find me cheek-by-jowl with Ursa
Major when you come back, make a pun and he
will go."

It was stiller than stillness upon the lake. Ripogenus, it seemed, had never listened to such
silence as this. Calm never could have been so
beyond the notion of calm. Stars in the empyrean
and stars in Ripogenus winked at each other across
ninety-nine billions of leagues as uninterruptedly
as boys at a boarding-school table.

I knelt amidships in the birch with gun and
rifle on either side. The pilot gave one stroke of
his paddle, and we floated out upon what seemed
the lake. Whatever we were poised and floating
upon he hesitated to shatter with another dip of
his paddle, lest he should shatter the thin basis and
sink toward heaven and the stars.

Presently the silence seemed to demand gentle
violence, and the unwavering water needed slight
tremors to teach it the tenderness of its calm ;
then my guide used his blade, and cut into glassiness. We crept noiselessly along by the lake-
edge, within the shadows of the pines. With
never a plash we slid. Rare drops fell from the
cautious paddle and tinkled on the surface, over-
shot, not parted by, our imponderable passage.
Sometimes from far within the forest would come

sounds of rustling branches or crackling twigs. Somebody of life approaches with stealthy tread. Gentlier, even gentlier, my steersman ! Take up no pearly drop from the lake, mother of pearliness, lest falling it sound too loudly. Somewhat comes. Let it come unterrified to our ambush among the shadows by the shore.

Somewhat, something, somebody was coming, perhaps, but some other thing or body thwarted it and it came not. To glide over glassiness while uneventful moments link themselves into hours is monotonous. Night and stillness laid their soothing spell upon me. I was entranced. I lost myself out of time and space, and seemed to be floating unimpelled and purposeless, nowhere in Forever.

Somewhere in Now I suddenly found myself.

There he was ! There was the moose trampling and snorting hard by, in the shallows of Ripogenus, trampling out of being the whole nadir of stars, making the world conscious of its lost silence by the death of silence in tumult.

I trembled with sudden eagerness. I seized my gun. In another instant I should have lodged the fatal pellet ! when a voice whispered over my shoulder, — " I kinder guess yer 've ben asleep an' dreamin', ha'n't yer ? "

So I had.

Never a moose came down to cool his clumsy snout in the water and swallow reflections of stars. Never a moose abandoned dry-browse in the bitter woods for succulent lily-pads, full in their cells and veins of water and sunlight. Till long past midnight we paddled and watched and listened, whisperless. In vain. At last, as we rounded a point, the level gleam of our dying camp-fire athwart the water reminded us of passing hours and traveller duties, of rest to-night and toil to-morrow.

My companions, fearless as if there were no bears this side of Ursa Major, were bivouacked in one of the barns. There I entered skulkingly, as a gameless hunter may, and hid my untrophied head beneath a mound of ancient hay, not without the mustiness of its age.

No one clawed us, no one chawed us, that night. A Ripogenus chill awaked the whole party with early dawn. We sprang from our nests, shook the hay-seed out of our hair, and were full-dressed without more ceremony, ready for whatever grand sensation Nature might purvey for our æsthetic breakfast.

Nothing is ever as we expect. When we stepped into out-of-doors, looking for Ripogenus, a lake of Maine, we found not a single aquatic fact in the landscape. Ripogenus, a lake, had mizzled, (as the Americans say,) literally mizzled. Our simplified view comprised a grassy hill with barns, and a stern positive pyramid, surely Katahdin ; aloft, beyond, above, below, thither, hither, and yon, Fog, — not fog, but FOG.

Ripogenus, the water-body, had had aspirations, and a boon of brief transfiguration into a cloud-body had been granted it by Nature, who grants

4 *

F

to every terrestrial essence prophetic experiences of what it one day would be.

In short, and to repeat, Ripogenus had transmuted itself into vapor, and filled the valley full to our feet. A faint wind had power to billow this mist-lake, and drive cresting surges up against the eastern hill-side, over which they sometimes broke, and, involving it totally, rolled clear and free toward Katahdin, where he stood hiding the glows of sunrise. Leagues higher up than the mountain rested a presence of cirri, already white and luminous with full daylight, and from them drooped linking wreaths of orange mist, clinging to the rosy-violet granite of the peak.

Up clomb and sailed Ripogenus and befogged the whole; then we condescended to breakfast.

CHAPTER XI.

TOWARD KATAHDIN.

SINGULARLY enough, mill-dams are always found below mill-ponds. Analogously in the Maine rivers, below the lakes, rapids are. Rapids too often compel carries. While we breakfasted without steak of bear or cutlet of moose, Ripogenus gradually retracted itself, and became conscious again of what poetry there is in a lake's pause and a rapid's flow. Fog condensed into water, and water submitting to its destiny went cascading down through a wild defile where no birch could follow.

The Ripogenus carry is three miles long, a faint path through thickets.

"First half," said Cancut, "'s plain enough; but after that 't would take a philosopher with his spectacles on to find it."

This was discouraging. Philosophers twain we might deem ourselves; but what is a craftsman without tools? And never a goggle had we.

But the trappers of muskrats had become our fast friends. They insisted upon lightening our loads over the brambly league. This was kindly. Cancut's elongated head-piece, the birch, was his share of the burden; and a bag of bread, a firkin of various grub, damp blankets for three, and multitudinous traps, seemed more than two could carry at one trip over this longest and roughest of portages.

We paddled from the camp to the lake-foot, and there, while the others compacted the portables for portage, Iglesias and I, at cost of a ducking with mist-drops from the thickets, scrambled up a crag for a supreme view of the fair lake and the clear mountain. And we did well. Katahdin, from the hill guarding the exit of the Penobscot from Ripogenus, is eminent and emphatic, a signal and solitary pyramid, grander than any below the realms of the unchangeable, more distinctly mountainous than any mountain of those that stop short of the venerable honors of eternal snow.

We trod the trail, we others, easier than Cancut. He found it hard to thread the mazes of an overgrown path and navigate his canoe at the same time. "Better," thought he, as he staggered and plunged and bumped along, extricating his boat-bonnet now from a bower of raspberry-bushes, now from the branches of a brotherly birch-tree, — "better," thought he, "were I seated in what I bear, and bounding gayly over the billow. Peril is better than pother."

Bushwhacking thus for a league, we circumvented the peril, and came upon the river flowing fair and free. The trappers said adieu, and launched us. Back then they went to consult their traps and flay their fragrant captives, and we shot forward.

That was a day all poetry and all music. Mountain airs bent and blunted the noonday sunbeams. There was shade of delicate birches on either hand, whenever we loved to linger. Our feather-shallop went dancing on, fleet as the current, and whenever a passion for speed came after moments of luxurious sloth, we could change floating at the river's will into leaps and chasing, with a few strokes of the paddle. All was untouched, unvisited wilderness, and we from bend to bend the first discoverers. So we might fancy ourselves; for civilization had been here only to cut pines, not to plant houses. Yet these fair curves, and liberal reaches, and bright rapids of the birchen-bowered river were only solitary, not lonely. It is never

lonely with Nature. Without unnatural men or
unnatural beasts, she is capital society by herself.
And so we found her, — a lovely being in perfect
toilet, which I describe, in an indiscriminating,
masculine way, by saying that it was a forest and
a river and lakes and a mountain and doubtless
sky, all made resplendent by her judicious disposition of a most becoming light. Iglesias and I,
being old friends, were received into close intimacy. She smiled upon us unaffectedly, and had
a thousand exquisite things to say, drawing us out
also, with feminine tact, to say our best things,
and teaching us to be conscious, in her presence,
of more delicate possibilities of refinement and a
tenderer poetic sense. So we voyaged through
the sunny hours, and were happy.

Yet there was no monotony in our progress.
We could not always drift and glide. Sometimes
we must fight our way. Below the placid reaches
were the inevitable "rips" and rapids : some we
could shoot without hitting anything ; some would
hit us heavily, did we try to shoot. Whenever
the rocks in the current were only as thick as the
plums in a boarding-school pudding, we could venture to run the gantlet ; whenever they multiplied
to a school-boy's ideal, we were arrested. Just at
the brink of peril we would sweep in by an eddy
into a shady pool by the shore. At such spots we
found a path across the carry. Cancut at once
proceeded to bonnet himself with the trickling
birch. Iglesias and I took up the packs and hur-

ried on with minds intent on berries. Berries we always found, — blueberries covered with a cloudy bloom, blueberries pulpy, saccharine, plenteous.

Often, when a portage was not quite necessary, a dangerous bit of white water would require the birch to be lightened. Cancut must steer her alone over the foam, while we, springing ashore, raced through the thick of the forest, tore through the briers, and plunged through the punk of trees older than history, now rotting where they fell, slain by Time the Giganticide. Cancut then had us at advantage. Sometimes we had laughed at him, when he, a good-humored malaprop, made vague clutches at the thread of discourse. Now suppose he should take a fancy to drop down stream and leave us. What then? Berries then, and little else, unless we had a chance at a trout or a partridge. It is not cheery, but dreary, to be left in pathlessness, blanketless, guideless, and with breadths of lake and mountain and Nature, shaggy and bearish, between man and man. With the consciousness of a latent shudder in our hearts at such a possibility, we parted brier and bramble until the rapid was passed, we scuffled hastily through to the river-bank, and there always, in some quiet nook, was a beacon of red-flannel shirt among the green leaves over the blue and shadowy water, and always the fast-sailing Cancut awaiting us, making the woods resound to amicable hails, and ready again to be joked and to retaliate.

Such alternations made our voyage a charming

olla. We had the placid glide, the fleet dash, the wild career, the pause, the landing, the agreeable interlude of a portage, and the unburdened stampede along-shore. Thus we won our way, or our way wooed us on, until, in early afternoon, a lovely lakelet opened before us. The fringed shores retired, and, as we shot forth upon wider calm, lo, Katahdin ! unlooked for, at last, as a revolution. Our boat ruffled its shadow, doing pretty violence to its dignity, that we might know the greater grandeur of the substance. There was a gentle agency of atmosphere softening the bold forms of this startling neighbor, and giving it distance, lest we might fear it would topple and crush us. Clouds, level below, hid the summit and towered aloft. Among them we might imagine the mountain rising with thousands more of feet of heaven-piercing height : there is one degree of sublimity in mystery, as there is another degree in certitude.

We lay to in a shady nook, just off Katahdin's reflection in the river, while Iglesias sketched him. Meanwhile I, analyzing my view, presently discovered a droll image in the track of a land-avalanche down the front. It was a comical fellow, a little giant, a colossal dwarf, six hundred feet high, and should have been thrice as tall, had it had any proper development, — for out of his head grew two misdirected skeleton legs, "hanging down and dangling." The countenance was long, elfin, sneering, solemn, as of a truculent demon, saddish for his trade, an ashamed, but unrepentant rascal. He had two immense erect ears, and in his boisterous position had suffered a loss of hair, wearing nothing save an impudent scalp-lock. A very grotesque personage. Was he the guardian imp, the legendary Eft of Katahdin, scoffing already at us as verdant, and warning that he would make us unhappy, if we essayed to appear in demon realms and on Brocken heights without initiation?

" A terrible pooty mountain," Cancut observed ; and so it is.

Not to fail in topographical duty, I record, that near this lakelet flows in the river Sowadehunk, and not far below, a sister streamlet, hardly less melodiously named Ayboljockameegus. Opposite the latter we landed and encamped, with Katahdin full in front, and broadly visible.

CHAPTER XII.

CAMP KATAHDIN.

OUR camping-place was worthy of its view. On the bank, high and dry, a noble yellow birch had been strong enough to thrust back the forest, making a glade for its own private abode. Other travellers had already been received in this natural pavilion. We had had predecessors, and they had built them a hut, a half roof of hemlock bark, resting on a frame. Time had developed the wrinkles in this covering into cracks, and cracks only wait to be leaks. First, then, we must mend our mansion. Material was at hand; hemlocks, with a back-load of bark, stood ready to be disburdened. In August they have worn their garment so long that they yield it unwillingly. Cancut's axe, however, was insinuating, not to say peremptory. He peeled off and brought great scales of rough purple roofing, and we disposed them, according to the laws of forest architecture, upon our cabin. It became a good example of the *renaissance*. Storm, if such a traveller were approaching, was shut out at top and sides; our blankets could become curtains in front and completely hide us from that unwelcome vagrant, should he peer about seeking whom he might duck and what he might damage.

Our lodge, built, must be furnished. We need a luxurious carpet, couch, and bed; and if we have these, will be content without secondary articles. Here, too, material was ready, and only the artist wanting, to use it. While Cancut peeled the hemlocks, Iglesias and I stripped off armfuls of boughs and twigs from the spruces to "bough down" our camp. "Boughing down" is shingling the floor elaborately with evergreen foliage; and when it is done well, the result counts among the high luxuries of the globe. As the feathers of this bed are harsh stems covered with leafage, the process of bed-making must be systematic, the stems thoroughly covered, and the surface smooth and elastic.

I have slept on the various beds of the world, — in a hammock, in a pew, on German feathers, on a bear-skin, on a mat, on a hide ; all, all give but a feeble, restless, unrecreating slumber, compared to the spruce or hemlock bed in a forest of Maine. This is fragrant, springy, soft, well-fitting, better than any Sybarite's couch of uncrumpled rose-leaves. It sweetly rustles when you roll, and, by a gentle titillation with the little javelin-leaves, keeps up a pleasant electricity over the cuticle. Rheumatism never, after nights on such a bed ; agues never ; vigor, ardor, fervor, always.

We despatched our camp-building and bed-making with speed, for we had a purpose. The Penobscot was a very beautiful river, and the Ayboljockameegus a very pretty stream ; and if there is one place in the world where trout, at certain seasons, are likely to be found, it is in a beautiful river at the mouth of a pretty stream. Now we wanted trout ; it was in the programme that something more delicate than salt-pork should grace our banquets before Katahdin. Cancut sustained our *a priori*, that trout were waiting for us over by the Aybol. By this time the tree-shadows, so stiff at noon, began to relax and drift down stream, cooling the surface. The trout could leave their shy lairs down in the chilly deeps, and come up without fear of being parboiled. Besides, as evening came, trout thought of their supper, as we did of ours.

Hereupon I had a new sensation. We made ready our flies and our rods, and embarked, as I supposed, to be ferried across and fish from *terra firma*. But no. Cancut dropped anchor very quietly opposite the Aybol's mouth. Iglesias, the man of Maine experience, seemed naught surprised. We were to throw our lines, as it appeared, from the birch; we were to peril our lives on the unsteady basis of a roly-poly vessel, — to keep our places and ballast our bowl, during the excitement of hooking pounds. Self-poise is an acrobatic feat, when a person, not loaded at the heels, undertakes trout-fishing from a birch.

We threw our flies. Instantly at the lucky hackle something darted, seized it, and whirled to fly, with the unwholesome bit in its mouth, up the peaceful Ayboljockameegus. But the lucky man, and he happened to be the novice, forgot, while giving the capturing jerk of his hook, that his fulcrum was not solid rock. The slight shell tilted, turned — over not quite, over enough to give everybody a start. One lesson teaches the docile. Caution thereafter presided over our fishing. She told us to sit low, keep cool, cast gently, strike firmly, play lightly, and pull in steadily. So we did. As the spotted sparklers were rapidly translated from water to a lighter element, a well-fed cheerfulness developed in our trio. We could not speak, for fear of breaking the spell; we smiled at each other. Twenty-three times the smile went round. Twenty-three trout, and not a pigmy among them, lay at our feet. More fish for one dinner and breakfast would be waste and wanton self-indulgence.   We stopped.   And I must avow, not to claim too much heroism, that the fish had also stopped.   So we paddled home contented.

Then, O Walton! O Davy! O Scrope! ye fishers hard by taverns! luxury was ours of which ye know no more than a Chinaman does of music. Under the noble yellow birch we cooked our own fish.   We used our scanty kitchen-battery with skill.   We cooked with the high art of simplicity. Where Nature has done her best, only fools rush in to improve : on the salmonids, fresh and salt; she has lavished her creative refinements ; cookery should only ripen and develop.   From our silver gleaming pile of pounders, we chose the larger and the smaller for appropriate experiments.   Then we tested our experiments ; we tasted our examples. Success.   And success in science proves knowledge and skill.   We feasted.   The delicacy of our food made each feaster a finer essence.

So we supped, reclined upon our couch of spruce-twigs.   In our good cheer we pitied the Eft of Katahdin : he might sneer, but he was supperless. We were grateful to Nature for the grand mountain, for the fair and sylvan woods, for the lovely river and what it had yielded us.

By the time we had finished our flaky fare and sipped our chocolate from the Magdalena, Night announced herself, — Night, a jealous, dark lady, eclipsed and made invisible all her rivals, that she might solely possess us.   Night's whispers lulled us.   The rippling river, the rustling leaves, the hum of insects, grew more audible ; and these are gentle sounds that prove wide quietude in Nature, and tell man that the burr and buzz in his day-laboring brain have ceased, and he had better be breathing deep in harmony. So we disposed our-selves upon the fragrant couch of spruce-boughs, and sank slowly and deeper into sleep, as divers sink into the thick waters down below, into the dreamy waters far below the plunge of sunshine.

By and by, as the time came for rising to the surface again, and the mind began to be half con-scious of facts without it, as the diver may half perceive light through thinning strata of sea, there penetrated through my last layers of slumber a pungent odor of wetted embers. It was raining quietly. Drip was the pervading sound, as if the rain-drops were counting aloud the leaves of the forest. Evidently a resolute and permanent wet-ting impended. On rainy days one does not climb Katahdin. Instead of rising by starlight, break-fasting by gray, and starting by rosy dawn, it would be policy to persuade night to linger long into the hours of a dull day. When daylight finally came, dim and sulky, there was no rivalry among us which should light the fire. We did not leap, but trickled slowly forth into the inhos-pitable morning, all forlorn. Wet days in camp try " grit." " Clear grit " brightens more crys-talline, the more it is rained upon ; sham grit dis-solves into mud and water.

Yankees, who take in pulverized granite with

every breath of their native dust, are not likely to
melt in a drizzle. We three certainly did not.
We reacted stoutly against the forlorn weather,
unpacking our internal stores of sunshine, as a
camel in a desert draws water from his inner tank
when outer water fails. We made the best of it.
A breakfast of trout and trimmings looks nearly
as well and tastes nearly as well in a fog as in a
glare : that we proved by experience at Camp
Katahdin.

We could not climb the mountain dark and dim ;
we would not be idle : what was to be done ?
Much. Much for sport and for use. We shouldered the axe and sallied into the dripping forest.
Only a faint smoke from the smouldering logs
curled up among the branches of the yellow birch
over camp. We wanted a big smoke, and chopped
at the woods for fuel. Speaking for myself, I
should say that our wood-work was ill done. Iglesias smiled at my axe-handling, and Cancut at his,
as chopping we sent chips far and wide.

The busy, keen, short strokes of the axe re-
sounded through the forest. When these had
done their work, and the bungler paused amid his
wasteful *débris* to watch his toil's result, first was
heard a rustle of leaves, as if a passing whirlwind
had alighted there ; next came the crack of bursting sinews ; then the groan of a great riving spasm,
and the tree, decapitated at its foot, crashed to
earth, with a vain attempt to clutch for support at
the stiff, unpitying arms of its woodland brotherhood.

Down was the tree, — fallen, but so it should not lie. This tree we proposed to promote from brute matter, mere lumber, downcast and dejected, into finer essence : fuel was to be made into fire.

First, however, the fuel must be put into portable shape. We top-sawyers went at our prostrate and vanquished non-resistant, and without mercy mangled and dismembered him, until he was merely a bare trunk, a torso incapable of restoration.

While we were thus busy, useful, and happy, the dripping rain, like a clepsydra, told off the morning moments. The dinner-hour drew nigh. We had determined on a feast, and trout were to be its daintiest dainty. But before we cooked our trout, we must, according to sage Kitchener's advice, catch our trout. They were, we felt confident, awaiting us in the refrigerate larder at hand. We waited until the confusing pepper of a shower had passed away and left the water calm. Then softly and deftly we propelled our bark across to the Ayboljockameegus. We tossed to the fish humbugs of wool, silk, and feathers, gauds such as captivate the greedy or the guileless. Again the " gobemouches " trout, the fellows on the look-out for novelty, dashed up and swallowed disappointing juiceless morsels, and with them swallowed hooks.

We caught an apostolic boat-load of beauties fresh and blooming as Aurora, silver as the morning star, gemmy with eye-spots as a tiger-lily.

O feast most festal! Iglesias, of course, was the great artist who devised and mainly executed it. As well as he could, he covered his pot and pan from the rain, admitting only enough to season each dish with gravy direct from the skies. As day had ripened, the banquet grew ripe. Then as day declined, we reclined on our triclinium of hemlock and spruce boughs, and made high festival, toasting each other in the uninebriating flow of our beverages. Jollity reigned. Cancut fattened, and visibly broadened. Toward the veriest end of the banquet, we seemed to feel that there had been a slight sameness in its courses. The Bill of Fare, however, proved the freest variety. And at the close we sat and sipped our chocolate with uttermost content. No *garçon*, cringing, but firm, would here intrude with the unhandsome bill. Nothing to pay is the rarest of pleasures. This dinner we had caught ourselves, we had cooked ourselves, and had eaten for the benefit of ourselves and no other. There was nothing to repent of afterwards in the way of extravagance, and certainly nothing of indigestion. Indigestion in the forest primeval, in the shadow of Katahdin, is impossible.

While we dined, we talked of our to-morrow's climb of Katahdin. We were hopeful. We disbelieved in obstacles. To-morrow would be fine. We would spring early from our elastic bed and stride topwards. Iglesias nerved himself and me with a history of his ascent some years before, up the eastern side of the mountain. He had left the house of Mr. Hunt, the outsider at that time of Eastern Maine, with a squad of lumbermen, and with them tramped up the furrow of a land-avalanche to the top, spending wet and ineffective days in the dripping woods, and vowing then to return and study the mountain from our present camping-spot. I recalled also the first recorded ascent of the Natardin or Catardin Mountain by Mr. Turner in 1804, printed in the Massachusetts Historical Society's Collections, and identified the stream up whose valley he climbed with the Ayboljockameegus. Cancut offered valuable contributions to our knowledge from his recent ascent with our Boston predecessors. To-morrow we would verify our recollections and our fancies.

And so good night, and to our spruce bed.

CHAPTER XIII.

UP KATAHDIN.

NEXT morning, when we awoke, just before the gray of dawn, the sky was clear and scintillating; but there was a white cotton night-cap on the head of Katahdin. As we inspected him, he drew his night-cap down farther, hinting that he did not wish to see the sun that day. When a mountain is thus in the sulks after a storm, it is as well not to disturb him : he will not offer the prize of a view.   Experience taught us this : but then experience is only an empiric at the best.

Besides, whether Katahdin were bare-headed or cloud-capped, it would be better to blunder upward than lounge all day in camp and eat Sybaritic dinners.   We longed for the nervy climb.   We must have it.   "Up!" said tingling blood to brain. "Dash through the forest!" Grasp the crag, and leap the cleft! Sweet flash forth the streamlets from granite fissures.   To breathe the winds that smite the peaks is life."

As soon as dawn bloomed in the woods we breakfasted, and ferried the river before sunrise. The ascent subdivides itself into five zones.   1. A scantily wooded acclivity, where bears abound. 2. A dense, swampy forest region. 3. Steep, mossy mountain-side, heavily wooded. 4. A belt of dwarf spruces, nearly impenetrable.   5. Ragged rock.

Cancut was our leader to-day.   There are by far too many blueberries in the first zone.   No one, of course, intends to dally, but the purple beauties tempted, and too often we were seduced.   Still such yielding spurred us on to hastier speed, when we looked up after delay and saw the self-denying far ahead.

To write an epic or climb a mountain is merely a dogged thing ; the result is more interesting to most than the process.   Mountains, being cloud-compellers, are rain-shedders, and the shed water

will not always flow with decorous gayety in dell
or glen. Sometimes it stays bewildered in a bog,
and here the climber must plunge. In the moist
places great trees grow, die, fall, rot, and barricade the way with their corpses. Katahdin has to
endure all the ills of mountain being, and we had
all the usual difficulties to fight through doggedly.
When we were clumsy, we tumbled and rose up
torn. Still we plodded on, following a path blazed
by the Bostonians, Cancut's late charge, and we
grumblingly thanked them.

Going up, we got higher and drier. The mountain-side became steeper than it could stay, and
several land-avalanches, ancient or modern, crossed
our path. It would be sad to think that all the
eternal hills were crumbling thus, outwardly, unless we knew that they bubble up inwardly as fast.
Posterity is thus cared for in regard to the picturesque. Cascading streams also shot by us, carrying light and music. From them we stole refresh-
ment, and did not find the waters mineral and astringent, as Mr. Turner, the first climber, calumni-
ously asserts.

The trees were still large and surprisingly parallel to the mountain wall. Deep soft moss covered
whatever was beneath, and sometimes this would
yield and let the foot measure a crevice. Perilous
pitfalls ; but we clambered unharmed. The moss,
so rich, deep, soft, and earthily fragrant, was a
springy stair-carpet of a steep stairway. And
sometimes when the carpet slipped and the state of

heels over head seemed imminent, we held to the baluster-trees, as one after wassail clings to the lamp-post.

Even on this minor mountain the law of diminishing vegetation can be studied. The great trees abandoned us, and stayed indolently down in shelter. Next the little wiry trees ceased to be the comrades of our climb. They were no longer to be seen planted upon jutting crags, and, bold as standard-bearers, inciting us to mount higher. Big spruces, knobby with balls of gum, dwindled away into little ugly dwarf spruces, hostile, as dwarfs are said to be always, to human comfort. They grew man-high, and hedged themselves together into a dense thicket. We could not go under, nor over, nor through. To traverse them at all, we must recall the period when we were squirrels or cats, in some former state of being.

Somehow we pierced, as man does ever, whether he owes it to the beast or the man in him. From time to time, when in this struggle we came to an open point of rock, we would remember that we were on high, and turn to assure ourselves that nether earth was where we had left it. We always found it *in situ*, in belts green, white, and blue, a tricolor of woods, water, and sky. Lakes were there without number, forest without limit. We could not analyze yet, for there was work to do. Also, whenever we paused, there was the old temptation, blueberries. Every outcropping ledge offered store of tonic, ozone-fed blueberries, or of mountain-cranberries, crimson and of concentrated flavor, or of the white snowberry, most delicate of fruits that grow.

As we were creeping over the top of the dwarf wood, Cancut, who was in advance, suddenly disappeared; he seemed to fall through a gap in the spruces, and we heard his voice calling in cavernous tones. We crawled forward and looked over. It was the upper camp of the Bostonians. They had profited by a hole in the rocks, and chopped away the stunted scrubs to enlarge it into a snug artificial abyss. It was snug, and so to the eye is a cell at Sing-Sing. If they were very misshapen Bostonians, they may have succeeded in lying there comfortably. I looked down ten feet into the rough chasm, and I saw, *Corpo di Bacco!* I saw a cork.

To this station our predecessors had come in an easy day's walk from the river; here they had tossed through a night, and given a whole day to finish the ascent, returning hither again for a second night. As we purposed to put all this travel within one day, we could not stay and sympathize with the late tenants. A little more squirrel-like skipping and cat-like creeping over the spruces, and we were out among bulky boulders and rough *débris* on a shoulder of the mountain. Alas! the higher, the more hopeless. Katahdin, as he had taken pains to inform us, meant to wear the veil all day. He was drawing down the white drapery about his throat and letting it fall over his shoulders. Sun and wind struggled mightily with his sulky fit ; sunshine rifted off bits of the veil, and wind seized, whirled them away, and, dragging them over the spruces below, tore them to rags. Evidently, if we wished to see the world, we must stop here and survey, before the growing vapor covered all. We climbed to the edge of Cloudland, and stood fronting the semicircle of southward view.

Katahdin's self is finer than what Katahdin sees. Katahdin is distinct, and its view is indistinct. It is a vague panorama, a mappy, unmethodic maze of water and woods, very roomy, very vast, very simple, — and these are capital qualities, but also quite monotonous. A lover of largeness and scope has the proper emotions stirred, but a lover of variety very soon finds himself counting the lakes. It is a wide view, and it is a proud thing for a man six feet or less high, to feel that he himself, standing on something he himself has climbed, and having Katahdin under his feet a mere convenience, can see all Maine. It does not make Maine less, but the spectator more, and that is a useful moral result. Maine's face, thus exposed, has almost no features ; there are no great mountains visible, none that seem more than green hillocks in the distance. Besides sky, Katahdin's view contains only the two primal necessities of wood and water. Nowhere have I seen such breadth of solemn forest, gloomy, were it not for the cheerful interruption of many fair lakes, and bright ways of river linking them.

Far away on the southern horizon we detected the heights of Mount Desert, our old familiar haunt. All the northern semicircle was lost to us by the fog. We lost also the view of the mountain itself. All the bleak, lonely, barren, ancient waste of the bare summit was shrouded in cold fog. The impressive gray ruin and Titanic havoc of a granite mountain-top, the heaped boulders, the crumbling crags, the crater-like depression, the long stern reaches of sierra, the dark curving slopes channelled and polished by the storms and fine drifting mists of æons, the downright plunge of precipices, all the savageness of harsh rock, unsoftened by other vegetation than rusty moss and the dull green splashes of lichen, all this was hidden, except when the mist, white and delicate where we stood, but thick and black above, opened whimsically and delusively, as mountain mists will do, and gave us vistas into the upper desolation. After such momentary rifts the mist thickened again, and swooped forward as if to involve our station ; but noon sunshine, reverberated from the plains and valleys and lakes below, was our ally ; sunshine checked the overcoming mist, and it stayed overhead, an unwelcome parasol, making our August a chilly November. Besides what our eyes lost, our minds lost, unless they had imagination enough to create it, the sentiment of triumph and valiant energy that the man of body and soul feels upon the windy heights, the highest, whence he looks far and wide, like a master of realms,

and knows that the world is his; and they lost
the sentiment of solemn joy that the man of soul
recognizes as one of the surest intimations of
immortality, stirring within him, whenever he is
in the unearthly regions, the higher world.

We stayed studying the pleasant solitude and
dreamy breadth of Katahdin's panorama for a long
time, and every moment the mystery of the mist
above grew more enticing. Pride also was awa-
kened. We turned from sunshine and Cosmos into
fog and Chaos. We made ourselves quite miserable for naught. We clambered up into Nowhere,
into a great, white, ghostly void. We saw nothing
but the rough surfaces we trod. We pressed along
crater-like edges, and all below was filled with mist,
troubled and rushing upward like the smoke of a
volcano. Up we went, — nothing but granite and
gray dimness. Where we arrived we know not.
It was a top, certainly: that was proved by the
fact that there was nothing within sight. We
cannot claim that it was the topmost top; Kim-
chinjinga might have towered within pistol-shot;
popgun-shot was our extremest range of vision,
except for one instant, when a kind-hearted sunbeam gave us a vanishing glimpse of a white lake
and breadth of forest far in the unknown North
toward Canada.

When we had thus reached the height of our
folly and made nothing by it, we addressed ourselves to the descent, no wiser for our pains.
Descent is always harder than ascent, for divine

ambitions are stronger and more prevalent than degrading passions. And when Katahdin is befogged, descent is much more perilous than ascent. We edged along very cautiously by remembered landmarks the way we had come, and so, after a dreary march of a mile or so through desolation, issued into welcome sunshine and warmth at our point of departure. When I said "we," I did not include the gravestone pedler. He, like a sensible fellow, had determined to stay and eat berries rather than breathe fog. While we wasted our time, he had made the most of his. He had cleared Katahdin's shoulders of fruit, and now, cuddled in a sunny cleft, slept the sleep of the well-fed. His red shirt was a cheerful beacon on our weary way. We took in the landscape with one slow, comprehensive look, and, waking Cancut suddenly, (who sprang to his feet amazed, and cried "Fire!") we dashed down the mountain-side.

It was long after noon; we were some dozen of miles from camp; we must speed. No glissade was possible, nor plunge such as travellers make down through the ash-heaps of Vesuvius; but, having once worried through the wretched little spruces, mean counterfeits of trees, we could fling ourselves down from mossy step to step, measuring off the distance by successive leaps of a second each, and alighting, sound after each, on moss yielding as a cushion.

On we hastened, retracing our footsteps of the morning across the avalanches of crumbled granite,

5 *

through the bogs, along the brooks ; undelayed by the beauty of sunny glade or shady dell, never stopping to botanize or to classify, we traversed zone⁻ after zone, and safely ran the gantlet of the possible bears on the last level.   We found lowland Nature still the same ; Ayboljockameegus was flowing still ; so was Penobscot ; no pirate had made way with the birch ; we embarked and paddled to camp.

The first thing, when we touched *terra firma,* was to look back regretfully toward the mountain. Regret changed to wrath, when we perceived its summit all clear and mistless, smiling warmly to the low summer's sun.   The rascal evidently had only waited until we were out of sight in the woods to throw away his night-cap.

One long rainy day had somewhat disgusted us with the old hemlock-covered camp in the glade of the yellow birch, and we were reasonably and not unreasonably morbid after our disappointment with Katahdin.   We resolved to decamp.   In the last hour of sunlight, floating pleasantly from lovely reach to reach, and view to view, we could choose a spot of bivouac where no home-scenery would recall any sorry fact of the past.   We loved this gentle gliding by the tender light of evening over the shadowy river, marking the rhythm of our musical progress by touches of the paddle.   We determined, too, that the balance of bodily forces should be preserved : legs had been well stretched over the bogs and boulders ; now for the arms.

Never did our sylvan sojourn look so fair as when we quitted it, and seemed to see among the streaming sunbeams in the shadows the Hamadryads of the spot returned, and waving us adieux. We forgot how damp and leaks and puddles had forced themselves upon our intimacy there; we remembered that we were gay, though wet, and there had known the perfection of Ayboljockameegus trout.

As we drifted along the winding river, between the shimmering birches on either bank, Katahdin watched us well. Sometimes he would show the point of his violet gray peak over the woods, and sometimes, at a broad bend of the water, he revealed himself fully, and threw his great image down beside for our nearer view. We began to forgive him, to disbelieve in any personal spite of his, and to recall that he himself, seen thus, was far more precious than any mappy dulness we could have seen from his summit. One great upright pyramid like this was worth a continent of grovelling acres.

Sunset came, and with it we landed at a point below a lake-like stretch of the river, where the charms of a neighbor and a distant view of the mountain combined. Cancut the Unwearied roofed with boughs an old frame for drying moose-hides, while Iglesias sketched, and I worshipped Katahdin. Has my reader heard enough of it, — a hillock only six thousand feet high? We are soon to drift away, and owe it here as kindly a farewell as it gave us in that radiant twilight by the river.

From our point of view we raked the long stern front tending westward. Just before sunset, from beneath a belt of clouds evanescing over the summit, an inconceivably tender, brilliant glow of rosy violet mantled downward, filling all the valley. Then the violet purpled richer and richer, and darkened slowly to solemn blue, that blended with the gloom of the pines and shadowy channelled gorges down the steep. The peak was still in sunlight, and suddenly, half-way down, a band of roseate clouds, twining and changing like a choir of Bacchantes, soared around the western edge and hung poised above the unillumined forests at the mountain-base; light as air they came and went and faded away, ghostly, after their work of momentary beauty was done. One slight maple, prematurely ripened to crimson and heralding the pomp of autumn, repeated the bright cloud-color amid the vivid verdure of a little island, and its image wavering in the water sent the flame floating nearly to our feet.

Such are the transcendent moments of Nature, unseen and disbelieved by the untaught. The poetic soul lays hold of every such tender pageant of beauty and keeps it forever. Iglesias, having an additional method of preservation, did not fail to pencil rapidly the wondrous scene. When he had finished his dashing sketch of this glory, so transitory, he peppered the whole with cabalistic cipher, which only he could interpret into beauty.

Cancut's camp-fire now began to overpower the

faint glimmers of twilight. The single-minded Cancut, little distracted by emotions, had heaped together logs enough to heat any mansion for a winter. The warmth was welcome, and the great flame, with its bright looks of familiar comradery, and its talk like the complex murmur of a throng, made a fourth in our party by no means terrible, as some other incorporeal visitors might have been. Fire was not only a talker, but an important actor : Fire cooked for us our evening chocolate ; Fire held the candlestick, while we, without much ceremony of undressing, disposed ourselves upon our spruce-twig couch ; and Fire watched over our slumbers, crouching now as if some stealthy step were approaching, now lifting up its head and peering across the river into some recess where the water gleamed and rustled under dark shadows, and now sending far and wide over the stream and the clearing and into every cleft of the forest a penetrating illumination, a blaze of light, death to all treacherous ambush. So Fire watched while we slept, and when safety came with the earliest gray of morning, it, too, covered itself with ashes and slept.

CHAPTER XIV.

HOMEWARD.

BEAUTIFUL, beautiful, beautiful is dawn in the woods. Sweet the first opalescent stir, as if the vanguard sunbeams shivered as they dashed along the chilly reaches of night. And the growth of day, through violet and rose and all its golden glow of promise, is tender and tenderly strong, as the deepening passions of dawning love. Presently up comes the sun very peremptory, and says to people, "Go about your business! Laggards not allowed in Maine! Nothing here to repent of, while you lie in bed and curse to-day because it cannot shake off the burden of yesterday; all clear the past here; all serene the future: into it at once!"

Birch was ready for us. Objects we travel on, if horses, often stampede or are stampeded; if wagons, they break down; if shanks, they stiffen; if feet, they chafe. No such trouble befalls Birch; leak, however, it will, as ours did this morning. We gently beguiled it into the position taken tearfully by unwhipped little boys, when they are about to receive birch. Then, with a firebrand, the pitch of the seams was easily persuaded to melt and spread a little over the leaky spot, and Birch was sound as a drum.

Staunch and sound Birch needed to be, for presently Penobscot, always a skittish young racer, began to grow lively after he had shaken off the weighty shadow of Katahdin, and, kicking up his heels, went galloping down hill, so furiously that we were at last, after sundry frantic plunges, compelled to get off his back before worse befell us. In the balmy morning we made our first portage through a wood of spruces. How light our firkin was growing! its pork, its hard-tack, and its condiments were diffused among us three, and had passed into muscle. Lake Degetus, as pretty a pocket lake as there is, followed the carry. Next came Lake Ambajeejus, larger, but hardly less lovely. Those who dislike long names may use its shorter Indian title, Umdo. We climbed a granite crag draped with moss long as the beard of a Druid, — a crag on the south side of Ambajeejus, or Umdo. Thence we saw Katahdin, noble as ever, unclouded in the sunny morning, near, and yet enchantingly vague, with the blue sky which surrounded it. It was still an isolate pyramid rising with no effect from the fair blue lakes and the fair green sea of the birch-forest, — a brilliant sea of woods, gay as the shallows of ocean shot through with sunbeams and sunlight reflected upward from golden sands.

We sped along all that exquisite day, best of all our poetic voyage. Sometimes we drifted and basked in sunshine, sometimes we lingered in the birchen shade ; we paddled from river to lake, from lake to river again ; the rapids whirled us along, surging and leaping under us with magnificent gal-

lop ; frequent carries struck in, that we might not
lose the forester in the waterman. It was a fresh
world that we traversed on our beautiful river-
path, — new as if no other had ever parted its over-
hanging bowers.

At noon we floated out upon Lakè Pemadum-
cook, the largest bulge of the Penobscot, and irregular as the verb To Be.   Lumbermen name it
Bammydumcook : Iglesias insisted upon this as the
proper reading ; and as he was the responsible
man of the party, I accepted it. Woods, woody
hills, and woody mountains surround Bammydumcook.   I have no doubt parts of it are pretty,
and will be famous in good time ; but we saw little.   By the time we were fairly out in the lake and
away from the sheltering shore, a black squall to
windward, hiding all the West, warned us to fly,
for birches swamp in squalls.   We deemed that
Birch, having brought us through handsomely, deserved a better fate : swamped it must not be. We
plied paddle valiantly, and were almost safe behind
an arm of the shore when the storm overtook us,
and in a moment more, safe, with a canoe only half-
full of Bammydumcook water.

It is easy to speak in scoffing tone ; but when
that great roaring blackness sprang upon us, and
the waves, showing their white teeth, snarled
around, we were far from being in the mood to
scoff. It is impossible to say too much of the
charm of this gentle scenery, mingled with the
charm of this adventurous sailing. And then there

were no mosquitoes, no alligators, no serpents
uncomfortably hugging the trees, no miasmas lurk-
ing near; and blueberries always. Dust there was
none, nor the things that make dust. But Iglesias
and I were breathing AIR, — Air sweet, tender,
strong, and 'pure as an ennobling love. It was a
day very happy, for Iglesias and I were near what
we both love almost best of all the dearly-beloveds.
It is such influence as this that rescues the thought
and the hand of an artist from enervating manner-
ism. He cannot be satisfied with vague blotches
of paint to convey impressions so distinct and vivid
as those he is forced to take direct from a Nature
like this. He must be true and powerful.

The storm rolled by and gave us a noble view of
Katahdin, beyond a broad, beautiful scope of water,
and rising seemingly directly from it. We fled before another squall, over another breadth of Bammydumcook, and made a portage around a great
dam below the lake. The world should know that
at this dam the reddest, spiciest, biggest, thickest
wintergreen-berries in the world are to be found,
beautiful as they are good.

Birch had hitherto conducted himself with perfect propriety. I, the novice, had acquired such
entire confidence in his stability of character that I
treated him with careless ease, and never listened
to the warnings of my comrades that he would
serve me a trick. Cancut navigated Birch through
some white water below the dam, and Birch went
curveting proudly and gracefully along, evidently

H

feeling his oats.   When Iglesias and I came to embark, I, the novice, perhaps a little intoxicated
with wintergreen-berries, stepped jauntily into the
laden boat.   Birch, alas ! failed me.   He tilted ; he
turned ; he took in Penobscot, — took it in by the
quart, by the gallon, by the barrel ; he would have
sunk without mercy, had not Iglesias and Cancut
succeeded in laying hold of a rock and restoring
equilibrium.   I could not have believed it of Birch.
I was disappointed, and in consternation ; and if I
had not known how entirely it was Birch's fault
that everybody was ducked and everybody now
had a wet blanket, I should have felt personally
foolish.   I punished myself for another's fault and
my own inexperience by assuming the wet blankets
as my share at the next carry.   I suppose few of
my readers imagine how many pounds of water a
blanket can absorb.

After camps at Katahdin any residence in the
woods without a stupendous mountain before the
door would have been tame.   It must have been
this, and not any wearying of sylvan life, that
made us hasten to reach the outermost log-house
at the Millinoket carry before nightfall.   The sensation of house and in-door life would be a new
one, and so satisfying in itself that we should not
demand beautiful objects to meet our first blink of
awakening eyes.

An hour before sunset, Cancut steered us toward
a beach, and pointed out a vista in the woods, evidently artificial, evidently a road trodden by feet

and hoofs, and ruled by parallel wheels. A road is one of the kindliest gifts of brother man to man : if a path in the wilderness, it comes forward like a friendly guide offering experience and proposing a comrade dash deeper into the unknown world ; if a highway, it is the great, bold, sweeping character with which civilization writes its autograph upon a continent. Leaving our plunder on the beach, beyond the reach of plunderers, whose great domain we were about to enter, we walked on toward the first house, compelled at parting to believe, that, though we did not love barbarism less, we loved civilization more. In the morning, Cancut should, with an ox-cart, bring Birch and our traps over the three miles of the carry.

CHAPTER XV.

OUT OF THE WOODS.

WHAT could society do without women and children ? Both we found at the first house, twenty miles from the second. The children buzzed about us ; the mother milked for us one of Maine's vanguard cows. She baked for us bread, fresh bread, — such bread ! not staff of life, — life's vaulting-pole. She gave us blueberries with cream of cream. Ah, what a change ! We sat on chairs, at a table,

and ate from plates.   There was a table-cloth, a
salt-cellar made of glass, of glass never seen at
camps near Katahdin.   There was a sugar-bowl, a
milk-jug, and other paraphernalia of civilization, including — O memories of Joseph Bourgogne ! — a
dome of baked beans, with a crag of pork project-
ing from the apex.   We partook decorously, with
controlled elbows, endeavoring to appear as if we
were accustomed to sit at tables and manage plates.
The men, women, and children of Millinoket were
hospitable and delighted to see strangers, and the
men, like all American men in the summer before a
Presidential election, wanted to talk politics.   Katahdin's last full-bodied appearance was here ; it
rises beyond a breadth of black forest, a bulkier
mass, but not so symmetrical as from the southern
points of view.   We slept that night on a feather-
bed, and took cold for want of air, beneath a
roof.

By the time we had breakfasted, Cancut arrived
with Birch on an ox-sledge.   Here our well-be-
loved west branch of the Penobscot, called of yore
Norimbagua, is married to the east branch, and of
course by marriage loses his identity, by and by,
changing from the wild, free, reckless rover of the
forest to a tamish family-man style of river, useful
to float rafts and turn mills.   However, during the
first moments of the honeymoon, the happy pair,
Mr. Penobscot and Miss Milly Noket, now a unit
under the marital name, are gay enough, and glide
along bowery reaches and in among fair islands,

with infinite endearments and smiles, making the
world very sparkling and musical there. By and
by they fall to romping, and, to avoid one of their
turbulent frolics, Cancut landed us, as he supposed, on the mainland, to lighten the canoe. Just
as he was sliding away down-stream, we discovered
that he had left us upon an island in the midst of
frantic, impassable rapids. "Stop, stop, John Gil-
pin!" and luckily he did stop, otherwise he would
have gone on to tide-water, ever thinking that we
were before him, while we, with our forest appetites, would have been glaring hungrily at each
other, or perhaps drawing lots for a cannibal doom.
Once again, as we were shooting a long rapid, a
table-top rock caught us in mid-current. We were
wrecked. It was critical. The waves swayed us
perilously this way and that. Birch would be full
of water, or overturned, in a moment. Small
chance for a swimmer in such maelstroms! All
this we saw, but had no time to shudder at. Aided
by the urgent stream, we carefully and delicately
— for a coarse movement would have been death
— wormed our boat off the rock, and went fleeting
through a labyrinth of new perils, onward, with a
wild exhilaration, like galloping through prairie on
fire. Of all the high distinctive national pleasures
of America, chasing buffalo, stump-speaking, and
the like, there is none so intense as shooting rapids in a birch. Whenever I recall our career down
the Penobscot, a longing comes over me to repeat it.

We dropped down stream without further adventures. We passed the second house, the first village, and other villages, very white and wide-awake, melodiously named Nickertow, Pattagumpus, and Mattascunk. We spent the first night at Mattawamkeag. We were again elbowed at a tavern table, and compelled to struggle with real and not ideal pioneers for fried beefsteak and soggy doughboys. The last river day was tame, but not tiresome. We paddled stoutly by relays, stopping only once, at the neatest of farm-houses, to lunch on the most airy-substantial bread and baked apples and cream. It is surprising how confidential a traveller always is on the subject of his gastronomic delights. He will have the world know how he enjoyed his dinner, perhaps hoping that the world by sympathy will enjoy its own.

Late in the afternoon of our eighth day from Greenville, Moosehead Lake, we reached the end of birch-navigation, the great mill-dams of Indian Oldtown, near Bangor. Acres of great pine logs, marked three crosses and a dash, were floating here at the boom; we saw what Maine men supposed timber was made for. According to the view acted upon at Oldtown, Senaglecouna has been for a century or centuries training up its lordly pines, that gang-saws, worked by Penobscot, should shriek through their helpless cylinders, gnashing them into boards and chewing them into sawdust.

Poor Birch! how out of its element it looked,

hoisted on a freight-car and travelling by rail to Bangor ! There we said adieu to Birch and Cancut. Peace and plenteous provender be with him ! Journeys make friends or foes ; and we remember our fat guide, not as one who from time to time just did not drown us, but as the jolly comrade of eight days crowded with novelty and beauty, and fine, vigorous, manly life.

LOVE AND SKATES.

6

LOVE AND SKATES.

CHAPTER I.

A KNOT AND A MAN TO CUT IT.

CONSTERNATION! Consternation in the back office of Benjamin Brummage, Esq., banker in Wall Street.

Yesterday down came Mr. Superintendent Whiffler, from Dunderbunk, up the North River, to say, that, "unless something be done, *at once*, the Dunderbunk Foundry and Iron-Works must wind up." President Brummage forthwith convoked his Directors. And here they sat around the green table, forlorn as the guests at a Barmecide feast.

Well they might be forlorn! It was the rosy summer solstice, the longest and fairest day of all the year. But rose-color and sunshine had fled from Wall Street. Noisy Crisis towing black Panic, as a puffing steam-tug drags a three-decker cocked and primed for destruction, had suddenly sailed in upon Credit.

As all the green inch-worms vanish on the tenth of every June, so on the tenth of that June all the

money in America had buried itself and was as if
it were not.   Everybody and everything was ready
to fail.   If the hindmost brick went, down would
go the whole file.

There were ten Directors of the Dunderbunk
Foundry.

Now, not seldom, of a Board of ten Directors,
five are wise and five are foolish : five wise, who
bag all the Company's funds in salaries and
commissions for indorsing its paper ; five foolish,
who get no salaries, no commissions, no dividends,
—— nothing, indeed, but abuse from the stock-
holders, and the reputation of thieves.   That is to
say, five of the ten are pickpockets ; the other five,
pockets to be picked.

It happened that the Dunderbunk Directors
were all honest and foolish but one.   He, John
Churm, honest and wise, was off at the West, with
his Herculean shoulders at the wheels of a dead-
locked railroad.   These honest fellows did not
wish Dunderbunk to fail for several reasons. First,
it was not pleasant to lose their investment.   Second, one important failure might betray Credit to
Crisis with Panic at its heels, whereupon every investment would be in danger.   Third, what would
become of their Directorial reputations ?   From
President Brummage down, each of these gentlemen was one of the pockets to be picked in a great
many companies.   Each was of the first Wall-
Street fashion, invited to lend his name and take
stock in every new enterprise.   Any one of them

might have walked down town in a long patch-
work toga made of the newspaper advertisements
of boards in which his name proudly figured.   If
Dunderbunk failed, the toga was torn, and might
presently go to rags beyond repair.   The first rent
would inaugurate universal rupture.   How to
avoid this disaster ? — that was the question.

"State the case, Mr. Superintendent Whiffler,"
said President Brummage, in his pompous manner,
with its pomp a little collapsed, *pro tempore.*

Inefficient Whiffler whimpered out his story.

The confessions of an impotent executive are
sorry stuff to read.   Whiffler's long, dismal com-
plaint shall not be repeated.   He had taken a prosperous concern, had carried on things in his own
way, and now failure was inevitable.   He had
bought raw material lavishly, and worked it badly
into half-ripe material, which nobody wanted to
buy.   He was in arrears to his hands.   He had tried
to bully them, when they asked for their money.
They had insulted him, and threatened to knock
off work, unless they were paid at once.   "A set
of horrid ruffians," Whiffler said, — "and his life
would n't be safe many days among them."

"Withdraw, if you please, Mr. Superintendent,"
President Brummage requested.   "The Board will
discuss measures of relief."

The more they discussed, the more consternation.
Nobody said anything to the purpose, except Mr.
Sam Gwelp, his late father's lubberly son and suc-
cessor.

"Blast!" said he; "we shall have to let it slide!"

Into this assembly of imbeciles unexpectedly entered Mr. John Churm. He had set his Western railroad trains rolling, and was just returned to town. Now he was ready to put those Herculean shoulders at any other bemired and rickety no-go-cart.

Mr. Churm was not accustomed to be a Director in feeble companies. He came into Dunderbunk recently as executor of his friend Damer, a year ago bored to death by a silly wife.

Churm's bristly aspect and incisive manner made him a sharp contrast to Brummage. The latter personage was flabby in flesh, and the oppressively civil counter-jumper style of his youth had grown naturally into a deportment of most imposing pomposity.

The Tenth Director listened to the President's recitative of their difficulties, chorused by the Board.

"Gentlemen," said Director Churm, "you want two things. The first is Money!"

He pronounced this cabalistic word with such magic power, that all the air seemed instantly filled with a cheerful flight of gold American eagles, each carrying a double eagle on its back and a silver dollar in its claws; and all the soil of America seemed to sprout with coin, as after a shower a meadow sprouts with the yellow buds of the dandelion.

"Money! yes, Money!" murmured the Directors.

It seemed a word of good omen, now.

"The second thing," resumed the new-comer, "is a Man!"

The Directors looked at each other and did not see such a being.

"The actual Superintendent of Dunderbunk is a dunderhead," said Churm.

"Pun!" cried Sam Gwelp, waking up from a snooze.

Several of the Directors, thus instructed, started a complimentary laugh.

"Order, gentlemen! Orrderr!" said the President, severely, rapping with a paper-cutter.

"We must have a Man, not a Whiffler!" Churm continued. "And I have one in my eye."

Everybody examined his eye.

"Would you be so good as to name him?" said Old Brummage, timidly.

He wanted to see a Man, but feared the strange creature might be dangerous.

"Richard Wade," says Churm.

They did not know him. The name sounded forcible.

"He has been in California," the nominator said.

A shudder ran around the green table. They seemed to see a frowzy desperado, shaggy as a bison, in a red shirt and jackboots, hung about the waist with an assortment of six-shooters and bowie-knives, and standing against a background of mustangs, monte-banks, and lynch-law.

"We must get Wade," Churm says, with authority. "He knows Iron by heart. He can handle Men. I will back him with my blank check, to any amount, to his order."

Here a murmur of applause, swelling to a cheer, burst from the Directors.

Everybody knew that the Geological Bank deemed Churm's deposits the fundamental stratum of its wealth. They lay there in the vaults, like underlying granite. When hot times came, they boiled up in a mountain to buttress the world.

Churm's blank check seemed to wave in the air like an oriflamme of victory. Its payee might come from Botany Bay; he might wear his beard to his knees, and his belt stuck full of howitzers and boomerangs; he might have been repeatedly hung by Vigilance Committees, and as often cut down and revived by galvanism; but brandishing that check, good for anything less than a million, every Director in Wall Street was his slave, his friend, and his brother.

"Let us vote Mr. Wade in by acclamation," cried the Directors.

"But, gentlemen," Churm interposed, "if I give him my blank check, he must have *carte blanche*, and no one to interfere in his management."

Every Director, from President Brummage down, drew a long face at this condition.

It was one of their great privileges to potter in

the Dunderbunk affairs and propose ludicrous impossibilities.

"Just as you please," Churm continued. "I name a competent man, a gentleman and fine fellow. I back him with all the cash he wants. But he must have his own way. Now take him, or leave him!"

Such despotic talk had never been heard before in that Directors' Room. They relucted a moment. But they thought of their togas of advertisements in danger. The blank check shook its blandishments before their eyes.

"We take him," they said, and Richard Wade was the new Superintendent unanimously.

"He shall be at Dunderbunk to take hold to-morrow morning," said Churm, and went off to notify him.

Upon this, Consternation sailed out of the hearts of Brummage and associates.

They lunched with good appetites over the green table, and the President confidently remarked, —

"I don't believe there is going to be much of a crisis, after all."

CHAPTER II.

BARRACKS FOR THE HERO.

WADE packed his kit, and took the Hudson River train for Dunderbunk the same afternoon.

He swallowed his dust, he gasped for his fresh air, he wept over his cinders, he refused his "lozengers," he was admired by all the pretty girls and detested by all the puny men in the train, and in good time got down at his station.

He stopped on the platform to survey the land-and water-privileges of his new abode.

"The June sunshine is unequalled," he soliloquized, "the river is splendid, the hills are pretty, and the Highlands, north, respectable ; but the village has gone to seed. Place and people look lazy, vicious, and ashamed. I suppose those chimneys are my Foundry. The smoke rises as if the furnaces were ill-fed and weak in the lungs. Nothing, I can see, looks alive, except that queer little steamboat coming in, — the 'I. Ambuster,' — jolly name for a boat ! "

Wade left his traps at the station, and walked through the village. All the gilding of a golden sunset of June could not make it anything but commonplace. It would be forlorn on a gray day, and utterly dismal in a storm.

"I must look up a civilized house to lodge in," thought the stranger. "I cannot possibly camp at

the tavern. Its offence is rum, and smells to
heaven."

Presently our explorer found a neat, white, two-
story, home-like abode on the upper street, over-
looking the river.

"This promises," he thought. "Here are roses
on the porch, a piano, or at least a melodeon, by
the parlor-window, and they are insured in the
Mutual, as the Mutual's plate announces. Now,
if that nice-looking person in black I see setting
a table in the back-room is a widow, I will camp
here."

Perry Purtett was the name on the door, and opposite the sign of an *omnium-gatherum* country-
store hinted that Perry was deceased. The hint
was a broad one. Wade read, "Ringdove, Successor to late P. Purtett."

"It's worth a try to get in here out of the pa-
gan barbarism around. I'll propose — as a lodger
— to the widow."

So said Wade, and rang the bell under the roses.
A pretty, slim, delicate, fair-haired maiden answered.

"This explains the roses and the melodeon,"
thought Wade, and asked, "Can I see your
mother?"

Mamma came. "Mild, timid, accustomed to
depend on the late Perry, and wants a friend,"
Wade analyzed, while he bowed. He proposed
himself as a lodger.

"I didn't know it was talked of generally,"

replied the widow, plaintively ; "but I *have* said
that we felt lonesome, Mr. Purtett bein' gone, and
if the new minister —"

Here she paused. The cut of Wade's jib was
unclerical. He did not stoop, like a new minister.
He was not pallid, meagre, and clad in unwhole
some black, like the same. His bronzed face was
frank and bold and unfamiliar with speculations on
Original Sin or Total Depravity.

"I am not the new minister," said Wade, smiling
slightly over his moustache ; "but a new Superintendent for the Foundry."

"Mr. Whiffler is goin' ?" exclaimed Mrs. Purtett.

She looked at her daughter, who gave a little
sob and ran out of the room.

"What makes my daughter Belle feel bad," says
the widow, "is, that she had a friend, — well, it
is n't too much to say that they was as good as
engaged, — and he was foreman of the Foundry
finishin'-shop. But somehow Whiffler spoilt him,
just as he spoils everything he touches ; and last
winter, when Belle was away, William Tarbox —
that 's his name, and his head is runnin' over with
inventions — took to spreein' and liquor, and got
ashamed of himself, and let down from a foreman
to a hand, and is all the while lettin' down lower."

The widow's heart thus opened, Wade walked
in as consoler. This also opened the lodgings to
him. He was presently installed in the large and
small front-rooms up-stairs, unpacking his traps,
and making himself permanently at home.

Superintendent Whiffler came over, by and by, to see his successor. He did not like his looks. The new man should have looked mean or weak or rascally, to suit the outgoer.

"How long do you expect to stay?" asks Whiffler, with a half-sneer, watching Wade hanging a map and a print *vis-à-vis*.

"Until the men and I, or the Company and I, cannot pull together."

"I'll give you a week to quarrel with both, and another to see the whole concern go to everlasting smash. And now, if you're ready, I'll go over the accounts with you and prove it."

Whiffler himself, insolent, cowardly, and a humbug, if not a swindler, was enough, Wade thought, to account for any failure. But he did not mention this conviction.

CHAPTER III.

HOW TO BEHEAD A HYDRA!

At ten next morning, Whiffler handed over the safe-key to Wade, and departed to ruin some other property, if he could get one to ruin. Wade walked with him to the gate.

"I'm glad to be out of a sinking ship," said the ex-boss. "The Works will go down, sure as shooting. And I think myself well out of the

clutches of these men.   They're a bullying,
swearing, drinking set of infernal ruffians.   Fore-
men are just as bad as hands.   I never felt safe of
my life with 'em.''

"A bad lot, are they?" mused Wade, as he
returned to the office.   " I must give them a little
sharp talk by way of Inaugural.''

He had the bell tapped and the men called together in the main building.

Much work was still going on in an inefficient,
unsystematic way.

While hot fires were roaring in the great furnaces, smoke rose from the dusty beds where
Titanic castings were cooling.   Great cranes, man-
acled with heavy chains, stood over the furnace-
doors, ready to lift steaming jorums of melted
metal, and pour out, hot and hot, for the moulds to
swallow.

Raw material in big heaps lay about, waiting
for the fire to ripen it.   Here was a stack of long,
rough, rusty pigs, clumsy as the shillelahs of the
Anakim.   There was a pile of short, thick masses,
lying higgledy-piggledy, stuff from the neighboring
mines, which needed to be crossed with foreign
stock before it could be of much use in civilization.

Here, too, was raw material organized: a fly-
wheel, large enough to keep the knobbiest of
asteroids revolving without a wabble ; a cross-
head, cross-tail, and piston-rod, to help a great sea-
going steamer breast the waves ; a light walking-
beam, to whirl the paddles of a fast boat on the

river ; and other members of machines, only asking to be put together and vivified by steam and they would go at their work with a will.

From the black rafters overhead hung the heavy folds of a dim atmosphere, half dust, half smoke. A dozen sunbeams, forcing their way through the grimy panes of the grimy upper windows, found this compound quite palpable and solid, and they moulded out of it a series of golden bars set side by side aloft, like the pipes of an organ out of its perpendicular.

Wade grew indignant, as he looked about him and saw so much good stuff and good force wasting for want of a little will and skill to train the force and manage the stuff. He abhorred bankruptcy and chaos.

"All they want here is a head," he thought.

He shook his own. The brain within was well developed with healthy exercise. It filled its case, and did not rattle like a withered kernel, or sound soft like a rotten one. It was a vigorous, muscular brain. The owner felt that he could trust it for an effort, as he could his lungs for a shout, his legs for a leap, or his fist for a knock-down argument.

At the tap of the bell, the "bad lot" of men came together. They numbered more than two hundred, though the Foundry was working short. They had been notified that "that gonoph of a Whiffler was kicked out, and a new feller was in, who looked cranky enough, and wanted to see 'em and tell 'em whether he was a damn' fool or not."

So all hands collected from the different parts of the Foundry to see the head.

They came up with easy and somewhat swaggering bearing, — a good many roughs, with here and there a ruffian. Several, as they approached, swung and tossed, for mere overplus of strength, the sledges with which they had been tapping at the bald shiny pates of their anvils. Several wielded their long pokers like lances,

Grimy chaps, all with their faces streaked, like Blackfeet in their war-paint. Their hairy chests showed, where some men parade elaborate shirt-bosoms. Some had their sleeves pushed up to the elbow to exhibit their compact flexors and extensors. Some had rolled their flannel up to the shoulder, above the bulging muscles of the upper arm. They wore aprons tied about the neck, like the bibs of our childhood, — or about the waist, like the coquettish articles which young house-wives affect. But there was no coquetry in these great flaps of leather or canvas, and they were besmeared and rust-stained quite beyond any bib that ever suffered under bread-and-molasses or mud-pie treatment.

They lounged and swaggered up, and stood at ease, not without rough grace, in a sinuous line, coiled and knotted like a snake.

Ten feet back stood the new Hercules who was to take down that Hydra's two hundred crests of insubordination.

They inspected him, and he them as coolly. He

read and ticketed each man, as he came up, —
good, bad, or on the fence, — and marked each so
that he would know him among a myriad.

The Hands faced the Head. It was a question
whether the two hundred or the one would be
master in Dunderbunk.

Which was boss? An old question. It has to
be settled whenever a new man claims power, and
there is always a struggle until it is fought out by
main force of brain or muscle.

Wade had made up his mind on this subject. He
waited a moment until the men were still. He was
a Saxon six-footer of thirty. He stood easily on
his pins, as if he had eyed men and facts before.
His mouth looked firm, his brow freighted, his nose
clipper, — that the hands could see. But clipper
noses are not always backed by a stout hull.
Seemingly freighted brows sometimes carry nothing
but ballast and dunnage. The firmness may be all
in the moustache, while the mouth hides beneath,
a mere silly slit. All which the hands knew.

Wade began, short and sharp as a trip-hammer,
when it has a bar to shape.

" I 'm the new Superintendent. Richard Wade
is my name. I rang the bell because I wanted to
see you and have you see me. You know as well
as I do that these Works are in a bad way. They
can't stay so. They must come up and pay you
regular wages and the Company profits. Every
man of you has got to be here on the spot when the
bell strikes, and up to the mark in his work. You

have n't been, — and you know it.   You 've turned
out rotten iron, — stuff that any honest shop would
be ashamed of.   Now there 's to be a new leaf
turned over here.   You 're to be paid on the nail ;
but you 've got to earn your money.   I won't have
any idlers or shirkers or rebels about me.   I shall
work hard myself, and every man of you will, or
he leaves the shop.   Now, if anybody has a com-
plaint to make, I 'll hear him before you all.''

The men were evidently impressed with Wade's
Inaugural.   It meant something.   But they were
not to be put down so easily, after long misrule.
There began to be a whisper, —

"B'il in, Bill Tarbox ! and talk up to him ! ''

Presently Bill shouldered forward and faced the
new ruler.

Since Bill took to drink and degradation, he
had been the but-end of riot and revolt at the
Foundry.   He had had his own way with Whiffler.
He did not like to abdicate and give in to this new
chap without testing him.

In a better mood, Bill would have liked Wade's
looks and words ; but to-day he had a sore head,
a sour face, and a bitter heart, from last night's
spree.   And then he had heard — it was as well
known already in Dunderbunk as if the town-crier
had cried it — that Wade was lodging at Mrs.
Purtett's, where poor Bill was excluded.   So Bill
stepped forward as spokesman of the ruffianly element, and the immoral force gathered behind and
backed him heavily.

Tarbox, too, was a Saxon six-footer of thirty. But he had sagged one inch for want of self-respect. He had spoilt his color and dyed his moustache. He wore foxy-black pantaloons tucked into red-topped boots, with the name of the maker on a gilt shield. His red-flannel shirt was open at the neck and caught with a black handkerchief. His damaged tile was in permanent crape for the late lamented Poole.

"We allow," says Bill, in a tone half-way between Lablache's *De profundis* and a burglar's bull-dog's snarl, "that we 've did our work as good as need to be did. We 'xpect we know our rights. We ha'n't ben treated fair, and I 'm damned if we 're go'n' to stan' it."

"Stop!" says Wade. "No swearing in this shop!"

"Who the Devil is go'n' to stop it?" growled Tarbox.

"I am. Do you step back now, and let some one come out who can talk like a gentleman!"

"I 'm damned if I stir till I 've had my say out," says Bill, shaking himself up and looking dangerous.

"Go back!"

Wade moved close to him, also looking dangerous.

"Don't tech me!" Bill threatened, squaring off.

He was not quick enough. Wade knocked him down flat on a heap of moulding-sand. The hat in mourning for Poole found its place in a puddle.

Bill did not like the new Emperor's method of

compelling *kotou*.   Round One of the mill had not given him enough.

He jumped up from his soft bed and made a vicious rush at Wade.   But he was damaged by evil courses.   He was fighting against law and order, on the side of wrong and bad manners.

The same fist met him again, and heavier.

Up went his heels!   Down went his head!   It struck the ragged edge of a fresh casting, and there he lay stunned and bleeding on his hard black pillow.

"Ring the bell to go to work!" said Wade, in a tone that made the ringer jump.   "Now, men, take hold and do your duty and everything will go smooth!"

The bell clanged in.   The line looked at its prostrate champion, then at the new boss standing there, cool and brave, and not afraid of a regiment of sledge-hammers.

They wanted an Executive.   They wanted to be well governed, as all men do.   They wanted disorder out and order in.   The new man looked like a man, talked fair, hit hard.   Why not all hands give in with a good grace and go to work like honest fellows?

The line broke up.   The hands went off to their duty.   And there was never any more insubordination at Dunderbunk.

This was June.

Skates in the next chapter.

Love in good time afterward shall glide upon the scene.

CHAPTER IV.

A CHRISTMAS GIFT.

THE pioneer sunbeam of next Christmas morning rattled over the Dunderbunk hills, flashed into Richard Wade's eyes, waked him, and was off, ricochetting across the black ice of the river.

Wade jumped up, electrified and jubilant. He had gone to bed feeling quite too despondent for so healthy a fellow. Christmas Eve, the time of family meetings, reminded him how lonely he was. He had not a relative in the world, except two little nieces, — one as tall as his knee, the other almost up to his waist; and them he had safely bestowed in a nook of New England, to gain wit and virtues as they gained inches.

"I have had a stern and lonely life," thought Wade, as he blew out his candle last night, "and what has it profited me?"

Perhaps the pioneer sunbeam answered this question with a truism, not always as applicable as in this case, — "A brave, able, self-respecting manhood is fair profit for any man's first thirty years of life."

But, answered or not, the question troubled Wade no more. He shot out of bed in tip-top spirits; shouted "Merry Christmas!" at the rising disk of the sun; looked over the black ice; thrilled with the thought of a long holiday for skating;

and proceeded to dress in a knowing suit of rough clothes, singing, "*Ah, non giunge!*" as he slid into them.

Presently, glancing from his south window, he observed several matinal smokes rising from the chimneys of a country-house a mile away, on a slope fronting the river.

"Peter Skerrett must be back from Europe at last," he thought. "I hope he is as fine a fellow as he was ten years ago. I hope marriage has not made him a muff, and wealth a weakling."

Wade went down to breakfast with an heroic appetite. His "Merry Christmas" to Mrs. Purtett was followed up by a ravished kiss and the gift of a silver butter-knife. The good widow did not know which to be most charmed with. The butter-knife was genuine, shining, solid silver, with her initials, M. B. P., Martha Bilsby Purtett, given in luxuriant flourishes; but then the kiss had such a fine twang, such an exhilarating titillation! The late Perry's kisses, from first to last, had wanted point. They were, as the Spanish proverb would put it, unsavory as unsalted eggs, for want of a moustache. The widow now perceived, with mild regret, how much she had missed when she married "a man all shaven and shorn." Her cheek, still fair, though forty, flushed with novel delight, and she appreciated her lodger more than ever.

Wade's salutation to Belle Purtett was more distant. There must be a little friendly reserve between a handsome young man and a pretty young woman several grades lower in the social scale, living in the same house. They were on the most cordial terms, however; and her gift — of course embroidered slippers — and his to her — of course "The Illustrated Poets," in Turkey morocco — were exchanged with tender good-will on both sides.

"We shall meet on the ice, Miss Belle," said Wade. "It is a day of a thousand for skating."

"Mr. Ringdove says you are a famous skater," Belle rejoined. "He saw you on the river yesterday evening."

"Yes; Tarbox and I were practising to exhibit to-day; but I could not do much with my dull old skates."

Wade breakfasted deliberately, as a holiday morning allowed, and then walked down to the Foundry. There would be no work done to-day, except by a small gang keeping up the fires. The Superintendent wished only to give his First Semi-Annual Report an hour's polishing, before he joined all Dunderbunk on the ice.

It was a halcyon day, worthy of its motto, "Peace on earth, good-will to men." The air was electric, the sun overflowing with jolly shine, the river smooth and sheeny from the hither bank to the snowy mountains opposite.

"I wish I were Rembrandt, to paint this grand shadowy interior," thought Wade, as he entered the silent, deserted Foundry. "With the gleam of the snow in my eyes, it looks deliciously warm and *chiaroscuro*.　When the men are here and '*fer-vet opus*,' — the pot boils, — I cannot stop to see the picturesque."

He opened his office, took his Report and began to complete it with ,s, ;s, and .s in the right places.

All at once the bell of the Works rang out loud and clear.　Presently the Superintendent became aware of a tramp and a bustle in the building. By and by came a tap at the office-door.

"Come in," said Wade, and, enter young Perry Purtett.

Perry was a boy of fifteen, with hair the color of fresh sawdust, white eyebrows, and an uncommonly wide-awake look.　Ringdove, his father's succes-sor, could never teach Perry the smirk, the grace, and the seductiveness of the counter, so the boy had found his place in the finishing-shop of the Foundry.

"Some of the hands would like to see you for half a jiff, Mr. Wade," said he.　"Will you come along, if you please?"

There was a good deal of easy swagger about Perry, as there is always in boys and men whose business is to watch the lunging of steam-engines. Wade followed him.　Perry led the way with a jaunty air that said, —

"Room here!　Out of the way, you lubberly bits of cast-iron!　Be careful, now, you big der-ricks, or I 'll walk right over you!　Room now for Me and My suite!"

This pompous usher conducted the Superintendent to the very spot in the main room of the Works where, six months before, the Inaugural had been pronounced and the first Veto spoken and enacted.

And there, as six months before, stood the Hands awaiting their Head. But the aprons, the red shirts, and the grime of working-days were off, and the whole were in holiday rig, — as black and smooth and shiny from top to toe as the members of a Congress of Undertakers.

Wade, following in the wake of Perry, took his stand facing the rank, and waited to see what he was summoned for. He had not long to wait.

To the front stepped Mr. William Tarbox, foreman of the finishing-shop, no longer a bhoy, but an erect, fine-looking fellow, with no nitrate in his moustache, and his hat permanently out of mourning for the late Mr. Poole.

" Gentlemen," said Bill, " I move that this meeting organize by appointing Mr. Smith Wheelwright Chairman. As many as are in favor of this motion, please to say, ' Ay.' "

" Ay ! " said the crowd, very loud and big. And then every man looked at his neighbor, a little abashed, as if he himself had made all the noise.

" This is a free country," continues Bill. " Every woter has a right to a fair shake. Contrary minds, ' No.' "

No contrary minds. The crowd uttered a great silence. Every man looked at his neighbor, surprised to find how well they agreed.

7

"Unanimous!" Tarbox pronounced. "No fractious minorities *here*, to block the wheels of legislation!"

The crowd burst into a roar at this significant remark, and, again abashed, dropped portcullis on its laughter, cutting off the flanks and tail of the sound.

"Mr. Purtett, will you please conduct the Chairman to the Chair," says Bill, very stately.

"Make way here!" cried Perry, with the manner of a man seven feet high. "Step out now, Mr. Chairman!"

He took a big, grizzled, docile-looking fellow patronizingly by the arm, led him forward, and chaired him on a large cylinder-head, in the rough, just hatched out of its mould.

"Bang away with that, and sing out 'Silence!'" says the knowing boy, handing Wheelwright an iron bolt, and taking his place beside him, as prompter.

The docile Chairman obeyed. At his breaking silence by hooting "Silence!" the audience had another mighty bobtailed laugh.

"Say, 'Will some honorable member state the object of this meeting?'" whispered the prompter.

"Will some honorable mumbler state the subject of this 'ere meetin'?" says Chair, a little bashful and confused.

Bill Tarbox advanced, and, with a formal bow, began, —

"Mr. Chairman — "

"Say, 'Mr. Tarbox has the floor,'" piped Perry.

"Mr. Tarbox has the floor," diapasoned the Chair.

"Mr. Chairman and Gentlemen—" Bill began, and stopped.

"Say, 'Proceed, Sir!'" suggested Perry, which the senior did, magnifying the boy's whisper a dozen times.

Again Bill began and stopped.

"Boys," said he, dropping grandiloquence, "when I accepted the office of Orator of the Day at our primary, and promised to bring forward our Resolutions in honor of Mr. Wade with my best speech, I did n't think I was going to have such a head of steam on that the walves would get stuck and the piston jammed and I could n't say a word.

"But," he continued, warming up, "when I think of the Indian powwow we had in this very spot six months ago,—and what a mean bloat I was, going to the stub-tail dogs with my hat over my eyes,—and what a hard lot we were all round, livin' on nothing but argee whiskey, and rampin' off on benders, instead of makin' good iron,—and how the Works was flat broke,—and how Dunderbunk was full of women crying over their husbands and mothers ashamed of their sons,—boys, when I think how things was, and see how they are, and look at Mr. Wade standing there like a—"

Bill hesitated for a comparison.

"Like a thousand of brick," Perry Purtett suggested, *sotto voce*.

The Chairman took this as a hint to himself.

"Like a thousand of brick," he said, with the voice of a Stentor.

Here the audience roared and cheered, and the Orator got a fresh start.

"When you came, Mr. Wade," he resumed, "we was about sick of putty-heads and sneaks that did n't know enough or did n't dare to make us stand round and bone in. You walked in, b'ilin' over with grit. You took hold as if you belonged here. You made things jump like a two-headed tarrier. All we wanted was a live man, to say, 'Here, boys, all together now! You 've got your stint, and I 've got mine. I 'm boss in this shop, — but I can't do the first thing, unless every man pulls his pound. Now, then, my hand is on the throttle, grease the wheels, oil the walves, poke the fires, hook on, and let 's yank her through with a will!' "

At this figure the meeting showed a tendency to cheer. "Silence!" Perry sternly suggested. "Silence!" repeated the Chair.

"Then," continued the Orator, "you was n't one of the uneasy kind, always fussin' and cussin' round. You was n't always spyin' to see we did n't take home a cross-tail or a hundred-weight of cast-iron in our pants' pockets, or go to swiggin' hot metal out of the ladles on the sly."

Here an enormous laugh requited Bill's joke. Perry prompted, the Chair banged with his bolt and cried, "Order!"

"Well, now, boys," Tarbox went on, "what has come of having one of the right sort to be boss? Why, this. The Works go ahead, stiddy as the North River. We work full time and full-handed. We turn out stuff that no shop needs to be ashamed of. Wages is on the nail. We have a good time generally. How is that, boys, — Mr. Chairman and Gentlemen?"

"That's so!" from everybody.

"And there's something better yet," Bill resumed. "Dunderbunk used to be full of crying women. They've stopped crying now."

Here the whole assemblage, Chairman and all, burst into an irrepressible cheer.

"But I'm making my speech as long as a lightning-rod," said the speaker. "I'll put on the brakes, short. I guess Mr. Wade understands pretty well, now, how we feel; and if he don't, here it all is in shape, in this document, with 'Whereas' at the top and 'Resolved' entered along down in five places. Mr. Purtett, will you hand the Resolutions to the Superintendent?"

Perry advanced and did his office loftily, much to the amusement of Wade and the workmen.

"Now," Bill resumed, "we wanted, besides, to make you a little gift, Mr. Wade, to remember the day by. So we got up a subscription, and every man put in his dime. Here's the present, — hand 'em over, Perry!

"There, Sir, is THE BEST PAIR OF SKATES to be had in York City, made for work, and no nonsense about 'em. We Dunderbunk boys give 'em to you, one for all, and hope you 'll like 'em and beat the world skating, as you do in all the things we 've knowed you try.

"Now, boys," Bill perorated, "before I retire to the shades of private life, I motion we give Three Cheers — regular Toplifters — for Richard Wade ! "

"Hurrah ! Wade and Good Government ! " "Hurrah ! Wade and Prosperity ! " "Hurrah ! Wade and the Women's Tears Dry ! "

Cheers like the shout of Achilles ! Wielding sledges is good for the bellows, it appears. Toplifters ! Why, the smoky black rafters overhead had to tug hard to hold the roof on. Hurrah ! From every corner of the vast building came back rattling echoes. The Works, the machinery, the furnaces, the stuff, all had their voice to add to the verdict.

Magnificent music ! and our Anglo-Saxon is the only race in the world civilized enough to join in singing it. We are the only hurrahing people, — the only brood hatched in a "Hurrah's nest."

Silence restored, the Chairman, prompted by Perry, said, "Gentlemen, Mr. Wade has the floor for a few remarks."

Of course Wade had to speak, and did. He would not have been an American in America else. But his heart was too full to say more than a few hearty and earnest words of good feeling.

"Now, men," he closed, "I want to get away

on the river and see if my skates will go as they look; so I'll end by proposing three cheers for Smith Wheelwright, our Chairman, three for our Orator, Tarbox, three for Old Dunderbunk, — Works, Men, Women, and Children; and one big cheer for Old Father Iron, as rousing a cheer as ever was roared."

So they gave their three times three with enormous enthusiasm. The roof shook, the furnaces rattled, Perry Purtett banged with the Chairman's hammer, the great echoes thundered through the Foundry.

And when they ended with one gigantic cheer for IRON, tough and true, the weapon, the tool, and the engine of all civilization, — it seemed as if the uproar would never cease until Father Iron himself heard the call in his smithy away under the magnetic pole, and came clanking up, to return thanks in person.

CHAPTER V.

SKATING AS A FINE ART.

OF all the plays that are played by this playful world on its play-days, there is no play like Skating.

To prepare a board for the moves of this game

of games, a panel for the drawings of this Fine
Art, a stage for the *entrechats* and *pirouettes* of its
graceful adepts, Zero, magical artificer, had been,
for the last two nights, sliding at full speed up
and down the North River.

We have heard of Midas, whose touch made
gold, and of the virgin under whose feet sprang
roses ; but Zero's heels and toes were armed with
more precious influences.   They left a diamond
way, where they slid, — a hundred and fifty miles
of diamond, half a mile wide and six inches thick.

Diamond can only reflect sunlight ; ice can con-
tain it.   Zero's product, finer even than diamond,
was filled — at the rate of a million to the square
foot — with bubbles immeasurably little, and yet
every one big enough to comprise the entire sun
in small, but without alteration or abridgment.
When the sun rose, each of these wonderful cells
was ready to catch the tip of a sunbeam and house
it in a shining abode.

Besides this, Zero had inlaid its work, all along
shore, with exquisite marquetry of leaves, brown
and evergreen, of sprays and twigs, reeds and
grasses.   No parquet in any palace from Fontaine-
bleau to St. Petersburg could show such delicate
patterns, or could gleam so brightly, though polished with all the wax in Christendom.

On this fine pavement, all the way from Cohoes
to Spuyten Duyvil, Jubilee was sliding without
friction, the Christmas morning of these adventures.

Navigation was closed.   Navigators had leisure.
The sloops and schooners were frozen in along
shore, the tugs and barges were laid up in basins,
the floating palaces were down at New York, de-
odorizing their bar-rooms, regilding their bridal
chambers, and enlarging their spittoon accommo-
dations alow and aloft, for next summer.   All the
population was out on the ice, skating, sliding,
sledding, slipping, tumbling, to its heart's content.

One person out of every Dunderbunk family was
of course at home, roasting Christmas turkey.
The rest were already at high jinks on Zero's
Christmas present, when Wade and the men came
down from the meeting.

Wade buckled on his new skates in a jiffy.   He
stamped to settle himself, and then flung off half a
dozen circles on the right leg, half a dozen with
the left, and the same with either leg backwards.

The ice, traced with these white peripheries,
showed like a blackboard where a school has been
chalking diagrams of Euclid, to point at with the
" slow unyielding finger " of demonstration.

" Hurrah ! " cries Wade, halting in front of the
men, who, some on the Foundry wharf, some on
the deck of our first acquaintance at Dunderbunk,
the tug " I. Ambuster," were putting on their
skates or watching him.   " Hurrah ! the skates
are perfection !   Are you ready, Bill ? "

" Yes," says Tarbox, whizzing off rings, as exact
as Giotto's autograph.

7 *

"Now, then," Wade said, "we'll give Dunderbunk a laugh, as we practised last night."

They got under full headway, Wade backwards, Bill forwards, holding hands. When they were near enough to the merry throng out in the stream, both dropped into a sitting posture, with the left knee bent, and each with his right leg stretched out parallel to the ice and fitting compactly by the other man's leg. In this queer figure they rushed through the laughing crowd.

Then all Dunderbunk formed a ring, agog for a grand show of

Skating as a Fine Art.

The world loves to see Great Artists, and expects them to do their duty.

It is hard to treat of this Fine Art by the Art of Fine Writing. Its eloquent motions must be seen.

To skate Fine Art, you must have a Body and a Soul, each of the First Order; otherwise you will never get out of coarse art and skating in one syllable. So much for yourself, the motive power. And your machinery, — your smooth-bottomed rockers, the same shape stem and stern, — this must be as perfect as the man it moves, and who moves it.

Now suppose you wish to skate so that the critics will say, "See! this athlete does his work as Church paints, as Darley draws, as Palmer chisels, as Whittier strikes the lyre, and Longfellow the dulcimer; he is as terse as Emerson, as clever as Holmes, as graceful as Curtis; he is as calm as

Seward, as keen as Phillips, as stalwart as Beecher; he is Garibaldi, he is Kit Carson, he is Blondin ; he is as complete as the steamboat Metropolis, as Steers's yacht, as Singer's sewing-machine, as Colt's revolver, as the steam-plough, as Civilization." You wish to be so ranked among the people and things that lead the age ; — consider the qualities you must have, and while you consider, keep your eye on Richard Wade, for he has them all in perfection.

First, — of your physical qualities. You must have lungs, not bellows ; and an active heart, not an assortment of sluggish auricles and ventricles. You must have legs, not shanks. Their shape is unimportant, except that they must not interfere at the knee. You must have muscles, not flabbiness ; sinews like wire ; nerves like sunbeams ; and a thin layer of flesh to cushion the gable-ends, where you will strike, if you tumble, — which, once for all be it said, you must never do. You must be all *momentum*, and no *inertia*. You must be one part grace, one force, one agility, and the rest caoutchouc, Manilla hemp, and watch-spring. Your machine, your body, must be thoroughly obedient. It must go just so far and no farther. You have got to be as unerring as a planet holding its own, emphatically, between forces centripetal and centrifugal. Your *aplomb* must be as absolute as the pounce of a falcon.

So much for a few of the physical qualities necessary to be a Great Artist in Skating. See Wade, how he shows them !

Now for the moral and intellectual. Pluck is the first ; — it always is the first quality. Then enthusiasm. Then patience. Then pertinacity. Then a fine æsthetic faculty, — in short, good taste. Then an orderly and submissive mind, that can consent to act in accordance with the laws of Art. Circumstances, too, must have been reasonably favorable. That well-known sceptic, the King of tropical Bantam, could not skate, because he had never seen ice and doubted even the existence of solid water. Widdrington, after the Battle of Chevy Chace, could not have skated, because he had no legs, — poor fellow !

But granted the ice and the legs, then if you begin in the elastic days of youth, when cold does not sting, tumbles do not bruise, and duckings do not wet ; if you have pluck and ardor enough to try everything ; if you work slowly ahead and stick to it ; if you have good taste and a lively invention ; if you are a man, and not a lubber ; — then, in fine, you may become a Great Skater, just as with equal power and equal pains you may put your grip on any kind of Greatness.

The technology of skating is imperfect. Few of the great feats, the Big Things, have admitted names. If I attempted to catalogue Wade's achievements, this chapter might become an unintelligible rhapsody. A sheet of paper and a penpoint cannot supply the place of a sheet of ice and a skate-edge. Geometry must have its diagrams, Anatomy its *corpus* to carve. Skating also refuses to be spiritualized into a Science; it remains an Art, and cannot be expressed in a formula.

Skating has its Little Go, its Great Go, its Baccalaureate, its M. A., its F. S. D. (Doctor of Frantic Skipping), its A. G. D. (Doctor of Airy Gliding), its N. T. D. (Doctor of No Tumbles), and finally its highest degree, U. P. (Unapproachable Podographer).

Wade was U. P.

There were a hundred of Dunderbunkers who had passed their Little Go and could skate forward and backward easily. A half-hundred, perhaps, were through the Great Go; these could do outer edge freely. A dozen had taken the Baccalaureate, and were proudly repeating the pirouettes and spread-eagles of that degree. A few could cross their feet, on the edge, forward and backward, and shift edge on the same foot, and so were *Magistri Artis*.

Wade, U. P., added to these an indefinite list of combinations and fresh contrivances. He spun spirals slow, and spirals neck or nothing. He pivoted on one toe, with the other foot cutting rings, inner and outer edge, forward and back. He skated on one foot better than the M. A.s could on both. He ran on his toes; he slid on his heels; he cut up shines like a sunbeam on a bender; he swung, light as if he could fly, if he pleased, like a wing-footed Mercury; he glided as if will, not muscle, moved him; he tore about in frenzies; his pivotal leg stood firm, his balance leg flapped like

a graceful pinion ; he turned somersets ; he jumped,
whirling backward as he went, over a platoon of
boys laid flat on the ice ; — the last boy winced,
and thought he was amputated ; but Wade flew
over, and the boy still holds together as well as
most boys.   Besides this, he could write his name,
with a flourish at the end, like the *rubrica* of a
Spanish *hidalgo*.   He could podograph any letter,
and multitudes of ingenious curlicues which might
pass for the alphabets of the unknown tongues.
He could *not* tumble.

It was Fine Art.

Bill Tarbox sometimes pressed the champion
hard.   But Bill stopped just short of Fine Art, in
High Artisanship.

How Dunderbunk cheered this wondrous dis-
play ! How delighted the whole population was
to believe they possessed the best skater on the
North River !   How they struggled to imitate !
How they tumbled, some on their backs, some on
their faces, some with dignity like the dying
Cæsar, some rebelliously like a cat thrown out of
a garret, some limp as an ancient acrobate !   How
they laughed at themselves and at each other !

"It's all in the new skates," says Wade,
apologizing for his unapproachable power and
finish.

"It's suthin' in the man," says Smith Wheelwright.

"Now chase me, everybody," said Wade.

And, for a quarter of an hour, he dodged the

merry crowd, until at last, breathless, he let himself be touched by pretty Belle Purtett, rosiest of all the Dunderbunk bevy of rosy maidens on the ice.

"He rayther beats Bosting," says Captain Isaac Ambuster to Smith Wheelwright. "It's so cold there that they can skate all the year round ; but he beats them, all the same."

The Captain was sitting in a queer little bowl of a skiff on the deck of his tug, and rocking it like a cradle, as he talked.

"Bosting's always hard to beat in anything," rejoined the ex-Chairman. "But if Bosting is to be beat, here's the man to do it."

And now, perhaps, gentle reader, you think I have said enough in behalf of a limited fraternity, the Skaters.

The next chapter, then, shall take up the cause of the Lovers, a more numerous body, and we will see whether True Love, which never makes "smooth running," can help its progress by a skate-blade.

CHAPTER VI.

"GO NOT, HAPPY DAY, TILL THE MAIDEN YIELDS."

CHRISTMAS noon at Dunderbunk. Every skater was in galloping glee, — as the electric air, and the sparkling sun, and the glinting ice had a right to expect that they all should be.

Belle Purtett, skating simply and well, had never looked so pretty and graceful. So thought Bill Tarbox.

He had not spoken to her, nor she to him, for more than six months. The poor fellow was ashamed of himself and penitent for his past bad courses. And so, though he longed to have his old flame recognize him again, and though he was bitterly jealous and miserably afraid he should lose her, he had kept away and consumed his heart like a true despairing lover.

But to-day Bill was a lion, only second to Wade, the unapproachable lion-in-chief. Bill was reinstated in public esteem, and had won back his standing in the Foundry. He had to-day made a speech which Perry Purtett gave everybody to understand "none of Senator Bill Seward's could hold the tallow to." Getting up the meeting and presenting Wade with the skates was Bill's own scheme, and it had turned out an eminent success. Everything began to look bright to him. His past life drifted out of his mind like the rowdy tales he used to read in the Sunday newspapers.

He had watched Belle Purtett all the morning, and saw that she distinguished nobody with her smiles, not even that *coq du village*, Ringdove. He also observed that she was furtively watching him.

By and by she sailed out of the crowd, and went off a little way to practise.

"Now," said he to himself, "sail in, Bill Tarbox!"

Belle heard the sharp strokes of a powerful skater coming after her. Her heart divined who this might be. She sped away like the swift Camilla, and her modest drapery showed just enough and "*ne quid nimis*" of her ankles.

Bill admired the grace and the ankles immensely. But his hopes sank a little at the flight, — for he thought she perceived his chase and meant to drop him. Bill had not had a classical education, and knew nothing of Galatea in the Eclogue, — how she did not hide, until she saw her swain was looking fondly after.

"She wants to get away," he thought. "But she sha'n't, — no, not if I have to follow her to Albany."

He struck out mightily. Presently the swift Camilla let herself be overtaken.

"Good morning, Miss Purtett." (Dogged air.)

"Good morning, Mr. Tarbox." (Taken-by-surprise air.)

"I've been admiring your skating," says Bill, trying to be cool.

K

"Have you ?" rejoins Belle, very cool and distant.

"Have you been long on the ice ?" he inquired, hypocritically.

"I came on two hours ago with Mr. Ringdove and the girls," returned she, with a twinkle which said, "Take that, Sir, for pretending you did not see me."

"You 've seen Mr. Wade skate, then," Bill said, ignoring Ringdove.

"Yes ; is n't it splendid ?" Belle replied, kindling.

"Tip-top !"

"But then he does everything better than anybody."

"So he does !" Bill said, — true to his friend, and yet beginning to be jealous of this enthusiasm. It was not the first time he had been jealous of Wade ; but he had quelled his fears, like a good fellow.

Belle perceived Bill's jealousy, and could have cried for joy. She had known as little of her once lover's heart as he of hers. She only knew that he stopped coming to see her when he fell, and had not renewed his visits now that he was risen again. If she had not been charmingly ruddy with the brisk air and exercise, she would have betrayed her pleasure at Bill's jealousy with a fine blush.

The sense of recovered power made her wish to use it again. She must tease him a little. So she continued, as they skated on in good rhythm, —

" Mother and I would n't know what to do without Mr. Wade. We like him *so* much," — said ardently.

What Bill feared was true, then, he thought. Wade, noble fellow, worthy to win any woman's heart, had fascinated his landlady's daughter.

" I don't wonder you like him," said he. " He deserves it."

Belle was touched by her old lover's forlorn tone.

" He does indeed," she said. " He has helped and taught us all so much. He has taken such good care of Perry. And then " — here she gave her companion a little look and a little smile — " he speaks so kindly of you, Mr. Tarbox."

Smile, look, and words electrified Bill. He gave such a spring on his skates that he shot far ahead of the lady. He brought himself back with a sharp turn.

" He has done kinder than he can speak," says Bill. " He has made a man of me again, Miss Belle."

" I know it. It makes me very happy to hear you able to say so of yourself." She spoke gravely.

" Very happy " — about anything that concerned him ? Bill had to work off his over-joy at this by an exuberant flourish. He whisked about Belle, — outer edge backward. She stopped to admire. He finished by describing on the virgin ice, before her, the letters B. P., in his neatest style of podography, — easy letters to make, luckily.

"Beautiful!" exclaimed Belle. "What are those letters? Oh! B. P.! What do they stand for?"

"Guess!"

"I'm so dull," said she, looking bright as a diamond. "Let me think! B. P.? British Poets, perhaps."

"Try nearer home!"

"What are you likely to be thinking of that begins with B. P.? — O, I know! Boiler Plates!"

She looked at him, — innocent as a lamb. Bill looked at her, delighted with her little coquetry. A woman without coquetry is insipid as a rose without scent, as Champagne without bubbles, or as corned beef without mustard.

"It's something I'm thinking of most of the time," says he; "but I hope it's softer than Boiler Plates. B. P. stands for Miss Isabella Purtett."

"Oh!" says Belle, and she skated on in silence.

"You came down with Alonzo Ringdove?" Bill asked, suddenly, aware of another pang after a moment of peace.

"He came with me and his sisters," she replied.

Yes; poor Ringdove had dressed himself in his shiniest black, put on his brightest patent-leather boots, with his new swan-necked skates newly strapped over them, and wore his new dove-colored overcoat with the long skirts, on purpose to be lovely in the eyes of Belle on this occasion. Alas, in vain!"

"Mr. Ringdove is a great friend of yours, is n't he?"

"If you ever came to see me now, you would know who my friends are, Mr. Tarbox."

"Would you be my friend again, if I came, Miss Belle?"

"Again? I have always been so, — always, Bill."

"Well, then, something more than my friend, — now that I am trying to be worthy of more, Belle?"

"What more can I be?" she said, softly.

"My wife."

She curved to the right. He followed. To the left. He was not to be shaken off.

"Will you promise me not to say *walves* instead of *valves*, Bill?" she said, looking pretty and saucy as could be. "I know, to say W for V is fashionable in the iron business; but I don't like it."

"What a thing a woman is to dodge!" says Bill. "Suppose I told you that men brought up inside of boilers, hammering on the inside against twenty hammering like Wulcans on the outside, get their ears so dumfounded that they can't tell whether they are saying *valves* or *walves*, *wice* or *virtue*, — suppose I told you that, — what would you say, Belle?"

"Perhaps I'd say that you pronounce *virtue* so well, and act it so sincerely, that I can't make any objection to your other words. If you'd asked me to be your *vife*, Bill, I might have said I did n't understand; but *wife* I do understand, and I say — "

She nodded, and tried to skate off. Bill stuck close to her side.

"Is this true, Belle?" he said, almost doubtfully.

"True as truth!"

She put out her hand. He took it, and they skated on together,— hearts beating to the rhythm of their movements. The uproar and merriment of the village came only faintly to them. It seemed as if all Nature was hushed to listen to their plighted troth, their words of love renewed, more earnest for long suppression. The beautiful ice spread before them, like their life to come, a pathway untouched by any sorrowful or weary footstep. The blue sky was cloudless. The keen air stirred the pulses like the vapor of frozen wine. The benignant mountains westward kindly surveyed the happy pair, and the sun seemed created to warm and cheer them.

"And you forgive me, Belle?" said the lover. "I feel as if I had only gone bad to make me know how much better going right is."

"I always knew you would find it out. I never stopped hoping and praying for it."

"That must have been what brought Mr. Wade here."

"Oh, I did hate him so, Bill, when I heard of something that happened between you and him! I thought him a brute and a tyrant. I never could get over it, until he told mother that you were the best machinist he ever knew, and would some time grow to be a great inventor."

"I'm glad you hated him. I suffered rattlesnakes and collapsed flues for fear you'd go and love him."

"My affections were engaged," she said with simple seriousness.

"Oh, if I'd only thought so long ago! How lovely you are!" exclaims Bill, in an ecstasy. "And how refined! And how good! God bless you!"

. He made up such a wishful mouth, — so wishful for one of the pleasurable duties of mouths, that Belle blushed, laughed, and looked down, and as she did so saw that one of her straps was trailing.

"Please fix it, Bill," she said, stopping and kneeling.

Bill also knelt, and his wishful mouth immediately took its chance.

A manly smack and sweet little feminine chirp sounded as their lips met.

Boom! twanging gay as the first tap of a marriage-bell, a loud crack in the ice rang musically for leagues up and down the river. "Bravo!" it seemed to say. "Well done, Bill Tarbox! Try again!" Which the happy fellow did, and the happy maiden permitted.

"Now," said Bill, "let us go and hug Mr. Wade!"

"What! Both of us?" Belle protested. "Mr. Tarbox, I am ashamed of you!"

CHAPTER VII.

WADE DOWN.

THE hugging of Wade by the happy pair had to be done metaphorically, since it was done in the sight of all Dunderbunk.

He had divined a happy result, when he missed Bill Tarbox from the arena, and saw him a furlong away, hand in hand with his reconciled sweetheart.

"I envy you, Bill," said he, "almost too much to put proper fervor into my congratulations."

"Your time will come," the foreman rejoined.

And says Belle, "I am sure there is a lady skating somewhere, and only waiting for you to follow her."

"I don't see her," Wade replied, looking with a mock-grave face up and down and athwart the river. "When you've all gone to dinner, I'll prospect ten miles up and down, and try to find a good matrimonial claim that's not taken."

"You will not come up to dinner?" Belle asked.

"I can hardly afford to make two bites of a holiday," said Wade. "I've sent Perry up for a luncheon. Here he comes with it. So I cede my quarter of your pie, Miss Belle, to a better fellow."

"Oh!" cries Perry, coming up and bowing elaborately. "Mr. and Mrs. Tarbox, I believe. Ah, yes! Well, I will mention it up at Albany. I am going to take my Guards up to call on the Governor."

Perry dashed off, followed by a score of Dunderbunk boys, organized by him as the Purtett Guards, and taught to salute him as Generalissimo with military honors.

So many hundreds of turkeys, done to a turn, now began to have an effect upon the atmosphere. Few odors are more subtile and pervading than this, and few more appetizing. Indeed, there is said to be an odd fellow, a strictly American gourmand, in New York, who sits from noon to dusk on Christmas-Day up in a tall steeple, merely to catch the aroma of roast-turkey floating over the city, — and much good, it is said, it does him.

Hard skating is nearly as effective to whet hunger as this gentleman's expedient. When the spicy breezes began to blow soft as those of Ceylon's isle over the river and every whiff talked Turkey, the population of Dunderbunk listened to the wooing and began to follow its several noses — snubs, beaks, blunts, sharps, piquants, dominants, fines, bulgies, and bifids — on the way to the several households which those noses adorned or defaced. Prosperous Dunderbunk had a Dinner, yes, a DINNER, that day, and Richard Wade was gratefully remembered by many over-fed foundry-men and their over-fed families.

Wade had not had half skating enough.

" I 'll time myself down to Skerrett's Point," he

8

thought, "and take my luncheon there among the hemlocks."

The Point was on the property of Peter Skerrett, Wade's friend and college comrade of ten years gone.   Peter had been an absentee in Europe, and smokes from his chimneys this morning had confirmed to Wade's eyes the rumor of his return.

Skerrett's Point was a mile below the Foundry. Our hero did his mile under three minutes.   How many seconds under, I will not say.   I do not wish to make other fellows unhappy.

The Point was a favorite spot of Wade's.   Many a twilight of last summer, tired with his fagging at the Works to make good the evil of Whiffler's rule, he had lain there on the rocks under the hemlocks, breathing the spicy methyl they poured into the air.   After his day's hard fight, in the dust and heat of the Foundry, with anarchy and unthrift, he used to take the quiet restoratives of Nature, until the murmur and fragrance of the woods, the cool wind, and the soothing loiter of the shining stream had purged him from the fevers of his task.

To this old haunt he skated, and kindling a little fire, as an old campaigner loves to do, he sat down and lunched heartily on Mrs. Purtett's cold leg, — cannibal thought ! — on the cold leg of Mrs. Purtett's yesterday's turkey.   Then lighting his weed, — dear ally of the lonely, — the Superintendent began to think of his foreman's bliss, and to long for something similar on his own plane.

"I hope the wish is father to its fulfilment," he

said. "But I must not stop here and be spooney. Such a halcyon day I may not have again in all my life, and I ought to make the best of it, with my New Skates."

So he dashed off, and filled the little cove above the Point with a labyrinth of curves and flourishes.

When that bit of crystal tablet was well covered, the podographer sighed for a new sheet to inscribe his intricate rubricas upon. Why not write more stanzas of the poetry of motion on the ice below the Point? Why not?

Braced by his lunch on the brown fibre of good Mrs. Purtett's cold drumstick and thigh, Wade was now in fine trim. The air was more glittering and electric than ever. It was triumph and victory and pæan in action to go flashing along over this footing, smoother than polished marble and sheenier than first-water gems.

Wade felt the high exhilaration of pure blood galloping through a body alive from top to toe. The rhythm of his movement was like music to him.

The Point ended in a sharp promontory. Just before he came abreast of it, Wade under mighty headway flung into his favorite corkscrew spiral on one foot, and went whirling dizzily along, round and round, in a straight line.

At the dizziest moment, he was suddenly aware of a figure, also turning the Point at full speed, and rushing to a collision.

He jerked aside to avoid it. He could not look

to his footing.   His skate struck a broken oar, imbedded in the ice.   He fell violently, and lay like a dead man.

His New Skates, Testimonial of Merit, seem to have served him a shabby trick.

CHAPTER VIII.

TÊTE-À-TÊTE.

SEEING Wade lie there motionless, the lady —

Took off her spectacles, blew her great red nose, and stiffly drew near.

Spectacles!   Nose!   No, — the latter feature of hers had never become acquainted with the former ; and there was as little stiffness as nasal redness about her.

A fresh start, then, — and this time accuracy!

Appalled by the loud thump of the stranger's skull upon the chief river of the State of New York, the lady — it was a young lady whom Wade had tumbled to avoid — turned, saw a human being lying motionless, and swept gracefully toward him, like a Good Samaritan, on the outer edge.   It was not her fault, but her destiny, that she had to be graceful even under these tragic circumstances.

"Dead!" she thought.   "Is he dead?"

The appalling thump had cracked the ice, and

she could not know how well the skull was cush-
ioned inside with brains to resist a blow.

She shuddered, as she swooped about toward
this possible corpse. It might be that he was
killed, and half the fault hers. No wonder her fine
color, shining in the right parts of an admirably
drawn face, all disappeared instantly.

But she evidently was not frightened. She halted, kneeled, looked curiously at the stranger, and
then proceeded, in a perfectly cool and self-possessed way, to pick him up.

A solid fellow, heavy to lift in his present lump-
ish condition of dead-weight! She had to tug
mightily to get him up into a sitting position.
When he was raised, all the backbone seemed gone
from his spine, and it took the whole force of her
vigorous arms to sustain him.

The effort was enough to account for the return
of her color. It came rushing back splendidly.
Cheeks, forehead, everything but nose, blushed.
The hard work of lifting so much avoirdupois, and
possibly, also, the novelty of supporting so much
handsome fellow, intensified all her hues. Her
eyes — blue, or that shade even more faithful than
blue — deepened ; and her pale golden hair grew
several carats — not carrots — brighter.

She was repaid for her active sympathy at once
by discovering that this big, awkward thing was
not a dead, but only a stunned body. It had an
ugly bump and a bleeding cut on its manly skull,
but otherwise was quite an agreeable object to

contemplate, and plainly on its "unembarrassed brow Nature had written 'Gentleman.'"

As this young lady had never had a fair, steady stare at a stunned hero before, she seized her advantage. She had hitherto been distant with the other sex. She had no brother. Not one of her male cousins had ever ventured near enough to get those cousinly privileges that timid cousins sigh for and plucky cousins take, if they are worth taking.

Wade's impressive face, though for the moment blind as a statue's, also seized its advantage and stared at her intently, with a pained and pleading look, new to those resolute features.

Wade was entirely unconscious of the great hit he had made by his tumble: plump into the arms of this heroine ! There were fellows extant who would have suffered any imaginable amputation, any conceivable mauling, any fling from the apex of anything into the lowest deeps of anywhere, for the honor he was now enjoying.

But all he knew was that his skull was a beehive in an uproar, and that one lobe of his brain was struggling to swarm off. His legs and arms felt as if they belonged to another man, and a very limp one at that. A ton of cast-iron seemed to be pressing his eyelids down, and a trickle of red-hot metal flowed from his cut forehead.

"I shall have to scream," thought the lady, after an instant of anxious waiting, "if he does not revive. I cannot leave him to go for help."

Not a prude, you see. A prude would have had cheap scruples about compromising herself by taking a man in her arms. Not a vulgar person, who would have required the stranger to be properly recommended by somebody who came over in the Mayflower, before she helped him. Not a feeble-minded damsel, who, if she had not fainted, would have fled away, gasping and in tears. No timidity or prudery or underbred doubts about this thorough creature. She knew she was in her right womanly place, and she meant to stay there.

But she began to need help, possibly a lancet, possibly a pocket-pistol, possibly hot blankets, possibly somebody to knead these lifeless lungs and pommel this flaccid body, until circulation was restored.

Just as she was making up her mind to scream, Wade stirred. He began to tingle as if a familiar of the Inquisition were slapping him all over with fine-toothed currycombs. He became half conscious of a woman supporting him. In a stammering and intoxicated voice he murmured, —

"Who ran to catch me when I fell,
And kissed the place to make it well?
My — "

He opened his eyes. It was not his mother ; for she was long since deceased. Nor was this non-mother kissing the place.

In fact, abashed at the blind eyes suddenly unclosing so near her, she was on the point of letting her burden drop. When dead men come to life in such a position, and begin to talk about "kissing the place," young ladies, however independent of conventions, may well grow uneasy.

But the stranger, though alive, was evidently in a molluscous, invertebrate condition. He could not sustain himself. She still held him up, a little more at arm's-length, and all at once the reaction from extreme anxiety brought a gush of tears to her eyes.

".Don't cry," says Wade, vaguely, and still only half conscious. "I promise never to do so again."

At this, said with a childlike earnestness, the lady smiled.

"Don't scalp me," Wade continued, in the same tone. "Squaws never scalp."

He raised his hand to his bleeding forehead.

She laughed outright at his queer plaintive tone and the new class he had placed her in.

Her laugh and his own movement brought Wade fully to himself. She perceived that his look was transferring her from the order of scalping squaws to her proper place as a beautiful young woman of the highest civilization, not smeared with vermilion, but blushing celestial rosy.

"Thank you," said Wade. "I can sit up now without assistance." And he regretted profoundly that good breeding obliged him to say so.

She withdrew her arms. He rested on the ice, — posture of the Dying Gladiator. She made an effort to be cool and distant as usual; but it would not do. This weak mighty man still interested her. It was still her business to be strength to him.

He made a feeble attempt to wipe away the drops of blood from his forehead with his handkerchief.

"Let me be your surgeon!" said she.

She produced her own folded handkerchief, — M. D. were the initials in the corner, — and neatly and tenderly turbaned him.

Wade submitted with delight to this treatment. A tumble with such trimmings was luxury indeed.

"Who would not break his head," he thought, "to have these delicate fingers plying about him, and this pure, noble face so close to his? What a queenly indifferent manner she has! What a calm brow! What honest eyes! What a firm nose! What equable cheeks! What a grand indignant mouth! Not a bit afraid of me! She feels that I am a gentleman and will not presume."

"There!" said she, drawing back. "Is that comfortable?"

"Luxury!" he ejaculated with fervor.

"I am afraid I am to blame for your terrible fall."

"No, — my own clumsiness and that oar-blade are in fault."

"If you feel well enough to be left alone, I will skate off and call my friends."

"Please do not leave me quite yet!" says Wade, entirely satisfied with the *tête-à-tête*.

"Ah! here comes Mr. Skerrett round the Point!" she said, — and sprang up, looking a little guilty.

8*　　　　　　　　　　　　　　　　L

CHAPTER IX.

LOVE IN THE FIRST DEGREE.

PETER SKERRETT came sailing round the purple rocks of his Point, skating like a man who has been in the South of Europe for two winters.

He was decidedly Anglicized in his whiskers, coat, and shoes. Otherwise he in all respects repeated his well-known ancestor, Skerrett of the Revolution; whose two portraits — 1. A ruddy hero in regimentals, in Gilbert Stuart's early brandy-and-water manner; 2. A rosy sage in senatorials, in Stuart's later claret-and-water manner — hang in his descendant's dining-room.

Peter's first look was a provokingly significant one at the confused and blushing young lady. Secondly he inspected the Dying Gladiator on the ice.

"Have you been tilting at this gentleman, Mary?" he asked, in the voice of a cheerful, friendly fellow. "Why! Hullo. Hooray! It's Wade, Richard Wade, Dick Wade! Don't look, Miss Mary, while I give him the grips of all the secret societies we belonged to in College."

Mary, however, did look on, pleased and amused, while Peter plumped down on the ice, shook his friend's hand, and examined him as if he were fine crockery, spilt and perhaps shattered.

"It's not a case of trepanning, Dick, my boy?" said he.

"No," said the other. "I tumbled in trying to dodge this lady. The ice thought my face ought to be scratched, because I had been scratching its face without mercy. My wits were knocked out of me; but they are tired of secession, and pleading to be let in again."

"Keep some of them out for our sake! We must have you at our commonplace level. Well, Miss Mary, I suppose this is the first time you have had the sensation of breaking a man's head. You generally hit lower." Peter tapped his heart.

"I'm all right now, thanks to my surgeon," says Wade. "Give me a lift, Peter." He pulled up and clung to his friend.

"You're the vine and I'm the lamp-post," Skerrett said. "Mary, do you know what a pocket-pistol is?"

"I have seen such weapons concealed about the persons of modern warriors."

"There's one in my overcoat-pocket, with a cup at the but and a cork at the muzzle. Skate off now, like an angel, and get it. Bring Fanny, too. She is restorative."

"Are you alive enough to admire that, Dick?" he continued, as she skimmed away.

"It would put a soul under the ribs of Death."

"I venerate that young woman," says Peter. "You see what a beauty she is, and just as unspoiled as this ice. Unspoiled beauties are rarer than rocs' eggs."

"She has a singularly true face," Wade replied,

" and that is the main thing, — the most excellent thing in man or woman."

" Yes, truth makes that nuisance, beauty, tolerable."

" You did not do me the honor to present me."

" I saw you had gone a great way beyond that, my boy. Have you not her initials in cambric on your brow ? Not M. T., which would n't apply ; but M. D."

" Mary —— ? "

" Damer."

" I like the name," says Wade, repeating it. " It sounds simple and thorough-bred."

" Just what she is. One of the nine simple-hearted and thorough-bred girls on this continent."

" Nine ? "

" Is that too many ? Three, then. That 's one in ten millions. The exact proportion of Poets, Painters, Orators, Statesmen, and all other Great Artists. Well, — three or nine, — Mary Damer is one of them. She never saw fear or jealousy, or knowingly allowed an ignoble thought or an ungentle word or an ungraceful act in herself. Her atmosphere does not tolerate flirtation. You must find out for yourself how much genius she has and has not. But I will say this, — that I think of puns two a minute faster when I 'm with her. Therefore she must be magnetic, and that is the first charm in a woman."

Wade laughed. " You have not lost your powers of analysis, Peter. But talking of this heroine, you have not told me anything about yourself, except *apropos* of punning."

"Come up and dine, and we'll fire away personal histories, broadside for broadside! I've been looking in vain for a worthy hero to set *vis-à-vis* to my fair kinswoman. But stop! perhaps you have a Christmas turkey at home, with a wife opposite, and a brace of boys waiting for drumsticks."

"No,—my boys, like cherubs, await their own drumsticks. They're not born, and I'm not married."

"I thought you looked incomplete and abnormal. Well, I will show you a model wife,—and here she comes!"

Here they came, the two ladies, gliding round the Point, with draperies floating as artlessly artful as the robes of Raphael's Hours, or a Pompeian Bacchante. For want of classic vase or *patera*, Miss Damer brandished Peter Skerrett's pocket-pistol.

Fanny Skerrett gave her hand cordially to Wade, and looked a little anxiously at his pale face.

"Now, M. D.," says Peter, "you have been surgeon, you shall be doctor and dose our patient. Now, then,—

'Hebe, pour free!
Quicken his eyes with mountain-dew,
That Styx, the detested,
No more he may view.'"

"Thanks, Hebe!"

Wade said, continuing the quotation,—

"I quaff it!
Io Pæan, I cry!
The whiskey of the Immortals
Forbids me to die."

"We effeminate women of the nineteenth century are afraid of broken heads," said Fanny. "But Mary Damer seems quite to enjoy your accident, Mr. Wade, as an adventure."

Miss Damer certainly did seem gay and exhilarated.

"I enjoy it," said Wade. "I perceive that I fell on my feet, when I fell on my crown. I tumbled among old friends, and I hope among new ones."

"I have been waiting to claim my place among your old friends," Mrs. Skerrett said, "ever since Peter told me you were one of his models."

She delivered this little speech with a caressing manner which totally fascinated Wade.

Nothing was ever so absolutely pretty as Mrs. Peter Skerrett. Her complete prettiness left nothing to be desired.

"Never," thought Wade, "did I see such a compact little casket of perfections. Every feature is thoroughly well done and none intrusively superior. Her little nose is a combination of all the amiabilities. Her black eyes sparkle with fun and mischief and wit, all playing over deep tenderness below. Her hair ripples itself full of gleams and shadows. The same coquetry of Nature that rippled her hair has dinted her cheeks with shifting dimples. Every time she smiles — and she smiles as if sixty an hour were not half-allowance — a dimple slides into view and vanishes like a dot in a flow of sunny water. And, O Peter Skerrett! if

you were not the best fellow in the world, I should
envy you that latent kiss of a mouth."

"You need not say it, Wade, — your broken
head exempts you from the business of compliments," said Peter ; "but I see you think my wife
perfection. You 'll think so the more, the more
you know her."

"Stop, Peter," said she, "or I shall have to
hide behind the superior charms of Mary Damer."

Miss Damer certainly was a woman of a grander
order. You might pull at the bells or knock at
the knockers and be introduced into the bou-
doirs of all the houses, villas, seats, chateaus,
and palaces in Christendom without seeing such
another. She belonged distinctly to the Northern
races, — the "brave and true and tender" women. There was, indeed, a trace of hauteur
and imperiousness in her look and manner; but
it did not ill become her distinguished figure
and face. Wade, however, remembered her sweet
earnestness when she was playing leech to his
wound, and chose to take that mood as her dominant one.

"She must have been desperately annoyed with
bores and boobies," he thought. "I do not wonder she protects herself by distance. I am afraid
I shall never get within her lines again, — not
even if I should try slow and regular approaches,
and bombard her with bouquets for a twelve-
month."

"But, Wade," says Peter, "all this time you

have not told us what good luck sends you here to be wrecked on the hospitable shores of my Point."

" I live here.   I am chief cook and confectioner where you see the smoking top of that tall chimney up-stream."

" Why, of course !   What a dolt I was, not to think of you, when Churm told us an Athlete, a Brave, a Sage, and a Gentleman was the Superintendent of Dunderbunk ; but said we must find his name out for ourselves.   You remember, Mary. Miss Damer is Mr. Churm's ward."

She acknowledged with a cool bow that she did remember her guardian's character of Wade.

" You do not say, Peter," says Mrs. Skerrett, with a bright little look at the other lady, " why Mr. Churm was so mysterious about Mr. Wade."

" Miss Damer shall tell us," Peter rejoined, repeating his wife's look of merry significance.

She looked somewhat teased.   Wade could divine easily the meaning of this little mischievous talk.   His friend Churm had no doubt puffed him furiously.

" All this time," said Miss Damer, evading a reply, " we are neglecting our skating privileges."

" Peter and I have a few grains of humanity in our souls," Fanny said.   " We should blush to sail away from Mr. Wade, while he carries the quarantine flag at his pale cheeks."

" I am almost ruddy again," says Wade.   " Your potion, Miss Damer, has completed the work of your surgery. I can afford to dismiss my lamp-post."

"Whereupon the post changes to a teetotum," Peter said, and spun off in an eccentric, ending in a tumble.

"I must have a share in your restoration, Mr. Wade," Fanny claimed. "I see you need a second dose of medicine. Hand me the flask, Mary. What shall I pour from this magic bottle ? juice of Rhine, blood of Burgundy, fire of Spain, bubble of Rheims, beeswing of Oporto, honey of Cyprus, nectar, or whiskey ? Whiskey is vulgar, but the proper thing, on the whole, for these occasions. I prescribe it." And she gave him another little draught to imbibe.

He took it kindly, for her sake, — and not alone for that, but for its own respectable sake. His recovery was complete. His head, to be sure, sang a little still, and ached not a little. Some fellows would have gone on the sick list with such a wound. Perhaps he would, if he had had a trouble to dodge. But here instead was a pleasure to follow. So he began to move about slowly, watching the ladies.

Fanny was a novice in the Art, and this was her first day this winter. She skated timidly, holding Peter very tightly. She went into the dearest little panics for fear of tumbles, and uttered the most musical screams and laughs. And if she succeeded in taking a few brave strokes and finished with a neat slide, she pleaded for a verdict of "Well done !" with such an appealing smile and such a fine show of dimples that every one was fascinated and applauded heartily.

Miss Damer skated as became her free and vigorous character. She had passed her Little Go as a scholar, and was now steadily winning her way through the list of achievements, before given, toward the Great Go. To-day she was at work at small circles backward. Presently she wound off a series of perfectly neat ones, and, looking up, pleased with her prowess, caught Wade's admiring eye. At this she smiled and gave an arch little womanly nod of self-approval, which also demanded masculine sympathy before it was quite a perfect emotion.

With this charming gesture, the alert feather in her Amazonian hat nodded, too, as if it admired its lovely mistress.

Wade was thrilled. " Brava ! " he cried, in answer to the part of her look which asked sympathy ; and then, in reply to the implied challenge, he forgot his hurt and his shock, and struck into the same figure.

He tried not to surpass his fair exemplar too cruelly. But he did his peripheries well enough to get a repetition of the captivating nod and a Bravo ! from the lady.

" Bravo ! " said she. " But do not tax your strength too soon."

She began to feel that she was expressing too much interest in the stranger. It was a new sensation for her to care whether men fell or got up.

A new sensation. She rather liked it. She was a trifle ashamed of it. In either case, she did not wish to show that it was in her heart. The consciousness of concealment flushed her damask cheek.

It was a damask cheek. All her hues were cool and pearly; while Wade, Saxon too, had hot golden tints in his hair and moustache, and his color, now returning, was good strong red with plenty of bronze in it.

"Thank you," he replied. "My force has all come back. You have electrified me."

A civil nothing; but meaning managed to get into his tone and look, whether he would or not.

Which he perceiving, on his part began to feel guilty.

Of what crime?

Of the very same crime as hers, — the most ancient and most pardonable crime of youth and maiden, — that sweet and guiltless crime of love in the first degree.

So, without troubling themselves to analyze their feelings, they found a piquant pleasure in skating together, — she in admiring his *tours de force*, and he in instructing her.

"Look, Peter!" said Mrs. Skerrett, pointing to the other pair skating, he on the backward roll, she on the forward, with hands crossed and locked; — such contacts are permitted in skating, as in dancing. "Your hero and my heroine have dropped into an intimacy."

"None but the Plucky deserve the Pretty," says Peter.

"But he seems to be such a fine fellow, — suppose she should n't — "

The pretty face looked anxious.

"Suppose *he* should n't," Peter on the masculine behalf returned.

"He cannot help it : Mary is so noble, — and so charming, when she does not disdain to be."

"I do not believe *she* can help it. She cannot disdain Wade. He carries too many guns for that. He is just as fine as she is. He was a hero when I first knew him. His face does not show an atom of change ; and you know what Mr. Churm told us of his chivalric deeds elsewhere, and how he tamed and reformed Dunderbunk. He is crystal grit, as crystalline and gritty as he can be."

"Grit seems to be your symbol of the highest qualities. It certainly is a better thing in man than in ice-cream. But, Peter, suppose this should be a true love and should not run smooth ? "

"What consequence is the smooth running, so long as there is strong running and a final getting in neck and neck at the winning-post ? "

"But," still pleaded the anxious soul, — having no anxieties of her own, she was always suffering for others, — "he seems to be such a fine fellow ! and she is so hard to win ! "

"Am I a fine fellow ? "

"No, — horrid ! "

"The truth, — or I let you tumble."

"Well, upon compulsion, I admit that you are."

"Then being a fine fellow does not diminish the said fellow's chances of being blessed with a wife quite superfine."

"If I thought you were personal, Peter, I should object to the mercantile adjective. 'Superfine,' indeed !"

"I am personal. I withdraw the obnoxious phrase, and substitute transcendent. No, Fanny dear, I read Wade's experience in my own. I do not feel very much concerned about him. He is big enough to take care of himself. A man who is sincere, self-possessed, and steady does not get into miseries with beautiful Amazons like our friend. He knows too much to try to make his love run up hill ; but let it once get started, rough running gives it *vim*. Wade will love like a deluge, when he sees that he may, and I'd advise obstacles to stand off."

"It was pretty, Peter, to see cold Mary Damer so gentle and almost tender."

"I always have loved to see the first beginnings of what looks like love, since I saw ours."

"Ours," she said, — "it seems like yesterday."

And then together they recalled that fair picture against its dark ground of sorrow, and so went on refreshing the emotions of that time until Fanny smiling said, —

"There must be something magical in skates, for here we are talking sentimentally like a pair of young lovers."

"Health and love are cause and effect," says Peter, sententiously.

Meanwhile Wade had been fast skating into the good graces of his companion. Perhaps the rap on his head had deranged him. He certainly tossed himself about in a reckless and insane way. Still he justified his conduct by never tumbling again, and by inventing new devices with bewildering rapidity.

This pair were not at all sentimental. Indeed, their talk was quite technical : all about rings and edges, and heel and toe, — what skates are best, and who best use them. There is an immense amount of sympathy to be exchanged on such topics, and it was somewhat significant that they avoided other themes where they might not sympathize so thoroughly. The negative part of a conversation is often as important as its positive.

So the four entertained themselves finely, sometimes as a quartette, sometimes as two duos with proper changes of partners, until the clear west began to grow golden and the clear east pink with sunset.

"It is a pity to go," said Peter Skerrett. "Everything here is perfection and Fine Art ; but we must not be unfaithful to dinner. Dinner would have a right to punish us, if we did not encourage its efforts to be Fine Art also."

"Now, Mr. Wade," Fanny commanded, "your most heroic series of exploits, to close this heroic day."

He nimbly dashed through his list. The ice was traced with a labyrinth of involuted convolutions.

Wade's last turn brought him to the very spot of his tumble.

" Ah ! " said he. " Here is the oar that tripped me, with ' Wade, his mark,' gashed into it. If I had not this " — he touched Miss Damer's handkerchief — " for a souvenir, I think I would dig up the oar and carry it home."

" Let it melt out and float away in the spring," Mary said. " It may be a perch for a sea-gull or a buoy for a drowning man."

Here, if this were a long story instead of a short one, might be given a description of Peter Skerrett's house and the *menu* of Mrs. Skerrett's dinner. Peter and his wife had both been to great pillory dinners, *ad nauseam*, and learnt what to avoid. How not to be bored is the object of all civilization, and the Skerretts had discovered the methods.

I must dismiss the dinner and the evening, stamped with the general epithet, Perfection.

" You will join us again to-morrow on the river," said Mrs. Skerrett, as Wade rose to go.

" To-morrow I go to town to report to my Directors."

" Then next day."

" Next day, with pleasure."

Wade departed and marked this halcyon day with white chalk, as the whitest, brightest, sweetest of his life.

CHAPTER X.

FOREBODINGS.

JUBILATION! Jubilation now, instead of Consternation, in the office of Mr. Benjamin Brummage in
Wall-Street.

President Brummage had convoked his Directors
to hear the First Semiannual Report of the new
Superintendent and Dictator of Dunderbunk.

And there they sat around the green table, no
longer forlorn and dreading a failure, but all chuck-
ling with satisfaction over their prosperity.

They were a happy and hilarious family now, —
so hilarious that the President was obliged to be
always rapping to Orderr with his paper-knife.

Every one of these gentlemen was proud of himself as a Director of so successful a Company.
The Dunderbunk advertisement might now consider itself as permanent in the newspapers, and
the Treasurer had very unnecessarily inserted the
notice of a dividend, which everybody knew of
already.

When Mr. Churm was not by, they all claimed
the honor of having discovered Wade, or at least
of having been the first to appreciate him.

They all invited him to dinner, — the others at
their houses, Sam Gwelp at his club.

They had not yet begun to wax fat and kick.
They still remembered the panic of last summer.

They passed a unanimous vote of the most complimentary confidence in Wade, approved of his system, forced upon him an increase of salary, and began to talk of "launching out" and doubling their capital. In short, they behaved as Directors do when all is serene.

Churm and Wade had a hearty laugh over the absurdities of the Board and all their vague propositions.

"Dunderbunk," said Churm, "was a company started on a sentimental basis, as many others are."

"Mr. Brummage fell in love with pig-iron?"

"Precisely. He had been a dry-goods jobber, risen from a retailer somewhere in the country. He felt a certain lack of dignity in his work. He wanted to deal in something more masculine than lace and ribbons. He read a sentimental article on Iron in the 'Journal of Commerce': how Iron held the world together; how it was nerve and sinew; how it was ductile and malleable and other things that sounded big; how without Iron civilization would stop, and New-Zealanders hunt rats among the ruins of London; how anybody who would make two tons of Iron grow where one grew before was a benefactor to the human race greater than Alexander, Cæsar, or Napoleon; and so on, — you know the eloquent style. Brummage's soul was fired. He determined to be greater than the three heroes named. He was oozing with unoccupied capital. He went about among the other rich jobbers, with the newspaper

9   N

article in his hand, and fired their souls. They determined to be great Iron-Kings, — magnificent thought ! They wanted to read in the newspapers, 'If all the iron rails made at the Dunderbunk Works in the last six months were put together in a straight line, they would reach twice round our terraqueous globe and seventy-three miles two rails over.' So on that poetic foundation they started the concern."

Wade laughed. " But how did you happen to be with them ? "

" Oh ! my friend Damer sold them the land for the shop and took stock in payment. I came into the Board as his executor. Did I never tell you so before ? "

" No."

" Well, then, be informed that it was in Miss Damer's behalf that you knocked down Friend Tarbox, and so got your skates for saving her property. It's quite a romance already, Richard, my boy ! and I suppose you feel immensely bored that you had to come down and meet us old chaps, instead of tumbling at her feet on the ice again to-day."

" A tumble in this wet day would be a cold bath to romance."

The Gulf Stream had sent up a warm spoil-sport rain that morning. It did not stop, but poured furiously the whole day.

From Cohoes to Spuyten Duyvil, on both sides of the river, all the skaters swore at the weather,

as profane persons no doubt did when the windows
of heaven were opened in Noah's time. The
skateresses did not swear, but savagely said, "It
is too bad," — and so it was.

Wade, loaded with the blessings of his Directors,
took the train next morning for Dunderbunk.

The weather was still mild and drizzly, but
promised to clear. As the train rattled along by
the river, Wade could see that the thin ice was
breaking up everywhere. In mid-stream a procession of blocks was steadily drifting along. Unless Zero came sliding down again pretty soon
from Boreal regions, the sheets that filled the coves
and clung to the shores would also sail away southward, and the whole Hudson be left clear as in mid-
summer.

At Yonkers a down train ranged by the side of
Wade's train, and, looking out he saw Mr. and
Mrs. Skerrett alighting.

He jumped down, rather surprised, to speak to
them.

"We have just been telegraphed here," said
Peter, gravely. "The son of a widow, a friend of
ours, was drowned this morning in the soft ice of
the river. He was a pet of mine, poor fellow! and
the mother depends upon me for advice. We have
come down to say a kind word. Why won't you
report us to the ladies at my house, and say we
shall not be at home until the evening train?
They do not know the cause of our journey except
that it is a sad one."

"Perhaps Mr. Wade will carve their turkey for them at dinner, Peter," Fanny suggested.

"Do, Wade, and keep their spirits up. Dinner's at six."

Here the engine whistled. Wade promised to "shine substitute" at his friend's board, and took his place again. The train galloped away.

Peter and his wife exchanged a bright look over the fortunate incident of this meeting, and went on their kind way to carry sympathy and such consolation as might be to the widow.

The train galloped northward. Until now, the beat of its wheels, like the click of an enormous metronome, had kept time to jubilant measures singing in Wade's brain. He was hurrying back, exhilarated with success, to the presence of a woman whose smile was finer exhilaration than any number of votes of confidence, passed unanimously by any number of conclaves of overjoyed Directors, and signed by Brummage after Brummage, with the signature of a capitalist in a flurry of delight at a ten per cent dividend.

But into this joyous mood of Wade's the thought of death suddenly intruded. He could not keep a picture of death and drowning out of his mind. As the train sprang along and opened gloomy breadth after breadth of the leaden river, clogged with slow-drifting files of ice-blocks, he found himself staring across the dreary waste and forever fancying some one sinking there, helpless and alone.

He seemed to see a brave, bright-eyed, ruddy

boy, venturing out carelessly along the edges of the weakened ice. Suddenly the ice gives way, the little figure sinks, rises, clutches desperately at a fragment, struggles a moment, is borne along in the relentless flow of the chilly water, stares in vain shoreward, and so sinks again with a look of agony, and is gone.

But whenever this inevitable picture grew before Wade's eyes, as the drowning figure of his fancy vanished, it suddenly changed features, and presented the face of Mary Damer, perishing beyond succor.

Of course he knew that this was but a morbid vision. Yet that it came at all, and that it so agonized him, proved the force of his new feeling.

He had not analyzed it before. This thought of death became its touchstone.

Men like Wade, strong, healthy, earnest, concentrated, straightforward, isolated, judge men and women as friends or foes at once and once for all. He had recognized in Mary Damer from the first a heart as true, whole, noble, and healthy as his own. A fine instinct had told him that she was waiting for her hero, as he was for his heroine.

So he suddenly loved her. And yet not suddenly ; for all his life, and all his lesser forgotten or discarded passions, had been training him for this master one.

He suddenly and strongly loved her ; and yet it had only been a beautiful bewilderment of uncomprehended delight, until this haunting vision of her fair face sinking amid the hungry ice beset him. Then he perceived what would be lost to him, if she were lost.

The thought of Death placed itself between him and Love. If the love had been merely a pretty remembrance of a charming woman, he might have dismissed his fancied drowning scene with a little emotion of regret. Now, the fancy was an agony.

He had too much power over himself to entertain it long. But the grisly thought came uninvited, returned undesired, and no resolute Avaunt, even backed by that magic wand, a cigar, availed to banish it wholly.

The sky cleared cold at eleven o'clock. A sharp wind drew through the Highlands. As the train rattled round the curve below the tunnel through Skerrett's Point, Wade could see his skating course of Christmas-Day with the ladies. Firm ice, glazed smooth by the sudden chill after the rain, filled the Cove and stretched beyond the Point into the river.

It was treacherous stuff, beautiful to the eyes of a skater, but sure to be weak, and likely to break up any moment and join the deliberate headlong drift of the masses in mid-current.

Wade almost dreaded lest his vision should suddenly realize itself, and he should see his enthusiastic companion of the other day sailing gracefully along to certain death.

Nothing living, however, was in sight, except here and there a crow, skipping about in the floating ice.

The lover was greatly relieved. He could now forewarn the lady against the peril he had imagined. The train in a moment dropped him at Dunderbunk. He hurried to the Foundry and wrote a note to Mrs. Damer.

" Mr. Wade presents his compliments to Mrs. Damer, and has the honor to inform her that Mr. Skerrett has nominated him carver to the ladies to-day in their host's place.

" Mr. Wade hopes that Miss Damer will excuse him from his engagement to skate with her this afternoon. The ice is dangerous, and Miss Damer should on no account venture upon it."

Perry Purtett was the bearer of this billet. He swaggered into Peter Skerrett's hall, and dreadfully alarmed the fresh-imported Englishman who answered the bell, by ordering him in a severe tone, —

" Hurry up now, White Cravat, with that answer! I 'm wanted down to the Works. Steam don't bile when I 'm off; and the fly-wheel will never buzz another turn, unless I 'm there to motion it to move on."

Mrs. Damer's gracious reply informed Wade " that she should be charmed to see him at dinner, etc., and would not fail to transmit his kind warning to Miss Damer, when she returned from her drive to make calls."

But when Miss Damer returned in the afternoon, her mother was taking a gentle nap over the violet, indigo, blue, green, yellow, orange, red stripes of a gorgeous Afghan she was knitting. The daughter

heard nothing of the billet.   The house was lonely
without Fanny Skerrett.   Mr. Wade did not come
at the appointed hour.   Mary was not willing to
say to herself how much she regretted his absence.

Had he forgotten the appointment ?

No, — that was a thought not to be tolerated.

" A gentleman does not forget," she thought.
And she had a thorough confidence, besides, that
this gentleman was very willing to remember.

She read a little, fitfully, sang fitfully, moved
about the house uneasily ; and at last, when it grew
late, and she was bored and Wade did not arrive,
she pronounced to herself that he had been detained
in town.

This point settled, she took her skates, put on
her pretty Amazonian hat with its alert feather,
and went down to waste her beauty and grace on
the ice, unattended and alone.

CHAPTER XI.

CAP'N AMBUSTER'S SKIFF.

It was a busy afternoon at the Dunderbunk
Foundry.

The Superintendent had come back with his
pocket full of orders.   Everybody, from the Czar
of Russia to the President of the Guano Republic,

was in the market for machinery. Crisis was gone
by.   Prosperity was come.   The world was all
ready to move, and only waited for a fresh supply
of wheels, cranks, side-levers, walking-beams, and
other such muscular creatures of iron, to push
and tug and swing and revolve and set Progress
a-going.

Dunderbunk was to have its full share in supply-
ing the demand.   It was well understood by this
time that the iron Wade made was as stanch as the
man who made it.   Dunderbunk, therefore, Head
and Hands, must despatch.

So it was a busy afternoon at the industrious
Foundry.   The men bestirred themselves.   The
furnaces rumbled.   The engine thumped.   The
drums in the finishing-shop hummed merrily their
lively song of labor.   The four trip-hammers —
two bull-headed, two calf-headed — champed, like
carnivorous maws, upon red bars of iron, and over
their banquet they roared the big-toned music of
the trip-hammer chorus, —

" Now then ! hit hard !

Strike while Iron 's hot.   Life 's short.   Art 's long."

By this massive refrain, ringing in at intervals above the ceaseless buzz, murmur, and clang
throughout the buildings, every man's work was
mightily nerved and inspired.   Everybody liked to
hear the sturdy song of these grim vocalists ; and
whenever they struck in, each solo or duo or qua-
tuor of men, playing Anvil Chorus, quickened time,
and all the action and rumor of the busy opera

9 *

went on more cheerily and lustily. So work kept astir like play.

An hour before sunset, Bill Tarbox stepped into Wade's office. Even oily and begrimed, Bill could be recognized as a favored lover. He looked more a man than ever before.

"I forgot to mention," says the foreman, "that Cap'n Ambuster was in, this morning, to see you. He says, that, if the river's clear enough for him to get away from our dock, he'll go down to the City to-morrow, and offers to take freight cheap. We might put that new walking-beam, we've just rough-finished for the 'Union,' aboard of him."

"Yes, — if he is sure to go to-morrow. It will not do to delay. The owners complained to me yesterday that the 'Union' was in a bad way for want of its new machinery. Tell your brother-in-law to come here, Bill."

Tarbox looked sheepishly pleased, and summoned Perry Purtett.

"Run down, Perry," said Wade, "to the 'Ambuster,' and ask Captain Isaac to step up here a moment. Tell him I have some freight to send by him."

Perry moved through the Foundry with his usual jaunty step, left his dignity at the door, and ran off to the dock.

The weather had grown fitful. Heavy clouds whirled over, trailing snow-flurries. Rarely the sun found a cleft in the black canopy to shoot a ray through and remind the world that he was still in his place and ready to shine when he was wanted.

Master Perry had a furlong to go before he reached the dock. He crossed the stream, kept unfrozen by the warm influences of the Foundry. He ran through a little dell hedged on each side by dull green cedars. It was severely cold now, and our young friend condescended to prance and jump over the ice-skimmed puddles to keep his blood in motion.

The little rusty, pudgy steamboat lay at the down-stream side of the Foundry wharf. Her name was so long and her paddle-box so short, that the painter, beginning with ambitious large letters, had been compelled to abbreviate the last syllable. Her title read thus : —

I. AMBUSTer.

Certainly a formidable inscription for a steamboat !

When she hove in sight, Perry halted, resumed his stately demeanor, and embarked as if he were a Doge entering a Bucentaur to wed a Sea.

There was nobody on deck to witness the arrival and salute the *magnifico*.

Perry looked in at the Cap'n's office. He beheld a three-legged stool, a hacked desk, an inky steel-pen, an inkless inkstand ; but no Cap'n Ambuster.

Perry inspected the Cap'n's state-room. There was a cracked looking-glass, into which he looked ; a hair-brush suspended by the glass, which he used ; a lair of blankets in a berth, which he had

no present use for; and a smell of musty boots,
which nobody with a nose could help smelling.
Still no Captain Ambuster, nor any of his crew.

Search in the unsavory kitchen revealed no cook,
coiled up in a corner, suffering nightmares for the
last greasy dinner he had brewed in his frying-
pan.   There were no deck hands bundled into
their bunks.   Perry rapped on the chain-box and
inquired if anybody was within, and nobody answering, he had to ventriloquize a negative.

The engine-room, too, was vacant, and quite as
unsavory as the other dens on board.   Perry pat-
ronized the engine by a pull or two at the valves,
and continued his tour of inspection.

The Ambuster's skiff, lying on her forward deck,
seemed to entertain him vastly.

"Jolly!" says Perry.   And so it was a jolly
boat in the literal, not the technical sense.

"The three wise men of Gotham went to sea in
a bowl; and here's the identical craft," says
Perry.

He gave the chubby little machine a push with
his foot.   It rolled and wallowed about grotesquely.
When it was still again, it looked so comic, lying
contentedly on its fat side like a pudgy baby, that
Perry had a roar of laughter, which, like other
laughter to one's self, did not sound very merry,
particularly as the north-wind was howling omi-
nously, and the broken ice, on its downward way,
was whispering and moaning and talking on in a
most mysterious and inarticulate manner.

" Those sheets of ice would crunch up this skiff, as pigs do a punkin," thinks Perry.

And with this thought in his head he looked out on the river, and fancied the foolish little vessel cast loose and buffeting helplessly about in the ice.

He had been so busy until now, in prying about the steamboat and making up his mind that Captain and men had all gone off for a comfortable supper on shore, that his eyes had not wandered toward the stream.

Now his glance began to follow the course of the icy current. He wondered where all this supply of cakes came from, and how many of them would escape the stems of ferry-boats below and get safe to sea.

All at once, as he looked lazily along the lazy files of ice, his eyes caught a black object drifting on a fragment in a wide way of open water opposite Skerrett's Point, a mile distant.

Perry's heart stopped beating. He uttered a little gasping cry. He sprang ashore, not at all like a Doge quitting a Bucentaur. He tore back to the Foundry, dashing through the puddles, and, never stopping to pick up his cap, burst in upon Wade and Bill Tarbox in the office.

The boy was splashed from head to foot with red mud. His light hair, blown wildly about, made his ashy face seem paler. He stood panting.

His dumb terror brought back to Wade's mind all the bad omens of the morning.

"Speak!" said he, seizing Perry fiercely by the shoulder.

The uproar of the Works seemed to hush for an instant, while the lad stammered faintly, —

"There's somebody carried off in the ice by Skerrett's Point. It looks like a woman. And there's nobody to help."

CHAPTER XII.

IN THE ICE.

"Help! help!" shouted the four trip-hammers, bursting in like a magnified echo of the boy's last word. "Help! help!" all the humming wheels and drums repeated more plaintively.

Wade made for the river.

This was the moment all his manhood had been training and saving for. For this he had kept sound and brave from his youth up.

As he ran, he felt that the only chance of instant help was in that queer little bowl-shaped skiff of the "Ambuster."

He had never been conscious that he had observed it; but the image had lain latent in his mind, biding its time. It might be ten, twenty precious moments before another boat could be found. This one was on the spot to do its duty at once.

"Somebody carried off, — perhaps a woman," Wade thought. " Not — No, she would not neglect my warning! Whoever it is, we must save her from this dreadful death! "

He sprang on board the little steamboat. She was swaying uneasily at her moorings, as the ice crowded along and hammered against her stem. Wade stared from her deck down the river, with all his life at his eyes.

More than a mile away, below the hemlock-crested point, was the dark object Perry had seen, still stirring along the edges of the floating ice. A broad avenue of leaden-green water wrinkled by the cold wind separated the field where this figure was moving from the shore. Dark object and its footing of gray ice were drifting deliberately farther and farther away.

For one instant Wade thought that the terrible dread in his heart would paralyze him. But in that one moment, while his blood stopped flowing and his nerves failed, Bill Tarbox overtook him and was there by his side.

" I brought your cap," says Bill, " and our two coats."

Wade put on his cap mechanically. This little action calmed him.

" Bill," said he, " I 'm afraid it is a woman, — a dear friend of mine, — a very dear friend."

Bill, a lover, understood the tone.

" We 'll take care of her between us," he said.

The two turned at once to the little tub of a boat.

Oars? Yes,—slung under the thwarts,—a pair of short sculls, worn and split, but with work in them still. There they hung ready,—and a rusty boat-hook, besides.

"Find the thole-pins, Bill, while I cut a plug for her bottom out of this broomstick," Wade said.

This was done in a moment. Bill threw in the coats.

"Now, together!"

They lifted the skiff to the gangway. Wade jumped down on the ice and received her carefully. They ran her along, as far as they could go, and launched her in the sludge.

"Take the sculls, Bill. I'll work the boat-hook in the bow."

Nothing more was said. They thrust out with their crazy little craft into the thick of the ice-flood. Bill, amidships, dug with his sculls in among the huddled cakes. It was clumsy pulling. Now this oar and now that would be thrown out. He could never get a full stroke.

Wade in the bow could do better. He jammed the blocks aside with his boat-hook. He dragged the skiff forward. He steered through the little open ways of water.

Sometimes they came to a broad sheet of solid ice. Then it was "Out with her, Bill!" and they were both out and sliding their bowl so quick over, that they had not time to go through the rotten surface. This was drowning business; but neither could be spared to drown yet.

In the leads of clear water, the oarsman got brave pulls and sent the boat on mightily. Then again in the thick porridge of brash ice they lost headway, or were baffled and stopped among the cakes. Slow work, slow and painful; and for many minutes they seemed to gain nothing upon the steady flow of the merciless current.

A frail craft for such a voyage, this queer little half-pumpkin! A frail and leaky shell. She bent and cracked from stem to stern among the nipping masses. Water oozed in through her dry seams. Any moment a rougher touch or a sharper edge might cut her through. But that was a risk they had accepted. They did not take time to think of it, nor to listen to the crunching and crackling of the hungry ice around. They urged straight on, steadily, eagerly, coolly, spending and saving strength.

Not one moment to lose! The shattering of broad sheets of ice around them was a warning of what might happen to the frail support of their chase. One thrust of the boat-hook sometimes cleft a cake that to the eye seemed stout enough to bear a heavier weight than a woman's.

Not one moment to spare! The dark figure, now drifted far below the hemlocks of the Point, no longer stirred. It seemed to have sunk upon the ice and to be resting there weary and helpless, on one side a wide way of lurid water, on the other half a mile of moving desolation.

Far to go, and no time to waste!

N

" Give way, Bill !   Give way !"

" Ay, ay !"

Both spoke in low tones, hardly louder than the whisper of the ice around them.

By this time hundreds from the Foundry and the village were swarming upon the wharf and the steamboat.

" A hundred tar-barrels would n't git up my steam in time to do any good," says Cap'n Ambuster. " If them two in my skiff don't overhaul the man, he 's gone."

" You 're sure it 's a man ? " says Smith Wheelwright.

" Take a squint through my glass.   I 'm drefful-ly afeard it 's a gal; but suthin' 's got into my eye, so I can't see."

Suthin' had got into the old fellow's eye, — suthin' saline and acrid, — namely, a tear.

" It 's a woman," says Wheelwright, — and suthin' of the same kind blinded him also.

Almost sunset now.   But the air was suddenly filled with perplexing snow-dust from a heavy squall.   A white curtain dropped between the anxious watchers on the wharf and the boatmen.

The same white curtain hid the dark floating object from its pursuers.   There was nothing in sight to steer by, now.

Wade steered by his last glimpse, — by the current, — by the rush of the roaring wind, — by instinct.

How merciful that in such a moment a man is

spared the agony of thought! His agony goes into action, intense as life.

It was bitterly cold. A swash of ice-water filled the bottom of the skiff. She was low enough down without that. They could not stop to bail, and the miniature icebergs they passed began to look significantly over the gunwale. Which would come to the point of foundering first, the boat or the little floe it aimed for?

Bitterly cold! The snow hardly melted upon Tarbox's bare hands. His fingers stiffened to the oars; but there was life in them still, and still he did his work, and never turned to see how the steersman was doing his.

A flight of crows came sailing with the snow-squall. They alighted all about on the hummocks, and curiously watched the two men battling to save life. One black impish bird, more malignant or more sympathetic than his fellows, ventured to poise on the skiff's stern!

Bill hissed off this third passenger. The crow rose on its toes, let the boat slide away from under him, and followed croaking dismal good wishes.

The last sunbeams were now cutting in everywhere. The thick snow-flurry was like a luminous cloud. Suddenly it drew aside.

The industrious skiff had steered so well and made such headway, that there, a hundred yards away, safe still, not gone, thank God! was the woman they sought.

A dusky mass flung together on a waning rood of ice, — Wade could see nothing more.

Weary or benumbed, or sick with pure forlorn-
ness and despair, she had drooped down and
showed no sign of life.

The great wind shook the river. Her waning
rood of ice narrowed, foot by foot, like an un-
thrifty man's heritage. Inch by inch its edges
wore away, until the little space that half sustained
the dark heap was no bigger than a coffin-lid.

Help, now ! — now, men, if you are to save !
Thrust, Richard Wade, with your boat-hook ! Pull,
Bill, till your oars snap ! Out with your last frenzies of vigor ! For the little raft of ice, even that
has crumbled beneath its burden, and she sinks, —
sinks, with succor close at hand !

Sinks ! No, — she rises and floats again.

She clasps something that holds her head just
above water. But the unmannerly ice has buffeted
her hat off. The fragments toss it about, — that
pretty Amazonian hat, with its alert feather, all
drooping and draggled. Her fair hair and pure
forehead are uncovered for an astonished sunbeam
to alight upon.

"It is my love, my life, Bill ! Give way, once
more !"

"Way enough ! Steady ! Sit where you are,
Bill, and trim boat, while I lift her out. We cannot risk capsizing."

He raised her carefully, tenderly, with his strong
arms.

A bit of wood had buoyed her up for that last
moment. It was a broken oar with a deep fresh
gash in it.

Wade knew his mark, — the cut of his own skate-iron. This busy oar was still resolved to play its part in the drama.

The round little skiff just bore the third person without sinking.

Wade laid Mary Damer against the thwart. She would not let go her buoy. He unclasped her stiffened hands. This friendly touch found its way to her heart. She opened her eyes and knew him.

"The ice shall not carry off her hat to frighten some mother, down stream," says Bill Tarbox, catching it.

All these proceedings Cap'n Ambuster's spy-glass announced to Dunderbunk.

"They 're h'istin' her up. They 've slumped her into the skiff. They 're puttin' for shore. Hooray!"

Pity a spy-glass cannot shoot cheers a mile and a half!

Perry Purtett instantly led a stampede of half Dunderbunk along the railroad-track to learn who it was and all about it.

All about it was, that Miss Damer was safe, and not dangerously frozen, — and that Wade and Tarbox had carried her up the hill to her mother at Peter Skerrett's.

Missing the heroes in chief, Dunderbunk made a hero of Cap'n Ambuster's skiff. It was transported back on the shoulders of the crowd in triumphal procession. Perry Purtett carried round the hat for a contribution to new paint it, new rib it, new gunwale it, give it new sculls and a new boat-hook, — indeed, to make a new vessel of the brave little bowl.

"I'm afeard," says Cap'n Ambuster, "that, when I git a harnsome new skiff, I shall want a harnsome new steamboat, and then the boat will go to cruisin' round for a harnsome new Cap'n."

And now for the end of this story.

Healthy love-stories always end in happy marriages.

So ends this story, begun as to its love portion by the little romance of a tumble, and continued by the bigger romance of a rescue.

Of course there were incidents enough to fill a volume, obstacles enough to fill a volume, and development of character enough to fill a tome thick as "Webster's Unabridged," before the happy end of the beginning of the Wade-Damer joint history.

But we can safely take for granted that, the lover being true and manly, and the lady true and womanly, and both possessed of the high moral qualities necessary to artistic skating, they will go on understanding each other better, until they are as one as two can be.

Masculine reader, attend to the moral of this tale : —

Skate well, be a hero, bravely deserve the fair, prove your deserts by your deeds, find your "perfect woman nobly planned to warm, to comfort, and command," catch her when found, and you are Blest.

Reader of the gentler sex, likewise attend :—

All the essential blessings of life accompany a true heart and a good complexion. Skate vigorously ; then your heart will beat true, your cheeks will bloom, your appointed lover will see your beautiful soul shining through your beautiful face, he will tell you so, and after sufficient circumlocution he will Pop, you will accept, and your lives will glide sweetly as skating on virgin ice to silver music.

NEW YORK SEVENTH REGIMENT.

OUR MARCH TO WASHINGTON.

10

NEW YORK SEVENTH REGIMENT.

OUR MARCH TO WASHINGTON.

THROUGH THE CITY.

At three o'clock in the afternoon of Friday, April 19th, we took our peacemaker, a neat twelve-pound brass howitzer, down from the Seventh Regiment Armory, and stationed it in the rear of the building. The twin peacemaker is somewhere near us, but entirely hidden by this enormous crowd.

An enormous crowd! of both sexes, of every age and condition. The men offer all kinds of truculent and patriotic hopes; the women shed tears, and say, "God bless you, boys!"

This is a part of the town where baddish cigars prevail. But good or bad, I am ordered to keep all away from the gun. So the throng stands back, peers curiously over the heads of its junior members, and seems to be taking the measure of my coffin.

After a patient hour of this, the word is given, we fall in, our two guns find their places at the right of the line of march, we move on through the thickening crowd.

At a great house on the left, as we pass the Astor Library, I see a handkerchief waving for me. Yes! it is she who made the sandwiches in my knapsack. They were a trifle too thick, as I afterwards discovered, but otherwise perfection. Be these my thanks and the thanks of hungry comrades who had bites of them!

At the corner of Great Jones Street we halted for half an hour, — then, everything ready, we marched down Broadway.

It was worth a life, that march. Only one who passed, as we did, through that tempest of cheers, two miles long, can know the terrible enthusiasm of the occasion. I could hardly hear the rattle of our own gun-carriages, and only once or twice the music of our band came to me muffled and quelled by the uproar. We knew now, if we had not before divined it, that our great city was with us as one man, utterly united in the great cause we were marching to sustain.

This grand fact I learned by two senses. If hundreds of thousands roared it into my ears, thousands slapped it into my back. My fellow-citizens smote me on the knapsack, as I went by at the gun-rope, and encouraged me each in his own dialect. "Bully for you!" alternated with benedictions, in the proportion of two "bullies" to one blessing.

I was not so fortunate as to receive more substantial tokens of sympathy. But there were parting gifts showered on the regiment, enough to establish a variety-shop. Handkerchiefs, of course, came floating down upon us from the windows, like a snow. Pretty little gloves pelted us with love-taps. The sterner sex forced upon us pocket-knives new and jagged, combs, soap, slippers, boxes of matches, cigars by the dozen and the hundred, pipes to smoke shag and pipes to smoke Latakia, fruit, eggs, and sandwiches. One fellow got a new purse with ten bright quarter-eagles.

At the corner of Grand Street, or thereabouts, a "bhoy" in red flannel shirt and black dress pantaloons, leaning back against the crowd with Herculean shoulders, called me, — "Saäy, bully! take my dorg! he's one of the kind that holds till he draps." This gentleman, with his animal, was instantly shoved back by the police, and the Seventh lost the "dorg."

These were the comic incidents of the march, but underlying all was the tragic sentiment that we might have tragic work presently to do. The news of the rascal attack in Baltimore on the Massachusetts Sixth had just come in. Ours might be the same chance. If there were any of us not in earnest before, the story of the day would steady us. So we said good-by to Broadway, moved down Cortlandt Street under a bower of flags, and at half past six shoved off in the ferry-boat.

Everybody has heard how Jersey City turned out and filled up the Railroad Station, like an opera-house, to give God-speed to us as a representative body, a guaranty of the unquestioning loyalty of the " conservative " class in New York. Everybody has heard how the State of New Jersey, along the railroad line, stood through the evening and the night to shout their quota of good wishes. At every station the Jerseymen were there, uproarious as Jerseymen, to shake our hands and wish us a happy despatch. I think I did not see a rod of ground without its man, from dusk till dawn, from the Hudson to the Delaware.

Upon the train we made a jolly night of it. All knew that the more a man sings, the better he is likely to fight. So we sang more than we slept, and, in fact, that has been our history ever since.

PHILADELPHIA.

At sunrise we were at the station in Philadelphia, and dismissed for an hour. Some hundreds of us made up Broad Street for the Lapierre House to breakfast. When I arrived, I found every place at table filled and every waiter ten deep with orders. So, being an old campaigner, I followed up the stream of provender to the fountain-head, the kitchen. Half a dozen other old campaigners were already there, most hospitably entertained by the cooks. They served us, hot and hot, with the best of their best, straight from the gridiron and the pan. I hope, if I live to breakfast again in the Lapierre House, that I may be allowed to help myself and choose for myself below-stairs.

When we rendezvoused at the train, we found

that the orders were for every man to provide himself three days' rations in the neighborhood, and be ready for a start at a moment's notice.

A mountain of bread was already piled up in the station. I stuck my bayonet through a stout loaf, and, with a dozen comrades armed in the same way, went foraging about for other *vivers*.

It is a poor part of Philadelphia; but whatever they had in the shops or the houses seemed to be at our disposition.

I stopped at a corner shop to ask for pork, and was amicably assailed by an earnest dame, — Irish, I am pleased to say. She thrust her last loaf upon me, and sighed that it was not baked that morning for my " honor's service."

A little farther on, two kindly Quaker ladies compelled me to step in. " What could they do ? " they asked eagerly. " They had no meat in the house ; but could we eat eggs ? They had in the house a dozen and a half, new-laid." So the pot to the fire, and the eggs boiled, and bagged by myself and that tall Saxon, my friend E., of the Sixth Company. While the eggs simmered, the two ladies thee-ed us prayerfully and tearfully, hoping that God would save our country from blood, unless blood must be shed to preserve Law and Liberty.

Nothing definite from Baltimore when we returned to the station. We stood by, waiting orders. About noon the Eighth Massachusetts Regiment took the train southward. Our regiment

was ready to a man to try its strength with the
Plug Uglies. If there had been any voting on the
subject, the plan to follow the straight road to
Washington would have been accepted by acclamation. But the higher powers deemed that "the
longest way round was the shortest way home,"
and no doubt their decision was wise. The event
proved it.

At two o'clock came the word to "fall in." We
handled our howitzers again, and marched down
Jefferson Avenue to the steamer "Boston" to embark.

To embark for what port? For Washington, of
course, finally; but by what route? That was to
remain in doubt to us privates for a day or two.

The Boston is a steamer of the outside line from
Philadelphia to New York. She just held our legion. We tramped on board, and were allotted
about the craft from the top to the bottom story.
We took tents, traps, and grub on board, and
steamed away down the Delaware in the sweet afternoon of April. If ever the heavens smiled fair
weather on any campaign, they have done so on
ours.

THE " BOSTON."

SOLDIERS on shipboard are proverbially fish out
of water. We could not be called by the good old
nickname of "lobsters" by the crew. Our gray
jackets saved the *sobriquet*. But we floundered
about the crowded vessel like boiling victims in a

pot. At last we found our places, and laid ourselves about the decks to tan or bronze or burn
scarlet, according to complexion. There were
plenty of cheeks of lobster-hue before next evening
on the Boston.

A thousand young fellows turned loose on shipboard were sure to make themselves merry. Let
the reader imagine that! We were like any other
excursionists, except that the stacks of bright guns
were always present to remind us of our errand,
and regular guard-mounting and drill went on all
the time. The young citizens growled or laughed
at the minor hardships of the hasty outfit, and
toughened rapidly to business.

Sunday, the 21st, was a long and somewhat anxious day. While we were bowling along in the
sweet sunshine and sweeter moonlight of the halcyon time, Uncle Sam might be dethroned by somebody in buckram, or Baltimore burnt by the boys
from Lynn or Marblehead, revenging the massacre
of their fellows. Every one begins to comprehend
the fiery eagerness of men who live in historic
times. "I wish I had control of chain-lightning
for a few minutes," says O., the droll fellow of our
company. "I'd make it come thick and heavy
and knock spots out of Secession."

At early dawn of Monday, the 22d, after feeling
along slowly all night, we see the harbor of Annapolis. A frigate with sails unbent lies at anchor.
She flies the stars and stripes. Hurrah!

A large steamboat is aground farther in. As

10 *   o

soon as we can see anything, we catch the glitter
of bayonets on board.

By and by boats come off, and we get news that
the steamer is the " Maryland," a ferry-boat of the
Philadelphia and Baltimore Railroad.   The Massachusetts Eighth Regiment had been just in time to
seize her on the north side of the Chesapeake.
They learned that she was to be carried off by the
crew and leave them blockaded.   So they shot their
Zouaves ahead as skirmishers.   The fine fellows
rattled on board, and before the steamboat had time
to take a turn or open a valve, she was held by
Massachusetts in trust for Uncle Sam.   Hurrah
for the most important prize thus far in the war!
It probably saved the " Constitution," " Old Ironsides," from capture by the traitors.   It probably
saved Annapolis, and kept Maryland open without
bloodshed.

As soon as the Massachusetts Regiment had
made prize of the ferry-boat, a call was made for
engineers to run her.   Some twenty men at once
stepped to the front.   We of the New York Seventh afterwards concluded that whatever was needed in the way of skill or handicraft could be found
among those brother Yankees.   They were the men
to make armies of.   They could tailor for themselves, shoe themselves, do their own blacksmith-
ing, gun-smithing, and all other work that calls for
sturdy arms and nimble fingers.   In fact, I have
such profound confidence in the universal accom-
plishment of the Massachusetts Eighth, that I have

no doubt, if the order were, "Poets to the front!"
"Painters present arms!" "Sculptors charge bag-
onets!" a baker's dozen out of every company
would respond.

Well, to go on with their story,— when they had
taken their prize, they drove her straight down-
stream to Annapolis, the nearest point to Washington. There they found the Naval Academy in danger of attack, and Old Ironsides — serving as a
practice-ship for the future midshipmen — also exposed. The call was now for seamen to man the
old craft and save her from a worse enemy than
her prototype met in the "Guerrière." Seamen?
Of course! They were Marblehead men, Glouces-
ter men, Beverly men, seamen all, *par excellence!*
They clapped on the frigate to aid the middies, and
by and by started her out into the stream. In doing this their own pilot took the chance to run them
purposely on a shoal in the intricate channel. A
great error of judgment on his part! as he perceived, when he found himself in irons and in con-
finement. "The days of trifling with traitors are
over!" think the Eighth Regiment of Massachusetts.

But there they were, hard and fast on the shoal,
when we came up. Nothing to nibble on but knobs
of anthracite. Nothing to sleep on softer or clean-
er than coal-dust. Nothing to drink but the brack-
ish water under their keel. "Rather rough!" so
they afterward patiently told us.

Meantime the Constitution had got hold of a tug,

and was making her way to an anchorage where her guns commanded everything and everybody. Good and true men chuckled greatly over this. The stars and stripes also were still up at the fort at the Naval Academy.

Our dread, that, while we were off at sea, some great and perhaps fatal harm had been suffered, was greatly lightened by these good omens. If Annapolis was safe, why not Washington safe also ? If treachery had got head at the capital, would not treachery have reached out its hand and snatched this doorway ? These were our speculations as we began to discern objects, before we heard news.

But news came presently. Boats pulled off to us. Our officers were put into communication with the shore. The scanty facts of our position became known from man to man. We privates have greatly the advantage in battling with the doubt of such a time. We know that we have nothing to do with rumors. Orders are what we go by. And orders are Facts.

We lay a long, lingering day, off Annapolis. The air was full of doubt, and we were eager to be let loose. All this while the Maryland stuck fast on the bar. We could see them, half a mile off, making every effort to lighten her. The soldiers tramped forward and aft, danced on her decks, shot overboard a heavy baggage-truck. We saw them start the truck for the stern with a cheer. It crashed down. One end stuck in the mud. The other fell back and rested on the boat. They went at it with axes, and presently it was clear.

As the tide rose, we gave our grounded friends a lift with a hawser. No go ! The Boston tugged in vain. We got near enough to see the whites of the Massachusetts eyes, and their unlucky faces and uniforms all grimy with their lodgings in the coal-dust. They could not have been blacker, if they had been breathing battle-smoke and dust all day. That experience was clear gain to them.

By and by, greatly to the delight of the impatient Seventh, the Boston was headed for shore. Never speak ill of the beast you bestraddle ! Therefore *requiescat* Boston ! may her ribs lie light on soft sand when she goes to pieces ! may her engines be cut up into bracelets for the arms of the patriotic fair ! good by to her, dear old, close, dirty, slow coach ! She served her country well in a moment of trial. Who knows but she saved it ? It was a race to see who should first get to Washington,— and we and the Virginia mob, in alliance with the District mob, were perhaps nip and tuck for the goal.

ANNAPOLIS.

So the Seventh Regiment landed and took Annapolis. We were the first troops ashore.

The middies of the Naval Academy no doubt believe that they had their quarters secure. The Massachusetts boys are satisfied that they first took the town in charge. And so they did.

But the Seventh took it a little more. Not, of

course, from its loyal men, but *for* its loyal men,—
for loyal Maryland, and for the Union.

Has anybody seen Annapolis? It is a picturesque old place, sleepy enough, and astonished to
find itself wide-awaked by a war, and obliged to
take responsibility and share for good and ill in the
movement of its time. The buildings of the Naval
Academy · stand parallel with the river Severn,
with a green plateau toward the water and a lovely
green lawn toward the town. All the scene was
fresh and fair with April, and I fancied, as the Boston touched the wharf, that I discerned the sweet
fragrance of apple-blossoms coming with the spring-
time airs.

I hope that the companies of the Seventh, should
the day arrive, will charge upon horrid batteries or
serried ranks with as much alacrity as they marched
ashore on the greensward of the Naval Academy.
We disembarked, and were halted in line between
the buildings and the river.

Presently, while we stood at ease, people began
to arrive, — some with smallish fruit to sell, some
with smaller news to give. Nobody knew whether
Washington was taken. Nobody knew whether
Jeff Davis was now spitting in the Presidential
spittoon, and scribbling his distiches with the nib
of the Presidential goose-quill. We were absolutely in doubt whether a seemingly inoffensive knot of
rustics, on a mound without the enclosure, might
not, at tap of drum, unmask a battery of giant co-
lumbiads, and belch blazes at us, raking our line.

Nothing so entertaining happened.   It was a parade, not a battle.   At sunset our band played strains sweet enough to pacify all Secession, if Secession had music in its soul.   Coffee, hot from the coppers of the Naval School, and biscuit were served out to us ; and while we supped, we talked with our visitors, such as were allowed to approach.

First the boys of the School — fine little bluejackets — had their story to tell.

"Do you see that white farm-house, across the river?" says a brave pigmy of a chap in navy uniform.   "That is head-quarters for Secession. They were going to take the School from us, Sir, and the frigate ; but we've got ahead of 'em, now you and the Massachusetts boys have come down," — and he twinkled all over with delight.   "We can't study any more.   We are on guard all the time.   We've got howitzers, too, and we'd like you to see, to-morrow, on drill, how we can handle 'em.   One of their boats came by our sentry last night," (a sentry probably five feet high,) "and he blazed away, Sir.   So they thought they wouldn't try us that time."

It was plain that these young souls had been well tried by the treachery about them.   They, too, had felt the pang of the disloyalty of comrades.   Nearly a hundred of the boys had been spoilt by the base example of their elders in the repudiating States, and had resigned.

After the middies, came anxious citizens from

the town.   Scared, all of them.   Now that we were come and assured them that persons and property were to be protected, they ventured to speak of the disgusting tyranny to which they, American citizens, had been subjected.   We came into contact here with utter social anarchy.   No man, unless he was ready to risk assault, loss of property, exile, dared to act or talk like a freeman. " This great wrong must be righted," think the Seventh Regiment, as one man.   So we tried to reassure the Annapolitans that we meant to do our duty as the nation's armed police, and mob-law was to be put down, so far as we could do it.

Here, too, voices of war met us.   The country was stirred up.   If the rural population did not give us a bastard imitation of Lexington and Concord, as we tried to gain Washington, all Pluguglydom would treat us à la Plugugly somewhere near the junction of the Annapolis and Baltimore and Washington Railroad.   The Seventh must be ready to shoot.

At dusk we were marched up to the Academy and quartered about in the buildings, — some in the fort, some in the recitation-halls.   We lay down on our blankets and knapsacks.   Up to this time our sleep and diet had been severely scanty.

We stayed all next day at Annapolis.   The Boston brought the Massachusetts Eighth ashore that night.   Poor fellows ! what a figure they cut, when we found them bivouacked on the Academy grounds next morning !   To begin : They had come off in hot patriotic haste, half-uniformed and half-outfitted. Finding that Baltimore had been taken by its own loafers and traitors, and that the Chesapeake ferry was impracticable, had obliged them to change line of march. They were out of grub. They were parched dry for want of water on the ferry-boat. Nobody could decipher Caucasian, much less Bunker-Hill Yankee, in their grimy visages.

But, hungry, thirsty, grimy, these fellows were GRIT.

Massachusetts ought to be proud of such hardy, cheerful, faithful sons.

We of the Seventh are proud, for our part, that it was our privilege to share our rations with them, and to begin a fraternization which grows closer every day and will be *historical.*

But I must make a shorter story. We drilled and were reviewed that morning on the Academy parade. In the afternoon the Naval School paraded their last before they gave up their barracks to the coming soldiery. So ended the 23d of April.

Midnight, 24th. We were rattled up by an alarm, — perhaps a sham one, to keep us awake and lively. In a moment, the whole regiment was in order of battle in the moonlight on the parade. It was a most brilliant spectacle, as company after company rushed forward, with rifles glittering, to take their places in the array.

After this pretty spirt, we were rationed with pork, beef, and bread for three days, and ordered to be ready to march on the instant.

WHAT THE MASSACHUSETTS EIGHTH HAD BEEN DOING.

MEANTIME General Butler's command, the Massachusetts Eighth, had been busy knocking disorder in the head.

Presently after their landing, and before they were refreshed, they pushed companies out to occupy the railroad-track beyond the town.

They found it torn up. No doubt the scamps who did the shabby job fancied that there would be no more travel that way until strawberry-time. They fancied the Yankees would sit down on the fences and begin to whittle white-oak toothpicks, darning the rebels, through their noses, meanwhile.

I know these men of the Eighth can whittle, and I presume they can say "Darn it," if occasion requires ; but just now track-laying was the business on hand.

"Wanted, experienced track-layers!" was the word along the files.

All at once the line of the road became densely populated with experienced track-layers, fresh from Massachusetts.

Presto change! the rails were relaid, spiked, and the roadway levelled and better ballasted than any road I ever saw south of Mason and Dixon's line. "We must leave a good job for these folks to model after," say the Massachusetts Eighth.

A track without a train is as useless as a gun without a man. Train and engine must be had. "Uncle Sam's mails and troops cannot be stopped another minute," our energetic friends conclude. So, — the railroad company's people being either frightened or false, — in marches Massachusetts to the station. "We, the People of the United States, want rolling-stock for the use of the Union," they said, or words to that effect.

The engine — a frowzy machine at the best — had been purposely disabled.

Here appeared the *deus ex machina*, Charles Homans, Beverly Light Guard, Company E, Eighth Massachusetts Regiment.

That is the man, name and titles in full, and he deserves well of his country.

He took a quiet squint at the engine, — it was as helpless as a boned turkey, — and he found " Charles Homans, his mark," written all over it.

The old rattletrap was an old friend. Charles Homans had had a share in building it. The machine and the man said, " How d'y' do ? " at once. Homans called for a gang of engine-builders. Of course they swarmed out of the ranks. They passed their hands over the locomotive a few times, and presently it was ready to whistle and wheeze and rumble and gallop, as if no traitor had ever tried to steal the go and the music out of it.

This had all been done during the afternoon of the 23d. During the night, the renovated engine was kept cruising up and down the track to see all clear. Guards of the Eighth were also posted to protect passage.

Our commander had, I presume, been co-operating with General Butler in this business. The Naval Academy authorities had given us every despatch and assistance, and the middies, frank, personal hospitality. The day was halcyon, the grass was green and soft, the apple-trees were just in blossom : it was a day to be remembered.

Many of us will remember it, and show the marks of it for months, as the day we had our heads cropped. By evening there was hardly one poll 'in the Seventh tenable by anybody's grip. Most sat in the shade and were shorn by a barber. A few were honored with a clip by the artist hand of the *petit caporal* of our Engineer Company.

While I rattle off these trifling details, let me not fail to call attention to the grave service done by our regiment, by its arrival, at the nick of time, at Annapolis. No clearer special Providence could have happened. The country-people of the traitor sort were aroused. Baltimore and its mob were but two hours away. The Constitution had been hauled out of reach of a rush by the Massachusetts men, — first on the ground, — but was half manned and not fully secure. And there lay the Maryland, helpless on the shoal, with six or seven hundred souls on board, so near the shore that the late Captain Rynders's gun could have sunk her from some ambush.

Yes ! the Seventh Regiment at Annapolis was the Right Man in the Right Place !

OUR MORNING MARCH.

REVEILLE.   As nobody pronounces this word
à la française, as everybody calls it " Revelee,"
why not drop it, as an affectation, and translate it
the " Stir your Stumps," the " Peel your Eyes,"
the " Tumble Up," or literally the " Wake " ?

Our snorers had kept up this call so lustily
since midnight, that, when the drums sounded it,
we were all ready.

The Sixth and Second Companies, under Captain
Nevers, are detached to lead the van.   I see my
brother Billy march off with the Sixth, into the
dusk, half moonlight, half dawn, and hope that no
beggar of a Secessionist will get a pat shot at him,
by the roadside, without his getting a chance to
let fly in return.   Such little possibilities intensify
the earnest detestation we feel for the treasons we
come to resist and to punish.   There will be some
bitter work done, if we ever get to blows in this
war, — this needless, reckless, brutal assault upon
the mildest of all governments.

Before the main body of the regiment marches,
we learn that the " Baltic " and other transports
came in last night with troops from New York and
New England, enough to hold Annapolis against a
square league of Plug Uglies.   We do not go on
without having our rear protected and our commu-
nications open.   It is strange to be compelled to
think of these things in peaceful America.   But
we really knew little more of the country before us

than Cortés knew of Mexico.   I have since learned
from a high official, that thirteen different messen-
gers were despatched from Washington in the in-
terval of anxiety while the Seventh was not forth-
coming, and only one got through.

At half past seven we take up our line of march,
pass out of the charming grounds of the Academy,
and move through the quiet, rusty, picturesque old
town.   It has a romantic dulness, — Annapolis, —
which deserves a parting compliment.

Although we deem ourselves a fine-looking set,
although our belts are blanched with pipe-clay and
our rifles shine sharp in the sun, yet the townspeo-
ple stare at us in a dismal silence.   They have already the air of men quelled by a despotism.   None
can trust his neighbor.   If he dares to be loyal, he
must take his life into his hands.   Most would be
loyal, if they dared.   But the system of society
which has ended in this present chaos has gradually eliminated the bravest and best men.   They
have gone in search of Freedom and Prosperity ;
and now the bullies cow the weaker brothers.
"There must be an end of this mean tyranny,"
think the Seventh, as they march through old Annapolis and see how sick the town is with doubt
and alarm.

Outside the town, we strike the railroad and
move along, the howitzers in front, bouncing over
the sleepers.   When our line is fully disengaged
from the town, we halt.

Here the scene is beautiful.   The van rests upon a high embankment, with a pool surrounded by pine-trees on the right, green fields on the left. Cattle are feeding quietly about. The air sings with birds. The chestnut-leaves sparkle. Frogs whistle in the warm spring morning. The regiment groups itself along the bank and the cutting. Several Marylanders of the half-price age — under twelve — come gaping up to see us harmless invaders. Each of these young gentry is armed with a dead spring frog, perhaps by way of tribute. And here — hollo! here comes Horace Greeley *in propria persona!* He marches through our groups with the Greeley walk, the Greeley hat on the back of his head, the Greeley white coat on his shoulders, his trousers much too short, and an absorbed, abstracted demeanor. Can it be Horace, reporting for himself? No; this is a Maryland production, and a little disposed to be sulky.

After a few minutes' halt, we hear the whistle of the engine. This machine is also an historic character in the war.

Remember it! "J. H. Nicholson" is its name. Charles Homans drives, and on either side stands a sentry with fixed bayonet. New spectacles for America! But it is grand to know that the bayonets are to protect, not to assail, Liberty and Law.

The train leads off. We follow, by the track. Presently the train returns. We pass it and trudge on in light marching order, carrying arms, blankets, haversacks, and canteens. Our knapsacks are upon the train.

Fortunate for our backs that they do not have to bear any more burden ! For the day grows sultry. It is one of those breezeless baking days which brew thunder-gusts. We march on for some four miles, when, coming upon the guards of the Massachusetts Eighth, our howitzer is ordered to fall out and wait for the train. With a comrade of the Artillery, I am placed on guard over it.

ON GUARD WITH HOWITZER NO. TWO.

HENRY BONNELL is my fellow-sentry. He, like myself, is an old campaigner in such campaigns as our generation has known. So we talk California, Oregon, Indian life, the Plains, keeping our eyes peeled meanwhile, and ranging the country. Men that will tear up track are quite capable of picking off a sentry. A giant chestnut gives us little dots of shade from its pigmy leaves. The country about us is open and newly ploughed. Some of the worm-fences are new, and ten rails high ; but the farming is careless, and the soil thin.

Two of the Massachusetts men come back to the gun while we are standing there. One is my friend Stephen Morris, of Marblehead, Sutton Light Infantry. I had shared my breakfast yesterday with Stephe. So we refraternize.

His business is, — " I make shoes in winter and fishin' in summer." He gives me a few facts, — suspicious persons seen about the track, men on horseback in the distance. One of the Massachusetts guard last night challenged his captain. Captain replied, " Officer of the night." Whereupon, says Stephe, " The recruit let squizzle and jest missed his ear." He then related to me the incident of the railroad station. " The first thing they know'd," says he, " we bit right into the depot and took charge." " I don't mind," Stephe remarked, — " I don't mind life, nor yit death ; but whenever I see a Massachusetts boy, I stick by him, and if them Secessionists attackt us to-night, or any other time, they 'll get in debt."

Whistle, again ! and the train appears. We are ordered to ship our howitzer on a platform car. The engine pushes us on. This train brings our light baggage and the rear guard.

A hundred yards farther on is a delicious fresh spring below the bank. While the train halts, Stephe Morris rushes down to fill my canteen. " This a'n't like Marblehead," says Stephe, panting up ; " but a man that can shin up *them* rocks can git right over *this* sand."

The train goes slowly on, as a rickety train should. At intervals we see the fresh spots of track just laid by our Yankee friends. Near the sixth mile, we began to overtake hot and uncomfortable squads of our fellows. The unseasonable heat of this most breathless day was too much for many of the younger men, unaccustomed to rough work, and weakened by want of sleep and irregular food in our hurried movements thus far.

Charles Homans's private carriage was, how-

11   P

ever, ready to pick up tired men, hot men, thirsty men, men with corns, or men with blisters. They tumbled into the train in considerable numbers.

An enemy that dared could have made a moderate bag of stragglers at this time. But they would not have been allowed to straggle, if any enemy had been about. By this time we were convinced that no attack was to be expected in this part of the way.

The main body of the regiment, under Major Shaler, a tall, soldierly fellow, with a moustache of the fighting color, tramped on their own pins to the watering-place, eight miles or so from Annapolis. There troops and train came to a halt, with the news that a bridge over a country·road was broken a mile farther on.

It had been distinctly insisted upon, in the usual Southern style, that we were not to be allowed to pass through Maryland, and that we were to be "welcomed to hospitable graves." The broken bridge was a capital spot for a skirmish. Why not look for it here?

We looked; but got nothing. The rascals could skulk about by night, tear up rails, and hide them where they might be found by a man with half an eye, or half destroy a bridge; but there was no shoot in them. They have not faith enough in their cause to risk their lives for it, even behind a tree or from one of these thickets, choice spots for ambush.

So we had no battle there, but a battle of the

elements. The volcanic heat of the morning was followed by a furious storm of wind and a smart shower. The regiment wrapped themselves in their blankets and took their wetting with more or less satisfaction. They were receiving samples of all the different little miseries of a campaign.

And here let me say a word to my fellow-volunteers, actual and prospective, in all the armies of all the States : —

A soldier needs, besides his soldierly drill,

I. Good FEET.

II. A good Stomach.

III. And after these, come the good Head and the good Heart.

But Good Feet are distinctly the first thing. Without them you cannot get to your duty. If a comrade, or a horse, or a locomotive, takes you on its back to the field, you are useless there. And when the field is lost, you cannot retire, run away, and save your bacon.

Good shoes and plenty of walking make good feet. A man who pretends to belong to an infantry company ought always to keep himself in training, so that any moment he can march twenty or thirty miles without feeling a pang or raising a blister. Was this the case with even a decimation of the army who rushed to defend Washington ? Were you so trained, my comrades of the Seventh ?

A captain of a company, who will let his men march with such shoes as I have seen on the feet of some poor fellows in this war, ought to be garroted with shoe-strings, or at least compelled to play Pope and wash the feet of the whole army of the Apostles of Liberty.

If you find a foot-soldier lying beat out by the roadside, desperate as a sea-sick man, five to one his heels are too high, or his soles too narrow or too thin, or his shoe is not made straight on the inside, so that the great toe can spread into its place as he treads.

I am an old walker over Alps across the water, and over Cordilleras, Sierras, Deserts, and Prairies at home ; I have done my near sixty miles a day without discomfort, — and speaking from large experience, and with painful recollections of the suffering and death I have known for want of good feet on the march, I say to every volunteer : —

Trust in God ; BUT KEEP YOUR SHOES EASY !

THE BRIDGE.

WHEN the frenzy of the brief tempest was over, it began to be a question, " What to do about the broken bridge ? " The gap was narrow ; but even Charles Homans could not promise to leap the " J. H. Nicholson " over it. Who was to be our Julius Cæsar in bridge-building? Who but Sergeant Scott, Armorer of the Regiment, with my fellow-sentry of the morning, Bonnell, as First Assistant ?

Scott called for a working party. There were plenty of handy fellows among our Engineers and in the Line. Tools were plenty in the Engineers' chest. We pushed the platform car upon which howitzer No. 1 was mounted down to the gap, and began operations.

" I wish," says the *petit caporal* of the Engineer Company, patting his howitzer gently on the back, " that I could get this Putty Blower pointed at the enemy, while you fellows are bridge-building."

The inefficient destructives of Maryland had only half spoilt the bridge. Some of the old timbers could be used, — and for new ones, there was the forest.

Scott and his party made a good and a quick job of it. Our friends of the Massachusetts Eighth had now come up. They lent a ready hand, as usual. The sun set brilliantly. By twilight there was a practicable bridge. The engine was despatched back to keep the road open. The two platform cars, freighted with our howitzers, were rigged with the gun-ropes for dragging along the rail. We passed through the files of the Massachusetts men, resting by the way, and eating by the fires of the evening the suppers we had in great part provided them ; and so begins our night-march.

THE NIGHT-MARCH.

O GOTTSCHALK ! what a poetic *Marche de Nuit* we then began to play, with our heels and toes, on the railroad track !

It was full-moonlight and the night inexpressibly sweet and serene. The air was cool and vivified

by the gust and shower of the afternoon. Fresh
spring was in every breath. Our fellows had forgotten that this morning they were hot and disgusted. Every one hugged his rifle as if it were
the arm of the Girl of his Heart, and stepped out
gayly for the promenade. Tired or foot-sore men,
or even lazy ones, could mount upon the two
freight-cars we were using for artillery-wagons.
There were stout arms enough to tow the whole.

The scouts went ahead under First Lieutenant
Farnham of the Second Company. We were at
school together, — I am afraid to say how many
years ago. He is just the same cool, dry, shrewd
fellow he was as a boy, and a most efficient officer.

It was an original kind of march. I suppose a
battery of howitzers never before found itself
mounted upon cars, ready to open fire at once and
bang away into the offing with shrapnel or into
the bushes with canister. Our line extended a
half-mile along the track. It was beautiful to
stand on the bank above a cutting, and watch the
files strike from the shadow of a wood into a broad
flame of moonlight, every rifle sparkling up alert
as it came forward. A beautiful sight to see the
barrels writing themselves upon the dimness, each
a silver flash.

By and by, " Halt ! " came, repeated along from
the front, company after company. " Halt ! a
rail gone."

It was found without difficulty. The imbeciles
who took it up probably supposed we would not

wish to wet our feet by searching for it in the dewy grass of the next field. With incredible doltishness they had also left the chairs and spikes beside the track. Bonnell took hold, and in a few minutes had the rail in place and firm enough to pass the engine. Remember, we were not only hurrying on to succor Washington, but opening the only convenient and practicable route between it and the loyal States.

A little farther on, we came to a village,— a rare sight in this scantily peopled region. Here Sergeant Keeler, of our company, the tallest man in the regiment, and one of the handiest, suggested that we should tear up the rails at a turnout by the station, and so be prepared for chances. So " Out crowbars ! " was the word. We tore up and bagged half a dozen rails, with chairs and spikes complete. Here, too, some of the engineers found a keg of spikes. This was also bagged and loaded on our cars. We fought the chaps with their own weapons, since they would not meet us with ours.

These things made delay, and by and by there was a long halt, while the Colonel communicated, by orders sounded along the line, with the engine. Homans's drag was hard after us, bringing our knapsacks and traps.

After I had admired for some time the beauty of our moonlit line, and listened to the orders as they grew or died along the distance, I began to want excitement. Bonnell suggested that he and I should scout up the road and see if any rails were wanting.   We travelled along into the quiet night.

A mile ahead of the line we suddenly caught the gleam of a rifle-barrel. "Who goes there?" one of our own scouts challenged smartly.

We had arrived at the nick of time. Three rails were up. Two of them were easily found. The third was discovered by beating the bush thoroughly. Bonnell and I ran back for tools, and returned at full trot with crowbar and sledge on our shoulders. There were plenty of willing hands to help, — too many, indeed, — and with the aid of a huge Massachusetts man we soon had the rail in place.

From this time on we were constantly interrupted. Not a half-mile passed without a rail up. Bonnell was always at the front laying track, and I am proud to say that he accepted me as aide-de-camp. Other fellows, unknown to me in the dark, gave hearty help. The Seventh showed that it could do something else than drill.

At one spot, on a high embankment over standing water, the rail was gone, sunk probably. Here we tried our rails brought from the turn-out. They were too short. We supplemented with a length of plank from our stores. We rolled our cars carefully over. They passed safe. But Homans shook his head. He could not venture a locomotive on that frail stuff. So we lost the society of the " J. H. Nicholson." Next day the Massachusetts commander called for some one to dive in the pool for the lost rail.   Plump into the water went a little wiry chap and grappled the rail.   "When I come up," says the brave fellow afterwards to me, " our officer out with a twenty-dollar gold-piece and wanted me to take it. 'That a'n't what I come for,' says I. 'Take it,' says he, 'and share with the others.'   'That a'n't what they come for,' says I.   But I took a big cold," the diver contin- ued, "and I 'm condemned hoarse yit," — which was the fact.

Farther on we found a whole length of track torn up, on both sides, sleepers and all, and the same thing repeated with alternations of breaks of sin- gle rails.   Our howitzer-ropes came into play to hoist and haul.   We were not going to be stopped.

But it was becoming a *Noche Triste* to some of our comrades.   We had now marched some sixteen miles.   The distance was trifling.   But the men had been on their legs pretty much all day and night.   Hardly any one had had any full or sub- stantial sleep or meal since we started from New York.   They napped off, standing, leaning on their guns, dropping down in their tracks on the wet ground, at every halt.   They were sleepy, but plucky.   As we passed through deep cuttings, places, as it were, built for defence, there was a general desire that the tedium of the night should be relieved by a shindy.

During the whole night I saw our officers mov- ing about the line, doing their duty vigorously, despite exhaustion, hunger, and sleeplessness.

11 *

About midnight our friends of the Eighth had joined us, and our whole little army struggled on together. I find that I have been rather understating the troubles of the march. It seems impossible that such difficulty could be encountered within twenty miles of the capital of our nation. But we were making a rush to put ourselves in that capital, and we could not proceed in the slow, systematic way of an advancing army. We must take the risk and stand the suffering, whatever it was. So the Seventh Regiment went through its bloodless *Noche Triste*.

MORNING.

At last we issued from the damp woods, two miles below the railroad junction. Here was an extensive farm. Our vanguard had halted and borrowed a few rails to make fires. These were, of course, carefully paid for at their proprietor's own price. The fires were bright in the gray dawn. About them the whole regiment was now halted. The men tumbled down to catch forty winks. Some, who were hungrier for food than sleep, went off foraging among the farm-houses. They returned with appetizing legends of hot breakfasts in hospitable abodes, or scanty fare given grudgingly in hostile ones. All meals, however, were paid for.

Here, as at other halts below, the country-people came up to talk to us. The traitors could easily be distinguished by their insolence disguised as obsequiousness. The loyal men were still timid, but more hopeful at last. All were very lavish with the monosyllable, Sir. It was an odd coincidence, that the vanguard, halting off at a farm in the morning, found it deserted for the moment by its tenants, and protected only by an engraved portrait of our (former) Colonel Duryea, serenely smiling over the mantel-piece.

From this point, the railroad was pretty much all gone. But we were warmed and refreshed by a nap and a bite, and besides had daylight and open country.

We put our guns on their own wheels, all dropped into ranks as if on parade, and marched the last two miles to the station. We still had no certain information. Until we actually saw the train awaiting us, and the Washington companies, who had come down to escort us, drawn up, we did not know whether our Uncle Sam was still a resident of the capital.

We packed into the train, and rolled away to Washington.

WASHINGTON.

WE marched up to the White House, showed ourselves to the President, made our bow to him as our host, and then marched up to the Capitol, our grand lodgings.

There we are now, quartered in the Representatives Chamber.

And here I must hastily end this first sketch of the Great Defence. May it continue to be as firm and faithful as it is this day!

I have scribbled my story with a thousand men stirring about me. If any of my sentences miss their aim, accuse my comrades and the bewilderment of this martial crowd. For here are four or five thousand others on the same business as ourselves, and drums are beating, guns are clanking, companies are tramping, all the while. Our friends of the Eighth Massachusetts are quartered under the dome, and cheer us whenever we pass.

Desks marked John Covode, John Cochran, and Anson Burlingame have allowed me to use them as I wrote.

WASHINGTON AS A CAMP.

WASHINGTON AS A CAMP.

OUR BARRACKS AT THE CAPITOL.

WE marched up the hill, and when the dust opened there was our Big Tent ready pitched.

It was an enormous tent, — the Sibley pattern modified. A simple soul in our ranks looked up and said, — "Tent! canvas! I don't see it: that's marble!" Whereupon a simpler soul informed us, — "Boys, that's the Capitol."

And so it was the Capitol, — as glad to see the New York Seventh Regiment as they to see it. The Capitol was to be our quarters, and I was pleased to notice that the top of the dome had been left off for ventilation.

The Seventh had had a wearisome and anxious progress from New York, as I have chronicled in the June "Atlantic." We had marched from Annapolis, while "rumors to right of us, rumors to left of us, volleyed and thundered." We had not expected that the attack upon us would be merely verbal. The truculent citizens of Maryland notified us that we were to find every barn a Concord and every hedge a Lexington. Our Southern breth-

ren at present repudiate their debts ; but we fancied they would keep their warlike promises.   At
least, everybody thought, " They will fire over our
heads, or bang blank cartridges at us."   Every
nose was sniffing for the smell of powder.   Vapor
instead of valor nobody looked for.   So the march
had been on the *qui vive*.   We were happy enough
that it was over, and successful.

Successful, because Mumbo Jumbo was not installed in the White House.   It is safe to call Jeff
Davis Mumbo Jumbo now.   But there is no doubt
that the luckless man had visions of himself receiving guests, repudiating debts, and distributing em-
bassies in Washington, May 1, 1861.   And as to
La' Davis, there seems to be documentary evidence
that she meant to be " At Home " in the capital,
bringing the first strawberries with her from Montgomery for her May-day *soirée*.   Bah ! one does
not like to sneer at people who have their necks in
the halter ; but one happy result of this disturbance
is that the disturbers have sent themselves to Cov-
entry.   The Lincoln party may be wanting in finish.   Finish comes with use.   A little roughness
of manner, the genuine simplicity of a true soul
like Lincoln, is attractive.   But what man of breeding could ever stand the type Southern Senator ?
But let him rest in such peace as he can find !   He
and his peers will not soon be seen where we of the
New York Seventh were now entering.

They gave us the Representatives Chamber for
quarters.   Without running the gantlet of caucus

primary and election, every one of us attained that sacred shrine.

In we marched, tramp, tramp. Bayonets took the place of buncombe. The frowzy creatures in ill-made dress-coats, shimmering satin waistcoats, and hats of the tile model, who lounge, spit, and vociferate there, and name themselves M. C., were off. Our neat uniforms and bright barrels showed to great advantage, compared with the usual costumes of the usual *dramatis personæ* of the scene.

It was dramatic business, our entrance there. The new Chamber is gorgeous, but ineffective. Its ceiling is flat, and panelled with transparencies. Each panel is the coat-of-arms of a State, painted on glass. I could not see that the impartial sunbeams, tempered by this skylight, had burned away the insignia of the malecontent States. Nor had any rampant Secessionist thought to punch any of the seven lost Pleiads out from that firmament with a long pole. Crimson and gold are the prevailing hues of the decorations. There is no unity and breadth of coloring. The desks of the members radiate in double files from a white marble tribune at the centre of the semicircle.

In came the new actors on this scene. Our presence here was the inevitable sequel of past events. We appeared with bayonets and bullets because of the bosh uttered on this floor ; because of the bills — with treasonable stump-speeches in their bellies — passed here ; because of the cowardice of the poltroons, the imbecility of the dodgers, and the

Q

arrogance of the bullies, who had here co-operated to blind and corrupt the minds of the people. Talk had made a miserable mess of it. The *ultima ratio* was now appealed to.

Some of our companies were marched up-stairs into the galleries. The sofas were to be their beds. With their white cross-belts and bright breast-plates, they made a very picturesque body of spectators for whatever happened in the Hall, and never failed to applaud in the right or the wrong place at will.

Most of us were bestowed in the amphitheatre. Each desk received its man. He was to scribble on it by day, and sleep under it by night. When the desks were all taken, the companies overflowed into the corners and into the lobbies. The staff took committee-rooms. The Colonel reigned in the Speaker's parlor.

Once in, firstly, we washed.

Such a wash merits a special paragraph. I compliment the M. C.s, our hosts, upon their water-privileges. How we welcomed this chief luxury after our march! And thenceforth how we prized it! For the clean face is an institution which requires perpetual renovation at Washington. "Constant vigilance is the price" of neatness. When the sky here is not travelling earthward in rain, earth is mounting skyward in dust. So much dirt must have an immoral effect.

After the wash we showed ourselves to the eyes of Washington, marching by companies, each to a different hotel, to dinner. This became one of the ceremonies of our barrack-life. We liked it. The Washingtonians were amused and encouraged by it. Three times a day, with marked punctuality, our lines formed and tramped down the hill to scuffle with awkward squads of waiters for fare more or less tolerable. In these little marches we encountered by and by the other regiments, and, most soldierly of all, the Rhode Island men, in blue flannel blouses and *bersaglière* hats. But of them hereafter.

It was a most attractive post of ours at the Capitol. Spring was at its freshest and fairest. Every day was more exquisite than its forerunner. We drilled morning, noon, and evening, almost hourly, in the pretty square east of the building. Old soldiers found that they rattled through the manual twice as alert as ever before. Recruits became old soldiers in a trice. And as to awkward squads, men that would have been the veriest louts and lubbers in the piping times of peace now learned to toe the mark, to whisk their eyes right and their eyes left, to drop the buts of their muskets without crushing their corns, and all the mysteries of flank and file, — and so became full-fledged heroes before they knew it.

In the rests between our drills we lay under the young shade on the sweet young grass, with the odors of snowballs and horse-chestnut blooms drifting to us with every whiff of breeze, and amused ourselves with watching the evolutions of our friends of the Massachusetts Eighth, and other less experienced soldiers, as they appeared upon the field. They too, like ourselves, were going through the transformations. These sturdy fellows were then in a rough enough chrysalis of uniform. That shed, they would look worthy of themselves.

But the best of the entertainment was within the Capitol. Some three thousand or more of us were now quartered there. The Massachusetts Eighth were under the dome. No fear of want of air for them. The Massachusetts Sixth were eloquent for their State in the Senate Chamber. It was singularly fitting, among the many coincidences in the history of this regiment, that they should be there, tacitly avenging the assault upon Sumner and the attempts to bully the impregnable Wilson.

In the recesses, caves, and crypts of the Capitol what other legions were bestowed I do not know. I daily lost myself, and sometimes when out of my reckoning was put on the way by sentries of strange corps, a Reading Light Infantry man, or some other. We all fraternized. There was a fine enthusiasm among us : not the soldierly rivalry in discipline that may grow up in future between men of different States acting together, but the brotherhood of ardent fellows first in the field and earnest in the cause.

All our life in the Capitol was most dramatic and sensational.

Before it was fairly light in the dim interior of the Representatives' Chamber, the *réveilles* of the different regiments came rattling through the corridors. Every snorer's trumpet suddenly paused. The impressive sound of the hushed breathing of a thousand sleepers, marking off the fleet moments of the night, gave way to a most vociferous uproar. The boy element is large in the Seventh Regiment. Its slang dictionary is peculiar and unabridged. As soon as we woke, the pit began to chaff the galleries, and the galleries the pit. We were allowed noise nearly *ad libitum*. Our riotous tendencies, if they existed, escaped by the safety-valve of the larynx. We joked, we shouted, we sang, we mounted the Speaker's desk and made speeches, — always to the point ; for if any but a wit ventured to give tongue, he was coughed down without ceremony. Let the M. C.s adopt this plan and silence their dunces.

With all our jollity we preserved very tolerable decorum. The regiment is *assez bien composé*. Many of its privates are distinctly gentlemen of breeding and character. The tone is mainly good, and the *esprit de corps* high. If the Colonel should say, "Up, boys, and at 'em!" I know that the Seventh would do brilliantly in the field. I speak now of its behavior in-doors. This certainly did it credit. Our thousand did the Capitol little harm that a corporal's guard of Biddies with mops and tubs could not repair in a forenoon's campaign.

Perhaps we should have served our country better by a little Vandalism. The decorations of the Capitol have a slight flavor of the Southwestern steamboat saloon. The pictures (now, by the way, carefully covered) would most of them be the better, if the figures were bayoneted and the backgrounds sabred out.   Both — pictures and decorations — belong to that bygone epoch of our country when men shaved the moustache, dressed like parsons, said "Sir," and chewed tobacco, — a transition epoch, now become an historic blank.

The home-correspondence of our legion of young heroes was illimitable.   Every one had his little tale of active service to relate.   A decimation of the regiment, more or less, had profited by the tender moment of departure to pop the question and to receive the dulcet "Yes."   These lucky fellows were of course writing to Dulcinea regularly, three meals of love a day.   Mr. Van Wyck, M. C., and a brace of colleagues, were kept hard at work all day giving franks and saving three-pennies to the ardent scribes.   Uncle Sam lost certainly three thousand cents a day in this manner.

What crypts and dens, caves and cellars, there are under that great structure!   And barrels of flour in every one of them this month of May, 1861.   Do civilians eat in this proportion?   Or does long standing in the "Position of a Soldier" (*vide* "Tactics" for a view of that graceful *pose*) increase a man's capacity for bread and beef so enormously?

It was infinitely picturesque in these dim vaults by night.   Sentries were posted at every turn. Their guns gleamed in the gaslight.   Sleepers were lying in their blankets wherever the stones were softest. Then in the guard-room the guard were waiting their turn. We have not had much of this scenery in America, and the physiognomy of volunteer military life is quite distinct from anything one sees in European service. The People have never had occasion until now to occupy their Palace with armed men.

THE FOLLOWING IS THE OATH.

WE were to be sworn into the service of the United States the afternoon of April 26th. All the Seventh, raw men and ripe men, marched out into the sweet spring sunshine. Every fellow had whitened his belts, burnished his arms, curled his moustache, and was scowling his manliest for Uncle Sam's approval.

We were drawn up by companies in the Capitol Square for mustering in.

Presently before us appeared a gorgeous officer, in full fig. "Major McDowell!" somebody whispered, as we presented arms. He is a General, or perhaps a Field Marshal, now. Promotions come with a hop, skip, and jump, in these times, when demerit resigns and merit stands ready to step to the front.

Major-Colonel-General McDowell, in a soldierly voice, now called the roll, and we all answered, "Here!" in voices more or less soldierly. He entertained himself with this ceremony for an hour. The roll over, we were marched and formed in three sides of a square along the turf. Again the handsome officer stepped forward, and recited to us the conditions of our service.   " In accordance with a special arrangement, made with the Governor of New York," says the Major, " you are now mustered into the service of the United States, to serve for thirty days, unless sooner discharged " ; and continues he, " the oath will now be read to you by the magistrate."

Hereupon a gentleman *en mufti*, but wearing a military cap with an oil-skin cover, was revealed. Until now he had seemed an impassive supernumerary.   But he was biding his time, and — with due respect be it said— saving his wind, and now in a Stentorian voice he ejaculated, —

" *The following is the oath !* "

Per se this remark was not comic.   But there was something in the dignitary's manner which tickled the regiment.   As one man the thousand smiled, and immediately adopted this new epigram among its private countersigns.

But the good-natured smile passed away as we listened to the impressive oath, following its title.

We raised our right hands, and, clause by clause, repeated the solemn obligation, in the name of God, to be faithful soldiers of our country.   It was not quite so comprehensive as the beautiful knightly pledge administered by King Arthur to his comrades, and transmitted to our time by Major-General Tennyson of the Parnassus Division.   We did not swear, as they did of yore, to be true lovers as well as loyal soldiers. *Ça va sans dire* in 1861, — particularly when you were engaged to your Amanda the evening before you started, as was the case with many a stalwart brave and many a mighty man of a corporal or sergeant in our ranks.

We were thrilled and solemnized by the stately ceremony of the oath. This again was most dramatic. A grand public recognition of a duty. A reavowal of the fundamental belief that our system was worthy of the support, and our Government of the confidence, of all loyal men. And there was danger in the middle distance of our view into the future, — danger of attack, or dangerous duty of advance, just enough to keep any trifler from feeling that his pledge was mere holiday business.

So, under the cloudless blue sky, we echoed in unison the sentences of the oath. A little low murmur of rattling arms, shaken with the hearty utterance, made itself heard in the pauses. Then the band crashed in magnificently.

We were now miserable mercenaries, serving for low pay and rough rations. Read the Southern papers and you will see us described. "Mudsills," — that, I believe, is the technical word. By repeating a form of words after a gentleman in a glazed cap and black raiment, we had suffered change into base assassins, the offscouring of society, starving for want of employment, and willing to "imbrue our coarse fists in fraternal blood" for the sum of eleven dollars a month, besides hard-

12

tack, salt junk, and the hope of a Confederate States bond apiece for bounty, or free loot in the treasuries of Florida, Mississippi, and Arkansas, after the war. How carefully from that day we watched the rise and fall of United States stocks! If they should go low among the nineties, we felt that our eleven dollars *per mensem* would be imperilled.

We stayed in our palace for a week or so after April 26th, the day of the oath. That was the most original part of our duty thus far. New York never had so unanimous a deputation on the floor of the Representatives Chamber before, and never a more patriotic one. Take care, Gentlemen Members of Congress! look to your words and your acts honestly and wisely in future! don't palter with Liberty again! it is not well that soldiers should get into the habit of thinking they are always to unravel the snarls and cut the knots twisted and tied by clumsy or crafty fingers. The traitor States already need the *main de fer*, — yes, and without the *gant de velours*. Let us beware, and keep ourselves worthy of the boon of self-government, man by man! I do not wish to hear, " Order arms ! " and " Charge bayonets !" in the Capitol. But this present defence of Free Speech and Free Thought ends, let us hope, that danger forever.

When we had been ten days in our showy barracks we began to quarrel with luxury. What had private soldiers to do with the desks of lawgivers ?

Why should we be allowed to revel longer in the dining-rooms of Washington hotels, partaking the admirable dainties there?

The May sunshine, the birds, and the breezes of May, invited us to Camp, — the genuine thing, under canvas. Besides, Uncles Sam and Abe wanted our room for other company. Washington was filling up fast with uniforms. It seemed as if all the able-bodied men in the country were moving, on the first of May, with all their property on their backs, to agreeable, but dusty, lodgings on the Potomac.

We also made our May move. One afternoon, my company, the Ninth, and the Engineers, the Tenth, were detailed to follow Captain Vielé, and lay out a camp on Meridian Hill.

CAMP CAMERON.

As we had the first choice, we got, on the whole, the best site for a camp. We occupy the villa and farm of Dr. Stone, two miles due north of Willard's Hotel. I assume that hotel as a peculiarly American point of departure, and also because it is the hub of Washington, — the centre of an eccentric, having the White House at the end of its shorter, and the Capitol at the end of its longer radius, — moral, so they say, as well as geometrical.

Sundry dignitaries, Presidents and what not, have lived here in times gone by. Whoever chose the site ought to be kindly remembered for his good taste. The house stands upon the pretty terrace commanding the plain of Washington. From the upper windows we can see the Potomac opening southward like a lake, and between us and the water ambitious Washington stretching itself along and along, like the shackly files of an army of recruits.

Oaks love the soil of this terrace. There are some noble ones on the undulations before the house. It may be permitted even for one who is supposed to think of nothing but powder and ball to notice one of these grand trees. Let the ivy-covered stem of the Big Oak of Camp Cameron take its place in literature! And now enough of scenery. The landscape will stay, but the troops will not. There are trees and slopes of greensward elsewhere, and shrubbery begins to blossom in these bright days of May before a thousand pretty homes. The tents and the tent-life are more interesting for the moment than objects which cannot decamp.

The old villa serves us for head-quarters. It is a respectable place, not without its pretensions. Four granite pillars, as true grit as if the two Presidents Adams had lugged them on their shoulders all the way from Quincy, Mass., make a carriage-porch. Here is the Colonel in the big west parlor, the Quartermaster and Commissary in the rooms with sliding-doors on the east, the Hospital up-stairs, and so on. Other rooms, numerous as the cells in a monastery, serve as quarters for the

Engineer Company. These dens are not monastic in aspect. The house is, of course, a Certosa, so far as the gentler sex are concerned ; but no anchorites dwell here at present. If the Seventh disdained everything but soldiers' fare, — which it does not, — common civility would require that it should do violence to its disinclination for comfort and luxury, and consume the stores sent down by ardent patriots in New York. The cellars of the villa overflow with edibles, and in the greenhouse is a most appetizing array of barrels, boxes, cans, and bottles, shipped here that our Sybarites might not sigh for the flesh-pots of home. Such trash may do very well to amuse the palate in these times of half peace, half hostility ; but when

> " war, which for a space does fail,
> Shall doubly thundering swell the gale,"

then every soldier should drop gracefully to the simple ration, and cease to dabble with frying-pans. Cooks to their aprons, and soldiers to their guns !

Our tents are pitched on a level clover-field sloping to the front for our parade-ground. We use the old wall tent without a fly. It is necessary to live in one of these awhile, to know the vast superiority of the Sibley pattern. Sibley's tent is a wrinkle taken from savage life. It is the Sioux buffalo-skin lodge, or *Tepee*, improved, — a cone truncated at the top and fitted with a movable apex for ventilation. A single tent-pole, supported upon a hinged tripod of iron, sustains the structure. It is compacter, more commodious, healthier, and

handsomer than the ancient models. None other
should be used in permanent encampments. For
marching troops, the French *Tente d'abri* is a capital shelter.

Still our fellows manage to be at home as they
are. Some of our model tents are types of the
best style of temporary cottages. Young house-
keepers of limited incomes would do well to visit
and take heed. A whole elysium of household
comfort can be had out of· a teapot, — tin ; a brace
of cups, — tin ; a brace of plates, — tin ; and a
frying-pan.

In these days of war everybody can see a camp.
Every one who stays at home has a brother or a
son or a lover quartered in one of the myriad tents
that have blossomed with the daffodil-season all over
our green fields of the North. I need not, then,
describe our encampment in detail, — its guard-
tent in advance, — its guns in battery, — its flag-
staff, — its companies quartered in streets with
droll and fanciful names, — its officers' tents in the
rear, at right angles to the lines of company tents,
— its kitchens, armed with Captain Vielé's capital
army cooking-stoves, — its big marquees, "The
White House" and "Fort Pickens," for the lodging and messing of the new artillery company, — its
barbers' shops, — its offices. The same, more or
less well arranged, can be seen in all the rendezvous
where the armies are now assembling. Instead of
such description, then, let me give the log of a
single day at our camp.

JOURNAL OF A DAY AT CAMP CAMERON, BY PRIVATE W., COMPANY L.

Boom!

I would rather not believe it ; but it is — yes, it is — the morning gun, uttering its surly "Hullo !" to sunrise.

Yes, — and, to confirm my suspicions, here rattle in the drums and pipe in the fifes, wooing us to get up, *get up*, with music too peremptory to be harmonious.

I rise up *sur mon séant* and glance about me. I, Private W., chance, by reason of sundry chances, to be a member of a company recently largely recruited and bestowed all together in a big marquee. As I lift myself up, I see others lift themselves up on those straw bags we kindly call our mattresses. The tallest man of the regiment, Sergeant K., is on one side of me. On the other side I am separated from two of the fattest men of the regiment by Sergeant M., another excellent fellow, prime cook and prime forager.

We are all presently on our pins, — K. on those lengthy continuations of his, and the two stout gentlemen on their stout supporters. The deep sleepers are pulled up from those abysses of slumber where they had been choking, gurgling, strangling, death-rattling all night. There is for a moment a sound of legs rushing into pantaloons and arms plunging into jackets.

Then, as the drums and fifes whine and clatter

their last notes, at the flap of our tent appears our orderly, and fierce in the morning sunshine gleams his moustache, — one month's growth this blessed day. "Fall in, for roll-call!" he cries, in a ringing voice. The orderly can speak sharp, if need be.

We obey. Not "Walk in!" "March in!" "Stand in!" is the order; but "Fall in!" as sleepy men must. Then the orderly calls off our hundred. There are several boyish voices which reply, several comic voices, a few mean voices, and some so earnest and manly and alert that one says to himself, "Those are the men for me, when work is to be done!" I read the character of my comrades every morning in each fellow's monosyllable "Here!"

When the orderly is satisfied that not one of us has run away and accepted a Colonelcy from the Confederate States since last roll-call, he notifies those unfortunates who are to be on guard for the next twenty-four hours of the honor and responsibility placed upon their shoulders. Next he tells us what are to be the drills of the day. Then, "Right face! Dismissed! Break ranks! March!"

With ardor we instantly seize tin basins, soap, and towels, and invade a lovely oak-grove at the rear and left of our camp. Here is a delicious spring into which we have fitted a pump. The sylvan scene becomes peopled with "National Guards Washing," — a scene meriting the notice of Art as much as any "Diana and her Nymphs." But we have no Poussin to paint us in the dewy sunlit grove.   Few of us, indeed, know how picturesque we are at all times and seasons.

After this *beau idéal* of a morning toilet comes the ante-prandial drill.   Lieutenant W. arrives, and gives us a little appetizing exercise in " Carry arms ! " " Support arms ! " " By the right flank, march ! " " Double quick ! "

Breakfast follows.   My company messes somewhat helter-skelter in a big tent.   We have very tolerable rations.   Sometimes luxuries appear of potted meats and hermetical vegetables, sent us by the fond New-Yorkers.   Each little knot of fellows, too, cooks something savory.   Our table-furniture is not elegant, our plates are tin, there is no silver in our forks ; but *à la guerre, comme à la guerre.* Let the scrubs growl ! Lucky fellows, if they suffer no worse hardships than this !

By and by, after breakfast, come company drills, bayonet practice, battalion drills, and the heavy work of the day.   Our handsome Colonel, on a nice black nag, manœuvres his thousand men of the line-companies on the parade for two or three hours.   Two thousand legs step off accurately together.   Two thousand pipe-clayed cross-belts — whitened with infinite pains and waste of time, and offering a most inviting mark to a foe — restrain the beating bosoms of a thousand braves, as they — the braves, not the belts — go through the most intricate evolutions unerringly.   Watching these battalion movements, Private W., perhaps, goes off and inscribes in his journal, — " Any clever, prompt man, with a mechanical turn, an eye for distance, a notion of time, and a voice of command, can be a tactician. It is pure pedantry to claim that the manœuvring of troops is difficult : it is not difficult, if the troops are quick and steady. But to be a general, with patience and purpose and initiative, — ah!" thinks Private W., "for that you must have the man of genius ; and in this war he already begins to appear out of Massachusetts and elsewhere."

Private W. avows without fear that about noon, at Camp Cameron, he takes a hearty dinner, and with satisfaction. Private W. has had his feasts in cot and chateau in Old World and New. It is the conviction of said private that nowhere and nowhen has he expected his ration with more interest, and remembered it with more affection, than here.

In the middle hours of the day, it is in order to get a pass to go to Washington, or to visit some of the camps, which now, in the middle of May, begin to form a cordon around the city. Some of these I may criticise before the end of this paper. Our capital seems arranged by nature to be protected by fortified camps on the circuit of its hills. It may be made almost a Verona, if need be. Our brother regiments have posts nearly as charming as our own, in these fair groves and on these fair slopes on either side of us.

In the afternoon comes target practice, skirmishing-drill, more company- or recruit-drill, and, at half past five, our evening parade. Let me not forget tent-inspection, at four, by the officer of the day, when our band plays deliciously.

At evening parade all Washington appears. A regiment of ladies, rather indisposed to beauty, observe us. Sometimes the Dons arrive, — Secretaries of State, of War, of Navy, — or military Dons, bestriding prancing steeds, but bestriding them as if " 't was *not* their habit often of an afternoon." All which, — the bad teeth, pallid skins, and rustic toilets of the fair, and the very moderate horsemanship of the brave, — privates, standing at ease in the ranks, take note of, not cynically, but as men of the world.

Wondrous gymnasts are some of the Seventh, and after evening parade they often give exhibitions of their prowess to circles of admirers. Muscle has not gone out, nor nerve, nor activity, if these athletes are to be taken as the types or even as the leaders of the young city-bred men of our time. All the feats of strength and grace of the gymnasiums are to be seen here, and show to double advantage in the open air.

Then comes sweet evening. The moon rises. It seems always full moon at Camp Cameron. Every tent becomes a little illuminated pyramid. Cooking-fires burn bright along the alleys. The boys lark, sing, shout, do all those merry things that make the entertainment of volunteer service. The gentle moon looks on, mild and amused, the fairest lady of all that visit us.

At last, when the songs have been sung and the hundred rumors of the day discussed, at ten the intrusive drums and scolding fifes get together and stir up a concert, always premature, called tattoo. The Seventh Regiment begins to peel for bed : at all events, Private W. does ; for said W. takes, when he can, precious good care of his cuticle, and never yields to the lazy and unwholesome habit of soldiers, — sleeping in the clothes. At taps — half past ten — out go the lights. If they do not, presently comes the sentry's peremptory command to put them out. Then, and until the dawn of another day, a cordon of snorers inside of a cordon of sentries surrounds our national capital. The outer cordon sounds its "All's well"; and the inner cordon, slumbering, echoes it.

And that is the history of any day at Camp Cameron. It is monotonous, it is not monotonous, it is laborious, it is lazy, it is a bore, it is a lark, it is half war, half peace, and totally attractive, and not to be dispensed with from one's experience in the nineteenth century.

OUR ADVANCE INTO VIRGINIA.

MEANTIME the weeks went on. May 23d arrived. Lovely creatures with their taper fingers had been brewing a flag for us. Shall I say that its red stripes were celestial rosy as their cheeks, its white stripes virgin white as their brows, its blue field cerulean as their eyes, and its stars scintillating as the beams of the said peepers ? Shall I say this ? If I were a poet, like Jeff Davis and each and every editor of each and every newspaper in our misbehaving States, I might say it. And involuntarily I have said it.

So the young ladies of New York — including, I hope, her who made my sandwiches for the march hither — had been making us a flag, as they have made us havelocks, pots of jelly, bundles of lint, flannel dressing-gowns, embroidered slippers for a rainy day in camp, and other necessaries of the soldier's life.

May 23d was the day we were to get this sweet symbol of good-will. At evening parade appeared General Thomas, as the agent of the ladies, the donors, with a neat speech on a clean sheet of paper. He read it with feeling ; and Private W., who has his sentimental moments, avows that he was touched by the General's earnest manner and patriotic words. Our Colonel responded with his neat speech, very *apropos*. The regiment then made its neat speech, nine cheers and a roar of tigers, — very brief and pointed.

There had been a note of preparation in General Thomas's remarks, — a *"Virginia, cave canem !"* And before parade was dismissed, we saw our officers holding parley with the Colonel.

Something in the wind ! As I was strolling off to see the sunset and the ladies on parade, I began to hear great irrepressible cheers bursting from the streets of the different companies.

" Orders to be ready to march at a moment's notice ! " — so I learned presently from-dozens of overjoyed fellows. " Harper's Ferry ! " says one.

"Alexandria!" shouts a second. "Richmond!" only Richmond will content a third. And some could hardly be satisfied short of the hope of a breakfast in Montgomery.

What a happy thousand were the line-companies! How their suppressed ardors stirred! No want of fight in these lads! They may be rather luxurious in their habits, for camp-life. They may be a little impatient of restraint. They may have — as the type regiment of militia — the type faults of militia on service. But a desire to dodge a fight is not one of these faults.

Every man in camp was merry, except two hundred who were grim. These were the two artillery companies, ordered to remain in guard of our camp. They swore as if Camp Cameron were Flanders.

I by rights belonged with these malecontent and objurgating gentlemen ; but a chronicler has privileges, and I got leave to count myself into the Eighth Company, my old friend Captain Shumway's. We were to move, about midnight, in light marching order, with one day's rations.

It has been always full moon at our camp. This night was full moon at its fullest, — a night more perfect than all perfection, mild, dewy, refulgent. At one o'clock the drum beat ; we fell into ranks, and marched quietly off through the shadowy trees of the lane, into the highway.

ACROSS THE LONG BRIDGE.

I HAVE heretofore been proud of my individuality, and resisted, so far as one may, all the world's attempts to merge me in the mass. *In pluribus unum* has been my motto. But whenever I march with the regiment, my pride is that I lose my individuality, that I am merged, that I become a part of a machine, a mere walking gentleman, a No. 1 or a No. 2, front rank or rear rank, file-leader or file-closer. The machine is so steady and so mighty, it moves with such musical cadence and such brilliant show, that I enjoy it entirely as the *unum* and lose myself gladly as a *pluribus.*

Night increases this fascination. The outer world is vague in the moonlight. Objects out of our ranks are lost. I see only glimmering steel and glittering buttons and the light-stepping forms of my comrades. Our array and our step connect us. We move as one man. A man made up of a thousand members and each member a man, is a grand creature, — particularly when you consider that he is self-made. And the object of this self-made giant, men-man, is to destroy another like himself, or the separate pigmy members of another such giant. We have failed to put ourselves — heads, arms, legs, and wills — together as a unit for any purpose so thoroughly as to snuff out a similar unit. Up to 1861, it seems that the business of war compacts men best.

Well, the Seventh, a compact projectile, was

now flinging itself along the road to Washington. Just a month ago, "in such a night as this," we made our first promenade through the enemy's country. The moon of Annapolis — why should we not have our ominous moon, as those other fellows had their sun of Austerlitz ? — the moon of Annapolis shone over us. No epithets are too fine or too complimentary for such a luminary, and there was no dust under her rays.

So we pegged along to Washington and across Washington, — which at that point consists of Willard's Hotel, few other buildings being in sight. A hag in a nightcap reviewed us from an upper window as we tramped by.

Opposite that bald block, the Washington Monument, and opposite what was of more importance to us, a drove of beeves putting beef on their bones in the seedy grounds of the Smithsonian Institution, we were halted while the New Jersey brigade — some three thousand of them — trudged by, receiving the complimentary fire of our line as they passed. New Jersey is not so far from New York but that the dialects of the two can understand each other. Their respective slangs, though peculiar, are of the same genus. By the end of this war, I trust that these distinctions of locality will be quite annulled.

We began to feel like an army as these thousands thronged by us. This was evidently a movement in force. We rested an hour or more by the road. Mounted officers galloping along down the lines kept up the excitement.

At last we had the word to fall in again and march. It is part of the simple perfection of the machine, a regiment, that, though it drops to pieces for a rest, it comes together instantly for a start, and nobody is confused or delayed. We moved half a mile farther, and presently a broad pathway of reflected moonlight shone up at us from the Potomac.

No orders, at this, came from the Colonel, "Attention, battalion! Be sentimental!" Perhaps privates have no right to perceive the beautiful. But the sections in my neighborhood murmured admiration. The utter serenity of the night was most impressive. Cool and quiet and tender the moon shone upon our ranks. She does not change her visage, whether it be lovers or burglars or soldiers who use her as a lantern to their feet.

The Long Bridge thus far has been merely a shabby causeway with water-ways and draws. Shabby, — let me here pause to say that in Virginia shabbiness is the grand universal law, and neatness the spasmodic exception, attained in rare spots, an æon beyond their Old Dominion age.

The Long Bridge has thus far been a totally unhistoric and prosaic bridge. Roads and bridges are making themselves of importance, and shining up into sudden renown in these times. The Long Bridge has done nothing hitherto except carry passengers on its back across the Potomac. Hucksters, planters, dry-goods drummers, members of Congress, *et ea genera omnia*, have here gone and come on their several mercenary errands, and, as it now appears, some sour little imp — the very reverse of a "sweet little cherub" — took toll of every man as he passed, — a heavy toll, namely, every man's whole store of Patriotism and Loyalty. Every man — so it seems — who passed the Long Bridge was stripped of his last dollar of *Amor Patriæ*, and came to Washington, or went home, with a waistcoat-pocket full of bogus in change. It was our business now to open the bridge and see it clear, and leave sentries along to keep it permanently free for Freedom.

There is a mile of this Long Bridge. We seemed to occupy the whole length of it, with our files opened to diffuse the weight of our column. We were not now the tired and sleepy squad which just a moon ago had trudged along the railroad to the Annapolis Junction, looking up a Capital and a Government, perhaps lost.

By the time we touched ground across the bridge, dawn was breaking, — a good omen for poor old sleepy Virginia. The moon, as bright and handsome as a new twenty-dollar piece, carried herself straight before us, — a splendid oriflamme.

Lucky is the private who marches with the van ! It may be the post of more danger, but it is also the post of less dust. My throat, therefore, and my eyes and beard, wore the less Southern soil when we halted half a mile beyond the bridge, and let sunrise overtake us.

Nothing men can do — except picnics, with ladies in straw flats with feathers — is so picturesque as soldiering. As soon as the Seventh.halt anywhere, or move anywhere, or camp anywhere, they resolve themselves into a grand *tableau*. Their own ranks should supply their own Horace Vernet. Our groups were never more entertaining than at this halt by the roadside on the Alexandria road. Stacks of guns make a capital framework for drapery, and red blankets dot in the lights most artistically. The fellows lined the road with their gay array, asleep on the rampage, on the lounge, and nibbling at their rations.

By and by, when my brain had taken in as much of the picturesque as it could stand, it suffered the brief congestion known as a nap. I was suddenly awaked by the rattle of a horse's hoofs. Before I had rubbed my eyes the rider was gone. His sharp tidings had stayed behind him. Ellsworth was dead, — so he said hurriedly, and rode on. Poor Ellsworth ! a fellow of genius and initiative ! He had still so much of the boy in him, that he rattled forward boyishly, and so died. *Si monumentum requiris*, look at his regiment. It was a brilliant stroke to levy it ; and if it does worthily, its young Colonel will not have lived in vain.

As the morning hours passed, we learned that we were the rear-guard of the left wing of the army advancing into Virginia. The Seventh, as the best organized body, acted as reserve to this force. It did n't wish to be in the rear ; but such is the penalty of being reliable for an emergency. Fellow-soldier, be a scalawag, be a bashi-bazouk, be a Billy-Wilsoneer, if you wish to see the fun in the van !

When the road grew too hot for us, on account of the fire of sunshine in our rear, we jumped over the fence into the Race-Course, a big field beside us, and there became squatter sovereigns all day. I shall be a bore if I say again what a pretty figure we cut in this military picnic, with two long lines of blankets draped on bayonets for parasols.

The New Jersey brigade were meanwhile doing workie work on the ridge just beyond us. The road and railroad to Alexandria follow the general course of the river southward along the level. This ridge to be fortified is at the point where the highway bends from west to south. The works were intended to serve as an advanced *tête du pont*,— a bridge-head, with a very long neck connecting it with the bridge. That fine old Fabius, General Scott, had no idea of flinging an army out broadcast into Virginia, and, in the insupposable case that it had turned tail, leaving it no defended passage to run away by.

This was my first view of a field-work in construction, — also, my first hand as a laborer at a field-work. I knew glacis and counterscarp on paper ; also, on paper, superior slope, banquette, and the other dirty parts of a redoubt. Here they were, not on paper. A slight wooden scaffolding determined the shape of the simple work ; and when I arrived, a thousand Jerseymen were working, not at all like Jerseymen, with picks, spades, and shovels, cutting into Virginia, digging into Virginia, shovelling up Virginia, for Virginia's protection against pseudo-Virginians.

I swarmed in for a little while with our Paymaster, picked a little, spaded a little, shovelled a little, took a hand to my great satisfaction at earth-works, and for my efforts I venture to suggest that Jersey City owes me its freedom in a box, and Jersey State a basket of its finest Clicquot.

Is my gentle reader tired of the short marches and frequent halts of the Seventh? Remember, gentle reader, that you must be schooled by such alphabetical exercises to spell bigger words — skirmish, battle, defeat, rout, massacre — by and by.

Well, — to be Xenophontic, — from the Race-Course that evening we marched one stadium, one parasang, to a cedar-grove up the road. In the grove is a spring worthy to be called a fountain, and what I determined by infallible indications to be a *lager-bier* saloon. Saloon no more! War is no respecter of localities. Be it Arlington House, the seedy palace of a Virginia Don, — be it the humbler, but seedy, pavilion where the tired Teuton washes the dust of Washington away from his tonsils, — each must surrender to the bold soldier-boy. Exit Champagne and its goblet; exit *lager* and its mug; enter whiskey-and-water in a tin pot. Such are the horrors of civil war!

And now I must cut short my story, for graver matters press. As to the residence of the Seventh

in the cedar-grove for two days and two nights, —
how they endured the hardship of a bivouac on soft
earth and the starvation ŏf coffee *sans* milk,— how
they digged manfully in the trenches by gangs all
these two laborious days, — with what supreme
artistic finish their work was achieved, — how they
chopped off their corns with axes, as they cleared
the brushwood from the glacis, — how they blis-
tered their hands, — how they chafed that they
were not lunging with battailous steel at the breasts
of the minions of the oligarchs, — how Washington,
seeing the smoke of burning rubbish, and hearing
dropping shots of target-practice, or of novices
with the musket shooting each other by accident,
— how Washington, alarmed, imagined a battle,
and went into panic accordingly, — all this, is it
not written in the daily papers ?

On the evening of the 26th, the Seventh travelled
back to Camp Cameron in a smart shower. Its service was over. Its month was expired. The troops
ordered to relieve it had arrived. It had given the
other volunteers the benefit of a month's education
at its drills and parades. It had enriched poor
Washington to the tune of fifty thousand dollars.
Ah, Washington ! that we, under Providence and
after General Butler, saved from the heel of Secession ! Ah, Washington, why did you charge us so
much for our milk and butter and strawberries ?
The Seventh, then, after a month of delightful
duty, was to be mustered out of service, and take
new measures, if it would, to have a longer and a
larger share in the war.

ARLINGTON HEIGHTS.

I took advantage of the day of rest after our return to have a gallop about the outposts. Arlington Heights had been the spot whence the alarmists threatened us daily with big thunder and bursting bombs. I was curious to see the region that had had Washington under its thumb.

So Private W., tired of his foot-soldiering, got a quadruped under him, and felt like a cavalier again. The horse took me along the tow-path of the Cumberland Canal, as far as the redoubts where we had worked our task. Then I turned up the hill, took a look at the camp of the New York Twenty-Fifth at the left, and rode along for Arlington House.

Grand name! and the domain is really quite grand, but ill-kept. Fine oaks make beauty without asking favors. Fine oaks and a fair view make all the beauty of Arlington. It seems that this old establishment, like many another old Virginian, had claimed its respectability for its antiquity, and failed to keep up to the level of the time. The road winds along through the trees, climbing to fairer and fairer reaches of view over the plain of Washington. I had not fancied that there was any such lovely site near the capital. But we have not yet appreciated what Nature has done for us there. When civilization once makes up its mind to colonize Washington, all this amphitheatre of hills will blossom with structures of sublimest gingerbread.

Arlington House is the antipodes of gingerbread, except that it is yellow, and disposed to crumble. It has a pompous propylon of enormous stuccoed columns. Any house smaller than Blenheim would tail on insignificantly after such a frontispiece. The interior has a certain careless, romantic, decayed-gentleman effect, wholly Virginian. It was enlivened by the uniforms of staff-officers just now, and as they rode through the trees of the approach and by the tents of the New York Eighth, encamped in the grove to the rear, the *tableau* was brilliantly warlike. Here, by the way, let me pause to ask, as a horseman, though a foot-soldier, why generals and other gorgeous fellows make such guys of their horses with trappings. If the horse is a screw, cover him thick with saddle-cloths, girths, cruppers, breast-bands, and as much brass and tinsel as your pay will enable you to buy; but if not a screw, let his fair proportions be seen as much as may be, and don't bother a lover of good horse-flesh to eliminate so much uniform before he can see what is beneath.

From Arlington I rode to the other encampments, — the Sixty-Ninth, Fifth, and Twenty-Eighth, all of New York, — and heard their several stories of alarms and adventures. This completed the circuit of the new fortification of the Great Camp. Washington was now a fortress. The capital was out of danger, and therefore of no further interest to anybody. The time had come for myself and my regiment to leave it by different ways.

" PARTANT POUR LA SYRIE."

I should have been glad to stay and see my comrades through to their departure ; but there was a Massachusetts man down at Fortress Monroe, Butler by name, — has any one heard of him ? — and to this gentleman it chanced that I was to report myself. So I packed my knapsack, got my furlough, shook hands with my fellows, said good by to Camp Cameron, and was off, two days after our month's service was done.

FAREWELL TO THE SEVENTH.

Under Providence, Washington owes its safety, 1st, To General Butler, whose genius devised the circumvention of Baltimore and its rascal rout, and whose utter bravery executed the plan ; — he is the Grand Yankee of this little period of the war. 2d, To the other Most Worshipful Grand Yankees of the Massachusetts regiment who followed their leader, as he knew they would, discovered a forgotten colony called Annapolis, and dashed in there, asking no questions. 3d, And while I gladly yield the first places to this General and his men, I put the Seventh in, as last, but not least, in saving the capital. Character always tells. The Seventh, by good, hard, faithful work at .drill, had established its fame as the most thorough militia regiment in existence. Its military and moral character were excellent. The mere name of the

13

regiment carried weight. It took the field as if
the field were a ball-room. There were myriads
eager to march ; but they had not made ready be-
forehand.   Yes, the Seventh had its important
share in the rescue.   Without our support, whether
our leaders tendered it eagerly or hesitatingly,
General Butler's position at Annapolis would have
been critical, and his forced march to the capital a
forlorn hope, — heroic, but desperate.

So, honor to whom honor is due.

Here I must cut short my story. So good by
to the Seventh, and thanks for the fascinating
month I have passed in their society. In this
pause of the war our camp-life has been to me
as brilliant as a permanent picnic.

Good by to Company I, and all the fine fellows,
rough and smooth, cool old hands and recruits verdant but ardent ! Good by to our Lieutenants, to
whom I owe much kindness ! Good by, the Orderly, so peremptory on parade, so indulgent off !
Good by, everybody !

And so in haste, I close.

FORTRESS MONROE.

FORTRESS MONROE.

[The sketches of the campaign in Virginia, which Winthrop had commenced in the "Atlantic Monthly," would have been continued, had he lived. Immediately upon his arrival at Fort Monroe he had commenced a third article. It is inserted here just as he left it, with one brief addition only to make his known meaning more clear. The part called "Voices of the Contraband" was written previously, and is not paged in the manuscript. It was to have been introduced into the article; but it is placed first here, that the sequence of the paper, as far as the author had written it, may remain undisturbed.]

VOICES OF THE CONTRABAND.

Solvuntur risu tabulæ. An epigram abolished slavery in the United States. Large wisdom, stated in fine wit, was the decision, "Negroes are contraband of war." "They are property," claim the owners. Very well! As General Butler takes contraband horses used in transport of munitions of war, so he takes contraband black creatures who tote the powder to the carts and flagellate the steeds. As he takes a spade used in hostile earthworks, so he goes a little farther off and takes the black muscle that wields the spade. As he takes the rations of the foe, so he takes the sable Soyer whose skilful hand makes those rations savory to the palates and digestible by the stomachs of the foe, and so puts blood and nerve into them. As he took the steam-gun, so he now takes what might become the stoker of the steam part of that machine and the aimer of its gun part. As he takes the musket, so he seizes the object who in the Virginia army carries that musket on its shoulder until its master is ready to reach out a lazy hand, nonchalantly lift the piece, and carelessly pop a Yankee.

[The third number of the author's Sketches of the Campaign in Virginia begins here.]

PHYSIOGNOMY OF FORTRESS MONROE.

THE "Adelaide" is a steamer plying between Baltimore and Norfolk. But as Norfolk has ceased to be a part of the United States, and is nowhere, the "Adelaide" goes no farther than Fortress Monroe, Old Point Comfort, the chief somewhere of this region. A lady, no doubt Adelaide herself, appears in *alto rilievo* on the paddle-box. She has a short waist, long skirt *sans* crinoline, leg-of-mutton sleeves, lofty bearing, and stands like Ariadne on an island of pedestal size, surrounded by two or more pre-Raphaelite trees. In the offing comes or goes a steamboat, also pre-Raphaelite ; and if Ariadne Adelaide's Bacchus is on board, he is out of sight at the bar.

Such an Adelaide brought me in sight of Fortress Monroe at sunrise, May 29, 1861. The fort, though old enough to be full-grown, has not grown very tall upon the low sands of Old Point Comfort. It is a big house with a basement story and a garret. The roof is left off, and stories between basement and garret have never been inserted.

But why not be technical ? For basement read a tier of casemates, each with a black Cyclops of a big gun peering out ; while above in the open air, with not even a parasol over their backs, lie the barbette guns, staring without a wink over sea and shore.

In peace, with a hundred or so soldiers here and there, this vast enclosure might seem a solitude. Now it is a busy city, — a city of one idea. I seem to recollect· that D'Israeli said somewhere that every great city was founded on one idea and existed to develop it. This city, into which we have improvised a population, has its idea, — a unit of an idea with two halves. The east half is the recovery of Norfolk, — the west half the occupation of Richmond ; and the idea complete is the education of Virginia's unmannerly and disloyal sons.

Why Secession did not take this great place when its defenders numbered a squad of officers and three hundred men, is mysterious. Floyd and his gang were treacherous enough. What was it? Were they imbecile? Were they timid? Was there, till too late, a doubt whether the traitors at home in Virginia would sustain them in an overt act of such big overture as an attempt here? But they lost the chance, and with it lost the key of Virginia, which General Butler now holds, this 30th day of May, and will presently begin to turn in the lock.

Three hundred men to guard a mile and a half of ramparts! Three hundred to protect some sixty-five broad acres within the walls! But the place was a Thermopylæ, and there was a fine old Leonidas at the head of its three hundred. He was enough to make Spartans of them. Colonel Dimmick was the man, — a quiet, modest, shrewd, faithful, Christian gentleman; and he held all Virginia at bay. The traitors knew, that, so long as the Colonel was here, these black muzzles with their white tompions, like a black eye with a white pupil, meant mischief. To him and his guns, flanking the approaches and ready to pile the moat full of Seceders, the country owes the safety of Fortress Monroe.

Within the walls are sundry nice old brick houses for officers' barracks. The jolly bachelors live in the casemates and the men in long barracks, now not so new or so convenient as they might be. In fact, the physiognomy of Fortress Monroe is not so neat, well-shorn, and elegant as a grand military post should be. Perhaps our Floyds, and the like, thought, if they kept everything in perfect order here, they, as Virginians, accustomed to general seediness, would not find themselves at home. But the new *régime* must change all this, and make this the biggest, the best equipped, and the model garrison of the country. For, of course, this must be strongly held for many, many years to come. It is idle to suppose that the dull louts we find here, not enlightened even enough to know that loyalty is the best policy, can be allowed the highest privilege of the moral, the intelligent, and the progressive, — self-government. Mind is said to march fast in our time ; but mind must put on steam hereabouts to think and act for itself, without stern schooling, in half a century.

But no digressing ! I have looked far away from the physiognomy of the fortress. Let us turn to the

PHYSIOGNOMY OF THE COUNTRY.

THE face of this county, Elizabeth City by name, is as flat as a Chinaman's. I can hardly wonder that the people here have retrograded, or rather, not advanced. This dull flat would make anybody dull and flat. I am no longer surprised at John Tyler. He has had a bare blank brick house, entitled sweetly Margarita Cottage, or some such ten-

13 *

der epithet, at Hampton, a mile and a half from the
fort. A summer in this site would make any man
a bore. And as something has done this favor for
His Accidency, I am willing to attribute it to the
influence of locality.

The country is flat ; the soil is fine sifted loam
running to dust, as the air of England runs to fog ;
the woods are dense and beautiful, and full of trees
unknown to the parallel of New York ; the roads
are miserable cart-paths ; the cattle are scalawags ;
so are the horses, not run away ; so are the people,
black and white, not run away ; the crops are tolerable, where the invaders have not trampled them.

Altogether the whole concern strikes me as a
failure. Captain John Smith & Co. might as well
have stayed at home, if this is the result of the two
hundred and thirty years' occupation. Apparent-
ly the colonists picked out a poor spot ; and the
longer they stayed, the worse fist they made of it.
Powhattan, Pocahontas, and the others without
pantaloons and petticoats, were really more service-
able colonists.

The farm-houses are mostly miserably mean habitations. I don't wonder the tenants were glad to
make our arrival the excuse for running off. Here
are men claiming to have been worth forty thousand dollars, half in biped property, half in all
other kinds, and they lived in dens such as a dray-
man would have disdained and a hod-carrier only
accepted on compulsion.

PHYSIOGNOMY OF WATER.

ALWAYS beautiful! the sea cannot be spoilt. Our fleet enlivens it greatly. Here is the flag-ship "Cumberland" *vis-à-vis* the fort. Off to the left are the prizes, unlucky schooners, which ought to be carrying pine wood to the kitchens of New York, and new potatoes and green peas for the wood to operate upon. This region, by the way, is New York's watermelon patch for early melons ; and if we do not conquer a peace here pretty soon, the Jersey fruit will have the market to itself.

Besides stately flag-ships and poor little bumboat schooners, transports are coming and going with regiments or provisions for the same. Here, too, are old acquaintances from the bay of New York, — the "Yankee," a lively tug, — the "Harriet Lane," coquettish and plucky, — the "Catiline," ready to reverse her name and put down conspiracy.

On the dock are munitions of war in heaps. Volunteer armies load themselves with things they do not need, and forget the essentials. The unlucky army-quartermaster's people, accustomed to the slow and systematic methods of the by-gone days at Fortress Monroe, fume terribly over these cargoes. The new men and the new manners of the new army do not altogether suit the actual men and manners of the obsolete army. The old men and the new must recombine. What we want now is the vigor of fresh people to utilize the experience of the experts. The Silver-Gray Army needs a frisky element interfused. On the other hand, the new army needs to be taught a lesson in *method* by the old ; and the two combined will make the grand army of civilization.

THE FORCES.

WHEN I arrived, Fort Monroe and the neighborhood were occupied by two armies.

1. General Butler.

2. About six thousand men, here and at Newport's News.

Making together more than twelve thousand men.

Of the first army, consisting of the General, I will not speak. Let his past supreme services speak for him, as I doubt not the future will.

Next to the army of a man comes the army of men. Regulars a few, with many post officers, among them some very fine and efficient fellows. These are within the post. Also within is the Third Regiment of Massachusetts, under Colonel Wardrop, the right kind of man to have, and commanding a capital regiment of three months' men, neatly uniformed in gray, with cocked felt hats.

Without the fort, across the moat, and across the bridge connecting this peninsula of sand with the nearest side of the mainland, are encamped three New York regiments. Each is in a wheat-field, up to its eyes in dust. In order of precedence they come One, Two, and Five ; in order of personal splendor of uniform, they come Five, One, Two ; in order of exploits they are all in the same negative position at present ; and the Second has done rather the most robbing of hen-roosts.

The Fifth, Duryea's Zouaves, lighten up the woods brilliantly with their scarlet legs and scarlet head-pieces.

[These last words were written upon the day that the. attack in which the author fell was arranged.]

BRIGHTLY'S ORPHAN.

A FRAGMENT.

[The author had only written two chapters of this story when he joined the Army. It was the last thing his hand was engaged upon when the call for volunteers summoned him to the field. He said of it, " I am tired of writing of crime and wrong ; this shall be cheerful and sunshiny, if I can make it so." In its unfinished state it has been thought worthy of preservation.]

BRIGHTLY'S ORPHAN.

CHAPTER I.

JOHN BRIGHTLY jumped out of bed. He filled his short and stout pantaloons with a pair of legs proportionable, and ran to the window.

Nothing to be seen through the thick frost upon the panes, until he had breathed himself a round eye-hole bearing upon his thermometer.

That erect little sentry had an emphatic fact to communicate to the scrutinizing eye of John Brightly. It was a very frigid fact, and made the eye that perceived it shiver a little. But the temperature of Brightly's mind was perpetual summer. The iciest ideas admitted into his brain became warmed and melted by the sunny spirits there; and so it was with this cold fact which the cold mercury fired at him through its cold glass barrel.

" Zero ! " said he, " a sharp zero, Mrs. Brightly ! "

A pretty, delicate, anxious face, lifted itself from the pillow by the side of its fellow, still depressed in the middle and high at the sides as her husband's head had left it.

" Zero ! " rejoined a voice sweet, but feeble. " I

T

should think by your tone that you had just seen the earliest bluebird. I have half a mind to go into a rage with you, John, for being so utterly contented."

"When you have your first rage, Mary Brightly, I shall have my first discontent. But I cannot scold 'Zero when I see what a wonderful artist he is. Look at this window. See this magic frost-landscape. It is a beautiful thought that such exquisite fancies are always in the air waiting to be discovered."

"The chill finds the latent pictures, as sorrow makes poets sing."

"Well said! We each owe the other one. And what did you dream of last night, Mrs. Brightly?"

"Nothing."

"Yes; you must have dreamed of the tropics, and breathed out palms and vines and tree-ferns in your dreams."

"As the girl in the fairy-tale dropped pearls and diamonds when she spoke. Perhaps I did. But how did you detect me?"

"Here they are all upon the window, just as you exhaled them. Here on this pane is a picture, crowded as a photograph of a jungle on the Amazon. Here are long feathery bamboos, drooping palms, stiff palms, and such a beautiful bewilderment of vines and creepers by a river sparkling in the sunshine. And here, hullo! here is an alligator done in ice, nabbing an iced boa-constrictor. Delicious! Do come and see, Mary!"

" Zero forbids," said she, with a pretty shiver.
" I 'll see them with your eyes, John."

" Well.   And while you were dreaming out this
enchanted vision, I must have been snoring forth
my recollections of the forests of Maine.   Here
they are on the next pane by way of pendant and
contrast.   'This is the forest primeval.'   Here
are pines in full feather and pines without a rag
on their poor bare branches, pines lying on the
ground, and pines that fell half-way and were
caught in the arms of brother pines.   Pines, hemlocks, and the finest arbor-vitæ I ever saw, all
crusted with glittering ice and hanging over a
mountain lake.   I think I like this better than the
tropics.   Do come, Mrs. Brightly."

" Zero doubly forbids my going to a colder
climate.   But it is delightful to be here, warm and
comfortable, and listen to your raptures."

" Mary," said Brightly, turning to her with a
grave and tender manner.

" What, John ? "

" I find a different picture on the next pane.   Do
you remember our two dear little ones ? "

" Do we remember them ? " she asked with tear-
ful eyes.

" God knows we do ! and here among these
lovely frost-pictures I find a memorial of them.
Shall I describe it ? "

" Yes, dear John," said she, by this time weeping abundantly.

" I see a little promontory jutting into a great

river.   Evergreens grow about the edges. The
top is nearly clear.   It is a graveyard, Mary.   In
one corner, under a hemlock heavy with snow, and
within a railing, I see two simple white stones,
such as are put over children's graves.   It is
strangely like a scene that we have looked at very
sadly together.   Shall I read the names I almost
fancy I decipher upon the stones ? ''

" Do, dear John," she said between her sobs.
" All memories of them are beautiful to me."

" John, son of John and Mary Brightly, drowned
at eight years of age, while endeavoring to rescue
his drowning sister Mary.   ' In death they were
not divided.' "

Brightly took his wife's hand very tenderly, as
in this grave, formal way he recalled their domestic
tragedy.

" We do not repine, my love," said he.

He was a singularly sturdy, bold, energetic-look-
ing man ; almost belligerent indeed, except that
an expression of frank good-nature showed that,
though warlike, he would not wage war unless on
compulsion, and when peace was impossible.   His
face was round and ruddy, his hair light, his eyes
dark blue, his figure of the middle height, and
solid as if he was built to carry weight.   Evidently a man to make himself heard and felt, one to
hit hard if he hit at all.   It was a shrewd and able
face, and if it had a weakness, it was that there
was too much frankness, too much trustfulness,
too little reserve in it.   A rough observer would

hardly have suspected this burly, boyish, exuberant man of thirty of so much delicacy of feeling and tenderness as he had shown in this interview with his wife.

"We do not repine, my love, for their loss," he repeated.

"I am sometimes very lonely, John," she hesitatingly said. "Our little Mary was growing just old enough to be a companion to me ; and John too, — I do not know which I loved best."

"I must find you," said Brightly, in his cheerful tone, "a nice little maiden or a fine little fellow to adopt."

"O if you would ! " she exclaimed.

"Which shall it be ? " he asked with a business air. He occupied himself in erasing with his breath the picture which had recalled their bereavement.

As the frost vanished, the scenery without appeared. No very vast or very attractive view. Most of the respectable citizens of New York have similar landscape privileges. Brightly's bedroom window was perforated in the front of a handsome precipice of brown freestone. It looked down upon a snowy ravine, planted alternately with lamp-posts and ailanthus-trees ; opposite was another long precipice of brown stone, evidently excavated into dwellings for the better class of troglodytes.

"Are you serious, John ? " asked Mrs. Brightly, drying her tears.

"Certainly," says he. "What do I live and work for except that my wife shall have everything she wants?"

"Don't claim to be too disinterested! I am sure you are dying to have me approve your scheme."

"I think we are both growing excited about it. But let us come to a conclusion. Which shall it be, boy or girl?"

"Boys are so merry and noisy in a solitary house," said Mrs. Brightly, thinking of her son.

"Girls are so gentle and quiet," Brightly returned.

"But then I am so afraid boys will get riotous companions, and be taught to smoke pipes."

"And girls must learn music and flirtation."

Each parent was evidently trifling away tears. The loss of their children was a bitter chapter in their history. They dared no more than glance at it, for fear their childless life should seem but idle, aimless business.

"We must draw lots," said Brightly, assuming a serio-comic air.

Mrs. Brightly, still couchant, watched smiling, while he took a clothes-broom and selected two straws.

"Graver matters have been decided by lot," said Brightly. "Draw, Mary. If you get the shorter straw, it's a girl; if the longer, a boy."

She coquetted a little, and finally selected her straw. They compared them carefully.

She had drawn a girl.

"I do hereby bind myself and mortgage my property," said Brightly, holding up his hand, as if he were taking a judicial oath, "to present to Mrs. John Brightly of the City of New York, on or before the 31st of December instant, one attractive and intelligent damsel not over fourteen years of age; to be by her, the said donee Brightly, adopted and brought up to the best of her knowledge and belief, either as daughter, step-daughter, companion, or handmaiden, as to the said Brightly may seem good. And thereto I plight thee my troth."

Mrs. Brightly laughed at this pledge. "But how are you going to find her, John?" she asked.

"I always find the things I look for; unless they find me as soon as they know I'm in search of them."

"Success will spoil you some of these days."

"Not if I lose what I prize success for. But this new child of ours shall be a new spur to me."

"She must be an orphan, John, or she will not love us as much as we shall love her."

"An orphan of course. I think I shall put an advertisement in the paper to this effect: — Wanted to adopt. An orphan of poor but respectable parentage, beautiful as a cherub, clean as a new-laid egg, with a character of docility and determination in equal parts; eyes blue, voice tranquil, laugh electric; one whose heart sings and heels dance spontaneously; a thing of beauty willing to be a joy forever in the house of a prosperous banker, where she will be spoiled all day by the mistress and spoiled from dinner to bedtime by the master.   No Irish, orange-girls, or rag-babies need apply."

"It is impossible not to be in good spirits where you are, John," said the little wife.   "How doleful I should be all day, unless you compelled me to begin my morning with a course of laughter!"

"I don't know any better medicine," said he. "I take all I can get, and give all I can.   Well; you approve of my advertisement?"

"As a description of what we want, it is perfect."

"I will pop it into the paper to-day, and to-morrow morning there will be a deadlock of dirty children in this street, and a deadlock of dirty parents up and down the cross streets, for half a dozen blocks, — parents and children all waiting to be adopted.   By the way, Mary," Brightly rattled on, "you must plunge into Zero, and dress and give me my breakfast in a hurry."

"O John, when will you have made money enough not to be in a hurry any more?"   •

"When I have hurried through my hurries.   But I must be early in Wall Street this morning, for another reason.   This talk about advertisements reminds me that I have advertised for an office-boy. I dare say there are a hundred juvenile noses flattening against my windows already.   It will be deadlock there, too, by the time I get down.   I am afraid poor Broke will be quite bewildered out of his wits, if he arrives first."

"Is Mr. Broke coming to dinner to-morrow?"

"Yes; he would not miss his Christmas with us. The others are all coming, I suppose?"

"Every one. The two Knightlys, Uncle Furbish and Amelia, Dr. Letherland, and Mrs. Purview and her son."

"And I hope you mean to have a good dinner for us, Mrs. Brightly."

"Certainly. Did I ever fail? And your Christmas dinners, John, for all the poor people that expect them from us, are they ordered?"

"Not yet. That is another reason for me to despatch. The pick of the market will be all gone, if I am late. Now, then, my dear, one spasm, and you are up."

CHAPTER II.

OF all the luxuries of town life on this globe, there is no luxury greater than a rattling walk down Broadway on a cold winter's morning.

So John Brightly thought as he strode along on that day before Christmas.

It was early, but the shops had all opened their eyes wide, and put on their most seductive smiles in honor of the season. Everything that the brain of man has fancied and the hands of man have contrived, had taken its stand at the windows to persuade passengers to stop and admire, and then to

14

enter and buy.   Even the mourning shops had hidden their gloomy merchandise under the counter for this day only, and displayed nothing but coquettish articles of half-mourning and the subdued purples of departing grief and awakening joy.   The toy-shop windows chuckled and grinned with jolly toys.   The print-shops had taken down their battle-scenes and death-bed scenes, and, instead of blood and tears, nothing but comedy and sentiment was to be seen.   The photographers exhibited their smuggest men and smirkiest women.   Nothing could be gayer or brighter or more party-colored than the confectioners' show-cases, where, under bowers of cornucopias, the tempting wares were arrayed, as if there was somewhere in fairy-land a planet all pink and white and blue and yellow sugar from centre to pole, and this was a geological cabinet of its specimens.

John Brightly ran this amicable gantlet at a great pace, conscious of its love-taps, but proof, as if he were a Princess Pari Banou, to its attempts to arrest him.

Only once he felt a little pang as he rattled along, electrified by the keen air.   A sharp sunbeam, reflected from a pair of skates, struck him in the eye. He thought of his drowned son, drowned last summer, and for an instant fancied him skimming along on the ice, as the father had taught him.   But Brightly, though greatly softened by this sorrow, was not a man to let it rankle in his heart and enfeeble him.

" I am very happy," said he to himself, " that Mary has so easily consented to this scheme of mine. I have long seen that her patient grief was wearing her away. Now, perhaps, if I can provide her a new object of interest and love, she will recover tone. Man can work ; but woman is in danger of brooding."

And so, with his busy brain full of schemes for his wife's happiness, full of schemes for comforting and helping all the people he knew who needed help and comfort, full of schemes for bringing the great powers and untiring energies he was conscious of to bear, to ease, speed, and better the world, Brightly hastened down Broadway.

The early clerks, seeing him pass, a knot an hour faster than they were travelling, nudged each other and said : " Hallo, there 's Brightly ! Early bird ! No wonder he 's making his fortune quicker than any man in Wall Street, lucky fellow !"

As everybody is aware, one end of Wall Street drowns itself in a river lately from Hellgate, the other end terminates in a church, and runs up a spire into heaven. Or it might be said that Wall Street, like many a man's career, begins with the sign of the cross up in the pure sky, tumbles down away from the church as fast as it can, and then rushes up hill and down, with Mammon on both sides of the way, until it suddenly finds itself plumped into a tide that is making full speed for Hellgate.

That ornate and flowery plant, the spire of Trinity, with its tap-root in a graveyard and its long radicles in the vaults of a dozen banks, besides its spiritual office of monitor, has a temporal office of time-keeper to perform. It certainly keeps the time of Wall Street; probably it keeps that Via Mala's conscience also, since kept in the street it evidently is not.

The clock of Trinity marked a quarter before nine, when Brightly could see its dial through the branches of the mean trees stunted by the unwholesome diet they found in the churchyard.

"I have beat Broke this morning by fifteen minutes," said he, and turned down the street.

A block before he arrived at his corner, he saw that a regiment of boys had collected in answer to his advertisement. "Wanted immediately, an office-boy, by John Brightly, Wall Street," — this notice had called out from their holes and caves fifty or sixty chaps of all sizes, shapes, tints, and toggery.

Brightly's office was on a corner, three steps below the level of the street. The throng of aspirants completely blockaded the door and filled the sidewalk. Brightly passed around them and took his stand on the high steps to the first floor of the building. From this vantage point he could inspect the troop he had evoked, and reduce it to manageable proportions, by mental subtractions.

It was an amusing sight, as all crowds are, unless the looker-on turns up his nose so much at vulgarity as to obstruct his vision.

It was a compact little crowd, well snugged together to keep warm. Plenty of good-natured hustle was going on in it. The hustle might have been ill-natured scuffle except for that spontaneous police which always keeps the peace and looks after fair-play in crowds that are not mobs. The brutal boys who would have pounded the weakly boys, and rendered them ineligible by black eyes and bloody noses, neutralized each other. Besides, emulation among so many could not develop into hostility. Every boy knew that he had only one fiftieth of one chance of success, and that each boy within reach had only a fiftieth. The natural dislike of competitors, subdivided into fractions with such a denominator, lost intensity, and expended itself in nudges of the elbows and shoves with the hips, instead of running down into the hands and electrifying them into pugilistic fists, or filling the boots with the idea, kick. It is not until two or three of a field distance the others, and are neck and neck within a dozen leaps of the winning-post, that hatred begins to expand in their souls, if they are hateful.

As Brightly had one boy to choose, and no time to spare to be philanthropic, he began to decimate the throng with his eye.

First, he rejected all who disdained or neglected the primal use of the pocket-handkerchief.

Second, he set aside all the irreclaimable ragamuffins.

Third, he counted out those who would be constitutionally unsavory.

Fourth, all who would fill their desks with pies, peanut-shells, and story-books to match.

Fifth, several who would drop in nonchalantly at irregular hours, and regard the office only as an agreeable lounging-place, which their presence honored.

Sixth, the sons or scholars of thieves.

Seventh, chronic upsetters of inkstands.

Eighth, a mean, stunted man of twenty-five, shaved close and disguised in jacket and turn-over collar, with forger and picklock in his face.

Ninth, a boy with a pipe, a boy with a "dorg," and a boy whistling as if his lungs could take breath only in the form of music.

By these successive expurgations, made rapidly by Brightly from his post on the steps, the number of applicants to be noticed was reduced to five or six, all decent, earnest little fellows, and clustered near the door as if they had come early.

One of these was seated against the door, with his head leaning upon the knob. For all the cold, he had dropped asleep in this position. His next neighbor was faithfully defending him from the pokes and pinches of the others.

"One or t' other of that pair will probably be the man," thought Brightly, descending the steps and elbowing his way toward the basement door.

The boys at once perceived that this gentleman, whom they had seen surveying them from above, was the advertiser. All felt a little detected. All made quick attempts to reform their manners and appearance. The inky boys doubled their inky thumbs under their fingers. The boy with a pipe pocketed it and bore the burn like a Spartan. The boy with a "dorg" obscured his bandy-legged comrade. The whistler shut his lips hard together, and breathed stertorously through his nose.

There were symptoms of a rush as Brightly unlocked his door. He repelled it, however, selected the most promising subjects for further examination, and dismissed the others. Most of them, conscious of demerit, abandoned the field at once. A few, with feeble pertinacity, remained sitting on the cold steps and hoping for another chance. The curious ones stayed about the windows peering in to watch who might be the successful candidate, and with a view, no doubt, of learning what was his peculiar charm. Two or three truculent urchins amused themselves with shaking their fists at the insiders, and ferociously threatening them, if they were preferred. The "dorg" boy, finding that he was a failure in his capacity of boy, presented himself as "dorg" merchant, and withdrew indignant when he learnt that dog spelt with an "r" was unsalable thereabouts.

Meantime Brightly had conducted his selection within, and after a question or two to each, had taken two of them into his inner office for closer examination. This was the pair who had been nearest the door.

The sleeper was now wide awake, and looking about observingly. No face could be honester or more freckled than his. Indeed, it seems to be a biological fact that the very red-haired and freckled tend to honesty. Nature compensates them by the gift of Worth for the want of Beauty. The brown splashes arranged themselves on this little chap's face as if each was a little muddy puddle to water the roots of a future hair of his future beard, and a series of them fell away from the bridge of his nose very dark and precisely drawn, and suggesting that his moustache, when it came, would come there instead of under his uplifted nostrils. A merry, trusty, busy fellow he was, and to see him was to like him.

" What is your name, my lad ? " asked Brightly.

" Doak, sir. Bevel Doak."

" And yours," continued the banker, turning to the other.

" Bozes, sir."

" Bozes ? " repeated Brightly.

" I did n't say, Bozes, sir. I said Bozes, —*Bozes.*"

" O Moses ! Well, Moses what ? "

" Dot Bozes Watt. By dabe is Shacob."

" Moses Jacob ? " says Brightly.

" Shacob Bozes, sir," replied the boy.

His speech bewrayed him. His name bewrayed him. His nose, his ruddy brown skin, his coarse black hair, his beady black eyes, his glass breast-pin, all bewrayed him.

" A Jew," thought Brightly, " and a shrewd one. A fellow with such a nose as that must open his way."

It was a droll nose. Side view or front view, his face seemed all nose. It was a nose well buttressed. His cheeks began at the ridge of it, and filled up the hollows on each side so that a straight-edge would have touched everywhere. This feature had absorbed the whole countenance. It was not large ; not a beak nor a snub, — in fact, not a classifiable nose ; its nostrils did not expand so as to promise a stereoscopic vision of its owner's brains. Indeed, taken *per se*, it was not unlike some other noses in Jewry or even in Christendom. But it refused to be taken *per se*. There was no isolating it. Every part of his face tended to nose. You could not say where it began, any more than you can say where Mount Etna begins on the landward side.

"Have n't I seen you before ? " said Brightly, trying to analyze the boy's chief feature as the last sentence has done.

"Yes," replied Moses. "I sold you thad dubbrella."

" And you propose to try a new business ? "

" Yes, sir. Gades is all out of fashion."

" What are ' gades ' ? "

" I did n't say gades ; I said gades, — *gades*."

"O, canes ! they are out of fashion, eh ? But how about umbrellas ? "

"The soft ads has put dowd the ubbrellas. Besides bed is gidding bore badly dow and does n't bind weddings."

" ' Men are more manly,' — that is good news.

14 *   U

But if they are, I should think they would mind their weddings all the more."

" I did n't mean weddings with wives ; I meant weddings with wader. But adyhow, tibes is dull, and bein' you wanted a boy, I thought I would like to go into business with you."

The boy's perfect simplicity, perfect self-possession, and an air of entire honesty and courage, greatly amused and pleased Brightly. He saw he had found a character.

" So you think you would like to go into business with me," he said.

" If agreeable."

" I cannot pay a boy much salary, you know."

" Id is n't the zalary ; id 's the coddection."

" You flatter me," said Brightly, his sense of humor more and more tickled with the other's seriousness.

" I speag the drooth. There 's dot mady med in the sdreet I 'd drust. I 've sold 'em all gades ad dubbrellas, ad I know 'em all."

" But you look pretty prosperous now, Moses. Why change ? "

" I have to dress well od aggout of the hodels."

He was attired to suit the hotel taste, in Chatham Street's most attractive styles. " Very neat," " Very chaste," and " Le bon ton," or some similar label, inscribed in gold on a handsome white card, had not long since decked each article of his raiment.

" But this bredspid," continued he, touching it,

" is n't diabod, — dode think id ; it 's glass, ad the chaids is pitchback."

Bevel Doak had been feeling his own hopes of employment dwindle while the pedler was stating his case. Poor Bevel had been greatly appalled by the fine jewel that glittered on the other's breast. What person of either sex could resist the gleam of that mountain of light, surrounded by knobs of light and secured in the flamboyant scarf of Mr. Bozes by a chain to the right, a chain to the left, and a chain aloft? Bevel brightened greatly as the breastpin under its wearer's avowal began to grow dim, — the diamonds dowsing their glim, and the mainstay, forestay, and bobstay transmuting themselves from gold to pinchbeck.

Brightly now thought it time to give the other the floor; so he said, " Well, Doak, Mr. Moses has told us the object of this call. How is it with you? Have you a fancy, too, for changing your business? "

" I want to make a little for mother and the children."

" You have no father? "

" No, sir. He was the carpenter that the other carpenter fell on from the top of the house in Trinity Place last summer."

" I saw 'em," Moses interjected. " Both was sbashed."

" I remember," said Brightly. " And how many children are there, Bevel? "

"There's me, sir, Bevel, — father gave us names out of the carpenter's trade, — and Plane and Dove ; — Dovetail was his name ; but we took off the tail. And then there's the two girls. Five, sir, besides mother."

"Are the girls named out of the carpenter's trade, too ? "

"No, sir. Mary and Jelling is their names."

"And you want to make a little money to help them ? "

"If mother was n't sick and the children was n't hungry, I should stick to my trade," replied Bevel, with an independent air. "I can handle tools already pretty well, for a boy. But times is dull, and 'prentices can't make money ; so last night, Mrs. Sassiger —"

"I 'be aggquainded with her," says Mr. Moses. "She zells the faddest durkeys in the Washington Market."

"That's her," rejoins Doak. "Well, Mrs. Sassiger showed mother the advertisement of 'Boy Wanted'; and says Mrs. Sassiger, 'Mrs. Doak, my eyes was drawed to that Wanted.' 'How?' says mother. 'By the name, Brightly,' says Mrs. Sassiger. 'A wide-awake kind of a name,' says mother. 'What you state is correct,' says Mrs. Sassiger ; 'but it 's suthin' else that drawed my eyes to that name. Do you remember the day Mr. Doak was fell on ? ' Mother, bein' weakly, could n't speak for crying, so says I, 'Yes, Mrs. Sassiger, she does remember it, and will remember it so long as she's under the canopy.' 'Well,' says Mrs. Sassiger, 'the day Mr. Doak was feil on, I got uneasy in my mind about the ways of Providence in puttin' so many burdings on one family. I felt as if things was n't equal, the way they ought to be. I don't say it was right, mind you,' says she, 'but that feelin' had got into my head. So, to see that the Doaks was n't the only people in affliction in the world, I took the paper and read about the great fire and loss of life, and about twelve persons killed or mutilated by the explosion of the steamboat Torpedo, and about the awful calamities and sudden deaths. By and by I come,' says she, 'to a teching tale how two children of Mr. John Brightly, up the North River, was drowned together, — the boy tryin' to save the girl. I cried a great deal over that,' says Mrs. Sassiger, 'and somehow it made me feel softer, and not so much of a rebel again' the Lord. Now, Mrs Doak,' says she, 'my eyes has been drawed to this call, "A boy wanted by John Brightly," and I motion that Bevel, not havin' any payin' work to do, and writin' a good hand, and a hard winter comin', — I motion,' says Mrs. Sassiger, 'that Bevel be the first boy at that John Brightly's door to-morrow morning.' That motion was kerried quite unanimous, and here I was, sir, at sunrise, and about three minutes before Moses, — Mr. Moses. That's a long story, sir," Bevel perorated, a little abashed at himself; "but I got going, and could n't stop."

Brightly looked very kindly at the earnest little

chap; then, turning to the other, who was listen-
ing with a critical ear, he asked: " Well, Moses,
what do you think of Doak's application ?"

" I reside," replied Moses.

" You resign ! "

" I reside," repeated the umbrella-merchant, with
composure. " The sbashed father is dothing. Like
as dot by father was sbashed. The sick bother is
dothing. By bother is dead — if I ever had ady.
The boys can take gare of theirselves. I 've toog
care of byself. If there was only one girl, I bight
insist. But there 's two. How old is Bary, Bister
Doak ! "

" Thirteen and a half."

" Thirdeen ad a alf. Just the age for the or-
ridge and apple business. I could set her up byself, if gapital is wanted. Id 's daggerous business for the borals ; but the borals of good girls
takes gare of theirselves. I could n't reside od
Bary's aggout. But there 's Jelling. How old is
she ? "

" Eight," replied Bevel.

" Eight is just the age for the batch business ;
ad id reguires very liddle gapidal, though the
profids is small. Batches without sulphur is dow
id deband. But the batch business is low and
ibboral. I dever dew a girl in the batch business
who got into good society, ad into the brown stode
Wards. Jelling had better be kepd ad hobe. I
reside id her favor.".

" What do you propose to do ? " asked Brightly,

keeping his gravity as well as he could. "Have you definitely abandoned the cane and umbrella business?"

"I have offered all my stock to my glerk. I shall spegulate around generally. I can always bake boney. I could go into Chaddam Sdreet, into the ready-made line. I'b thought to have a had-some taste in gents' clothing."

Mr. Moses glanced at his own habiliments. They were, as was before suggested, somewhat more showy than our grave and colorless civilization approves. His race still retains much of the Oriental love for what we name barbaric splendors.

"Or," continued he, "I could do a good thing id watches and chewelry. Young bed of good badders are always wanted to attract young ladies."

"How old are you?" asked Brightly, all the while amazed and amused at the calm, precocious youth.

"By barber thinks I bust be about sixteed by the dowd od my chid. I'b probised a beard by dext winter."

"Now, Doak," said Brightly, "what do you think of Jacob's resignation in your favor for Jelling's sake, subject to my approval, — for I must be allowed a voice in the matter?"

"It's very generous, sir."

"It is gederous!" said Moses, loftily. "I abaddon, dot the chadce of baking by fortune, — thad is a drifle. I cad bake fortunes without drubble. Bud

social bosition is whad I abe at, ad Bister Brightly's office-boy has a social bosition whidg all the
ready-made id Chaddam Sdreet ad all the chewelry
of the origidal Zhacobs caddot cobbad.''

All these speeches of the young Jew were delivered with entire self-possession, seriousness, and
good-faith.

THE HEART OF THE ANDES.'

" Eye to eye we look
On knowledge, under whose command
Is Earth and Earth's, and in whose hand
Is Nature like an open book."

"THE HEART OF THE ANDES."

We of the northern hemisphere have a geographical belief in the Andes as an unsteady family of mountains in South America, — a continent where earthquakes shake the peaks and revolutions the people, where giant condors soar and swoop, where volcanoes hurl up orbed masses of fiery smoke by day· and flare luridly by night, where silver may hang in tubers-at the roots of any bush, and where statesmen protocol, and soldiers keep up a runaway fight, for the honor and profit of administering guano. Long ago, in the dim cycles, Incas watched the snowy Andes for the daily coming of their God, the Sun. Then the barbaric music of those morning oblations died away, and, except for Potosi, the Andes might have been quite forgotten. First again we hear of them as a scientific convenience. That mysterious entity, the Equator, hung, like a more tenacious Atlantic cable, from peak to peak. French savans climbed and measured it, and found it droll to stand at noon on their own shadows no bigger than dinner-plates. The world began to respect these mountains as pedestals for science ; but later, as the Himalayas went up, the Andes went down.   Chimborazo dwindled sadly in public esteem when it was proved that Kunchinjinga and Gaourichanka could rest their chins upon its crown without tiptoeing.   By and by came Humboldt and lifted the Andes again.   He proclaimed anew their marvellous wealth of vegetation, and how they carry on their shoulders the forests and gardens of all climes.   He told, also, of their grandeur, and invited mankind to recognize it.   But their transcendent glory, as the triumph of Nature working splendid harmony out of brilliant contrast, remained only a doubt and a dream, until Mr. Church became its interpreter to the Northern world.

A great work of art is a delight and a lesson. A great artist owes a mighty debt to mankind for their labor and thought, since thought and toil began.   He must give token that he is no thankless heritor of the sum of human knowledge, no selfish or indolent possessor of man's purest ideals of beauty.   The world is very tender, but very. exacting with genius.   True genius accepts its duty, and will not rest short of the highest truth of its age.   A master artist works his way to the core of Nature, because he demands not husks nor pith, but kernel.   The inmost spirit of beauty is not to be discerned by dodging about and waiting until the doors of her enchanted castle shall stand ajar. The true knight must wind the horn of challenge, chop down the ogre, garrote the griffon, hoist the portcullis with a petard, and pierce to the shrine, deaf to the blandishments of the sirens. Then when he has won his bride, the queen, he must lead her beauty forth for the world's wonderment, to dazzle and inspire.

Recipients of the boons of Art have their duty co-ordinate with the artist's. Art gives a bounty or a pittance, as we have the will or the capacity to receive, — copper to the blind, silver to the fond, red gold to the passionate, dense light of diamond to the faithful lover. We gain from a noble picture according to our serenity, our pureness, our docility, our elevation of mind. Dolts, fools, and triflers do not get much from Art, unless Art may perchance seize the moment to illuminate them through and through, and pierce their pachyderms with thrills of indignant self-contempt and awakening love. For divine Art has power to confound conceit into humility, and shame the unwashed into purifying their hearts. Clown Cymon saw Iphigenia, and presently the clown was a gentleman. Even if we have a neat love for the beautiful, and call ourselves by the pretty, modest title of amateurs, we have a large choice of degrees of benefit. We may see the first picture of our cycle, and receive a butterfly pleasure, a sniff of half-sensual emotion ; or we may transmute our butterfly into a bird of paradise, may educate our slight pleasure into a permanent joy, and sweetly discipline our passion of the finer senses into a love and a wor-

ship.   We can be vulgar admirers of novelty with
no pains, or refined lovers of the beautiful with
moderate pains.   Let no one be diffident.   Eyes
are twice as numerous as men ; and if we look we
must see, unless we are timid and blink.   We must
outgrow childish fancies, — we must banish to the
garret our pre-Praxitelite clay-josses, and dismiss
our pre-Giottesque ligneous daubs to the flames.
We may safely let ourselves grow, and never fear
overgrowth.   Why should not men become too
large for " creeds outworn " !

    " The Heart of the Andes " demands far more
than a vague confidence that we can safely admire
without committing ourselves.   It is not enough
to look awhile and like a little, and evade discrimination with easy commonplaces.   Here is a strange
picture evidently believing itself to be good ; if
not so, it must be elaborately bad, and should be
massacred.   If good and great, let it have the
crown of unfading bays ; but the world cannot
toss its laurels lightly about to bristle on every
ambitious pate.   If we want noble pictures and
progress to nobler, let us recognize them heartily
when they come.   An artist feels the warmth of
intelligent sympathy, as a peach feels sunshine.
The applause of a mob has a noisy charm, like the
flapping of wings in an army of wild-pigeons, but
the tidal sympathy of a throng of brother men
stirs the life-blood.   When a man of genius asks
if he speak the truth, and the world responds with
a magnificent " Ay ! " thenceforth his impulses

move with the momentum of mankind. Appreciation is the cause and the consequence of excellence.

As a contribution toward the understanding of Mr. Church's great work, I propose in the following pages to analyze its subject and manner of treatment. I shall eschew technicality of thought and phrase. The subject is new, the scenes are strange, the facts are amazing. People in the United States are familiar with solemn pine woods and jocund plains and valleys, and have studied the bridal-cottage picturesque everywhere ; but Cordilleras, and the calm of uppermost peaks of snow, and the wealth of tropic forests, they know not. Some commentary, then, on this novel work, seems not impertinent. I am obliged to execute my task in the few last days while the picture ripens rapidly under the final brilliant touches of its creator ; and the necessity of haste must be my excuse for any roughness of style or opacity of condensation.

Before proceeding to the direct analysis, let us notice the strength of our position as American thinkers on Art. Generally with the boons of the past we have to accept the burdens of the past. But only a withered incubus, moribund with an atrophy, squats upon our healthy growth in Art. We may have much to learn, but we have little to unlearn. Young artists, errant with Nature, are not caught and cuffed by the despotism of effete schools, nor sneered down into inanity by conservative dilettantism. Superstition for the past is feeble here, to-day. We might tend to irreverence, but irreverence is soon scourged out of every sincere life. We have a nearly clear field for Art, and no rubbish to be burned. Europe has been wretchedly impeded and futilized in Art by worshipping men rather than God, finite works rather than infinite Nature, and is now at pains to raze and reconstruct its theories. Our business is simpler, and this picture is a token of inevitable success, — a proof and a promise, a lesson and a standard. The American landscape-artist marches at Nature with immense civilization to back him. The trophies of old triumph are not disdained, but they are behind him. He is not compelled to serve apprenticeship in the world's garrets of trash for inspiration, nor to kotou to any fetish, whether set up on the Acropolis, or the Capitoline, in the Court of the Louvre, or under the pepper-boxes in Trafalgar Square.

No lover of Art should be bullied out of his faith in his own instincts and independent culture by impertinencies about old masters and antique schools. Remember that Nature is the mistress of all masters, and founder of all schools. Nature makes Art possible straightway, everywhere, always.

Habits of mind are in every man's power which will make him an infallible judge of artistic excellence at once. Does some one ask how to form those habits for comprehending landscape Art? If we are pure lovers of the world of God; if we have recognized the palpitating infinite of blue sky, and loved to name it Heaven; if we have been thrilled with the solemnity of violet dawn, and are rich with remembered pageantries of sunrise, and have known the calm and the promise of twilight glories over twilight glooms, and have chosen clouds to be the companions of our brightest earthly fancies; if we have studied the modesty, the stateliness, and the delicate fiery quietness of the world of flowers, and have been showered with sunbeams and shadows in the tremulous woods; if we have watched where surges come, with a gleam on their crest, to be lavish of light and music on glittering crags; if, with the simple manly singer of old Greece, we deem "water best,"— best for its majesty in Ocean, best in the brave dashes and massy plunge of a waterfall, best in every shady dingle where it drifts dimples full of sweet sunlight, and best in twinkling dew-drops on a lily tossed into showers of sparkles by a humming-bird; if we have felt the large grandeur of plains sweeping up to sudden lifts of mountain, and if mountains have taught us their power and energy, and the topmost snow-peaks their transcendent holy calm; if we have loved and studied Nature thus, and kept our hearts undebased by sense and unbewildered by mammon, — then it is to us that noblest Art appeals, and we are its scholars and its tribunal. Then we have no mundane errors to recant, and will not keep up a shabby scuffle with our convictions, and chuckle punily over some pinch-

15   v

beck treasure-trove of our conceit, some minor
fault in a noble work ; but, finding that a bold lover
has gone nearer to Nature than we, will choose
him for our guide, and follow straight in his track
to the penetralia of beauty.

There are two questions to be asked regarding
" The Heart of the Andes." 1. Is it a subject fit
to be painted ? 2. Is it well done ? Genius should
not choose for its theme, The Model Frog-Pond,
and revel there in the clammy ooze. And if Genius
paints the Portals of Paradise, they must not be
rusty, repulsive, and baleful as the Infernal doors.
This picture is a new-comer of imposing port
When a supernatural guest enters, the first question is, — " Ho, the Great Unknown ! Art thou
Archangel, or Ogre, or overgrown Scarecrow ? "
Which of these personages have we here ?

" Why paint the Andes ? " says anybody. " Are
not Abana and Pharpar, rivers of Damascus, better
than all the waters of Israel ? Why go among the
condors and centipedes for beauty ? Cannot Mr.
Church stay at home and paint Niagaras ? Or the
White Mountains, — they are a mile high ? "

Why paint the tropics ? Every passionate soul
longs to be with Nature in her fervor underneath
the palms. Must we know the torrid zone only
through travelled bananas, plucked too soon and
pithy ? or by bottled anacondas ? or by the tarry-
flavored slang of forecastle-bred paroquets ? Rosy
summer dwells fair and winning beyond our Northern wastes, where winter has been and will be, and

we sigh for days of basking in perpetual sunshine. Warmth is the cheer, and sunshine the charm of Nature. Without warmth, we become Esquimaux nibbling at a tallow dip. Without sunshine, color fades away into Arctic pallors. All the blush and bloom and winy ripeness of earthly beauty are the gifts of sunshine. Upon the tropics those gifts are poured out most lavishly.

For some years past, Mr. Church has been helping us to a complete knowledge of the exciting and yet indolent beauty of the tropics. He has learned the passion of those Southern climes, while he has not unlearned the energy of his own. He has painted the dreamy haste of the Magdalena, the cataract of Tequendama, temperate uplands where spring abides forever, and scene after scene of sunny noon and tender evening, with river and plain watched by distant snow-peaks. He has given us already other noble smaller pictures of the Andes, prototypes of the present work.

Men of science have sighed over their bewilderment in tropic zones, where every novelty of vegetation is a phenomenon. Botanists sit there among the ruins of their burst herbariums, and bewail the lack of polysyllabic misnomers for beautiful strangers in the world of flowers. But Art should sing pæans, when it discovers the poetry of form and color entangled among those labyrinths, and hasten to be its interpreter to the world. Mr. Church has attempted to fulfil this duty already, and has painted rich forests by rivers near the sea, where

files of graceful cocoa-palms stand above the leggy
mangroves, — luxuriant copses where the crimson
orchis glows among inland palms, — pulpy-leaved
trees all abloom with purple flowers, — delicate
mimosas, — ceibas like mounds of verdure, — bowers of morning-glories, so dense that humming-
birds cannot enter, and glades where lianas hang
their cables and cords, bearing festoons of large
leaves and blossoms with tropic blood shining
through their veins. He has happily avoided any
feeling of the rank and poisonous. No one calls
for quinine after seeing his pictures, or has nightmares filled with caymans and vampires.

So much for the tropical lowlands. " The Heart
of the Andes " takes us to the tropical highlands.
It claims to convey the sentiment of the grandest
scenery on the globe. Through a mighty rift of
the South American continent parallel with the
Pacific, the Andes have boiled up and crystallized.
Under the equator, this Titanic upheaval was
mightiest. According to some cosmical law, power worked most vigorously where beauty could
afterward decorate most lovingly. Here narrow
upright belts of climate are substituted for the
breadths of zone after zone from torrid to frozen
regions. All the garden wealth of the tropics, all
the domestic charm of Northern plain and field and
grove, dashed with a richer splendor than their
own, are here combined and grouped at the base
and along the flanks of bulky ranges topped with
snow and fire. Polar scenes are here colonized

under the hot equator. Eternal snows climb out of eternal summer. The eye may catch a beam from the scarlet orchis, child of fiery climes, and glance before that rosy light is lost to the solemn white dome of Chimborazo. We can look at the North Pole through the crest of a palm, and cool the fire in our brain by the vision of a frostier than the "frosty Caucasus." Symbols of passion and of peace face each other. We can see at once what the world is worth. What Nature has deemed man fit to receive, is here bestowed in one largess. All earth's riches are compacted into one many-sided crystal.

In "The Heart of the Andes," Mr. Church has condensed the condensation of Nature. It is not an actual scene, but the subtle essence of many scenes combined into a typical picture. A man of genius, painter, poet, organizer in any domain of thought, works with larger joy and impulse when he obeys his creative imagination. Life is too short for descriptive painting ; we want dramatic painting. We want to know from a master what are the essentials, the compact, capital, memorable facts which he has had eyes to see and heart to understand in Nature. We should have asked of Mr. Church, after the elaborate studies of his two visits among the Andes, to give us what he has given here, — the vital spirit of these new glorious regions, so that their beauty could become a part of our minds, and all our future conceptions be larger and richer for this new possession.

The first question, then, as to the subject of this picture, is answered. The theme is worthy to be treated. Let us proceed, secondly, to the special analysis.

The picture may be roughly divided into different regions, as follows : —

The Sky.
The Snow Dome.
The Llano, or central plain.
The Cordillera.
The Clouds, their shadows and the atmosphere.
The Hamlet.
The Montaña, or central forest.
The Cataract and its Basin.
The Glade on the right foreground.
The Road and left foreground.

Each of these regions I will take up in order.

The Scene is an elevated valley in the Andes, six thousand feet above the sea ; the Time, an hour or two before sunset.

The artist might have chosen an enthusiastic moment of dawn, when peaks of snow over purple shoulders of porphyry confront the coming day. Or he might have exhibited a sunset pageant with marshalling of fiery clouds. Handled with his ability of color, such would have been electrifying effects of power in passionate action. But this picture is to teach the majesty of Power in Repose. The day's labor is over. High noon is long past, but " gray-hooded even " not yet come. There is rich accumulation of sunshine, and withal an un-

dertone of pensive shadow answering to that consciousness of past and possible sorrow which so
deepens every present joy. In a previous great
picture, "The Andes of Ecuador," painted after
Mr. Church's first visit, he has depicted the glory
of sunset flooding a broad wild valley. There the
sun is master, and its atmosphere almost dazzles
us away from simple study of the mountain forms.
In "The Heart of the Andes" the great snow-peak
is master, and its solemn, peaceful light the illumi-
nator of the scene. Any land can see the sun occa-
sionally, but any land cannot see dome mountains
of snow. Therefore let the sun retire from this
picture, and stand, as we do, spectator; and let us
have that moment of day when light is strong and
quiet, and shadows deep but not despotic.

The blue sky is the first region of the picture for
our study. Unless a landscape conveys a feeling
of the infinite, it is not good for immortals. This
sky is no brazen canopy, no lustrous burnished
screen, no opaque turquoise surface. It is pure,
penetrable, lucent in every tremulous atom of its
substance, and as the eye pierces its depths, it feels
the same vital quiver thrilling through a boundless
calm. Without an atmosphere of joy, earthly triumphs and splendid successes are naught. As fully is pure sky a necessary condition of delight in
the glories of Nature. Could that divine presence
of the snow-peak dwell in regions less clear and
radiant than those we are viewing? Blue sky
melting into a warmer glow overhangs, surrounds,

tenderly enfolds, and rests upon the mountain's golden crown and silvery-shadowed heights. No blank wall thrusts us back as we seek an egress from the picture, but blue sky clinging and closing about our way leads us on, sphere after sphere into the infinite.

A few motionless cirri lie like wreaths of foam flung together by meeting ripples on this aerial ocean. Pellucid creatures of air are they, dwelling in mid ether from which they came and into which they will presently be transfigured after moments of brilliant incarnation. They seem emanations from the mountain, a film of its own substance, light snow-drifts whirled up into the blue. Their spiritual flakes lift the peak and intensify the hue of the sky. Their white upon the azure is as delicate as the mingling of erect white blossoms and violet-blue wreaths of flowers in the right-hand foreground, which in fact recalls and is a memorial of them. Of the other clouds I will speak as I come to their proper aerial region in the picture.

Next let our thoughts come down from these supernal regions, and pause "new-lighted on a heaven-kissing hill." A man becomes exalted to a demigod, more nobly divine than any of the Olympians, when he can soar to such a summit as this. An isolated snow-peak is the sublimest of material objects, and worthiest of daring Art, if Art but dare. Here it has dared and done.

This mountain is a type, not a portrait. If the

reader insists.upon a name, he may call it Cayambe, and fancy he sees the ghost of La Condamine stepping off an arc of the Equator on its shoulders, and blowing his icy fingers as he parts the snow to find the line. But Cayambe perhaps does its share in carrying the girdle of the world. It has been useful enough in a scientific way, and need not take the artistic responsibility of resembling this pictured peak. Besides, compared to this, Cayambe is but a stunted hillock, being only some nineteen thousand feet high. The snow line of the equatorial Andes is at sixteen thousand feet, and Cayambe's three thousand feet of snow would be but a narrow belt on this mountain's breadth of golden fields of winter. Chimborazo then! — *clarum et venerabile nomen* — is it Chimborazo? Alas those revolutionary South American republics! — they have allowed El Chimborazo to be dethroned. Once he was chieftain of the long line from Tierra del Fuego to Arctic ice. Then fickle men revolted and set up two temporary bullies, a doubtful duumvirate, Sorato and Illimani. Finally, some uneasy radical rummaged out Aconcagua from modest retirement in the Chilian Andes, and pronounced his ermine to be broadest, unless his brother Tupungato should pretend to rival him. This mountain, dominant at the "Heart of the Andes," is not then Cayambe or Chimborazo, or any other peak of the equatorial group. It is each and all of them, and more than any. It is the type of the great trachytic domes of the Andes, which stand in such solemn

15*

repose beside the fiery vigor of volcanic cones like
Cotopaxi, and the terrible ghastly ruin of a gulf of
burning craters like Sangay.

And now, let us dally no more with questions,
but look and wonder before the supreme object of
the picture, — this miracle of vastness, and peace,
and beauty, not merely white snow against blue
sky, but Light against Heaven. No poetry of
words can fitly paint its symmetry, its stateliness,
the power of its rising slowly and strongly, from
chasm and cloud, up with pearly shadows and co-
ruscating lights, up with golden sunshine upon its
crown, up into the empyrean. The poetry is before our eyes. A look can read it. For this is
what great Art alone can do, and triumphs in
doing. It gives a vision of glory, and every one
who beholds it is a poet.

But we can study the architecture of this firm
fabric. Consider on what a base it stands, — what
buttresses it has. No threatening crag is this that
may be sapped. Here toppling ruin will never be-
fall. We are safe in our Paradise at the Heart of
the Andes.

Observe the method of its growth. First, across
and closing the purple glen to the left, rises a
rosy purple mountain, as it were an experiment
of form toward the grander edifice. A few spots
of snow rest among its tyro domes and pinnacles.
It is not, then, a petty structure. The snow tells
us that, if it stood where stands the shadowy
mountain of the middle background, it would rise
far above that cloud-compelling height.

Behind this disrobed model of the grander forms above, rises another experimental mountain, climbing up to the regions where snow gives roundness and softness to anatomical lines of rock. It leans upon the dome, and bears it up with stalwart breadth of shoulder. Separated from its younger brother by profound ravines, it grows up a mighty concave mass, a slow, majestic upward surge, with a sweep, and sway, and climb in every portion of its substance and its surface, and yet so broken by insurgent crests of cliff, paly purple over opalescent shadows, and so varied by slopes of snow, and wreath, and drift, and dimple, and bend, and rounded angle everywhere, that there is no monotony in its solemn curve towards the dome. Faint shadows of clouds dim its lustre. It has not yet attained to the uppermost cloudlessness. A delicate drapery of blue mistiness over its swelling reaches is rendered with masterly refinement.

Two essays have thus been made in mountain building, and two degrees of elevation overcome. Now the vigor of the first purple cliffs, and the broad sweep of the snowy shoulder, are combined in the Dome. Suddenly, across its chasm of isolation, the Dome mounts upward, and marks its firm outlines against the sky. Its convex lines of ascent are bold as the lines of the first model, while its calm, rounded summit repeats the deliberate curves of the snow-clad terrace beneath. There is no insubordination among the parts, nothing careless or temporary in the work. Skill and plan have

built up a mass, harmonious, steadfast, and ada-
mantine.   This is a firm head upon firm shoulders,
whatever else may crumble in a century, and fall to
ruin in an æon. Cities of men may sink through
the clefts of an earthquake, but this mountain is
set up to be a symbol of power for the world's life.

Observe further the effect of orderly vastness
given by the nearly parallel lines of the ridges upholding the Dome.   The uppermost of these is a
complete system of mutually sustaining buttresses.
Up from crag to crag of this ridge, the eye climbs
easily ; dashing up the shady purple precipices,
resting in each gray shadow, speeding across the
snowy levels, leaping crevice, and pausing at each
fair dimple until it has measured its way up to the
specular summit.   If colossal peaks rose, naked
rock, against the sky, their gloom would be over-
powering.   And if fiends had the making of worlds,
mountains would be dreadful bulks of black porphyry, the flame-born rock, — monuments and por-
tents of malignity.   Cyclops and gnomes, to say
nothing of more demoniac craftsmen, would never
have capped their domes and pyramids with lightsome snow.   But mountains, the most signal of
earthly facts, are transfigured from gloom to glory
by the gentlest creature of all that float and fall, —
the snow-flake.   It is not enough that air should
lie in clouds, and float in mists, and linger in violet
haze in every dell of the lower mountains, but there
must be a grander beauty than bare mountains, rich
with play of strong color, and softened with shad-

ow, can express. High above the strength of his
earth God has set the beauty of his earth, — glory
of snow above the might of adamant.

When the observer estimates that the Dome is at
least sixty miles from his point of view, he will be
able to measure the power of its mass and the proportions of its details. Each sunny dimple thus
expands to an abyss. Seeming ripples on the
snow-fields become enormous mounds heaped up
by the whirlwinds that riot forever among those
dry, unfathomable drifts, the accumulation of ages.
Below the first sheer slope on the front of the summit is a chasm between the precipice and a bare
elbow of rock, — a lovely spot of pearly shadow.
Measure that chasm with the eye ; — into it you
might toss Ossa and see it flounder through the
snow and drown ; and Pelion upon Ossa would only
protrude a patch of its dishevelled poll. Things
are done in the large among the Andes.

Clouds close the view on each slope of the
Dome ; on the left touched with orange, where
they reflect the glow of the peak ; on the right
gray and shadowy. They half disclose and half
conceal a mysterious infinite on either side. An
isolated silvery aiguille juts out of this obscure, a
contrast in its color and keen form to the Dome,
and hinting at successions of unseen peaks beyond.
A slender stratus cloud comes in with subtle effect
across the vapors below the summit, — a quiet level
for the eye, where all the lines are curved and tending upward.

The Dome is the Alpha and the Omega of the picture, — first to take the eye as the principal light, and the last object of recurring thought when study proves that all the wealth below lies tribute at its feet, and every minor light only recalls its mild benignancy.

It is hard to put the essence of a volume into a few paragraphs. This mountain is a marvel, and merits silent study of hours ; I have endeavored to point out briefly its great qualities of construction. The reader must remember that the beauty of snowy mountains is a recent discovery. An age ago, poets had nothing to say of them but a shiver, and painters skulked away and painted " bits." The sublimity of snow-peaks should underlie all our feeling for the lesser charms of Nature. Yet many people of considerable sentiment still shiver and skulk before these great white thrones of the Almighty. But yet not every one who would, can be a pilgrim to Mecca. Not every one can kneel at the holiest shrines of Nature. Let us be thankful to Mr. Church that he has brought the snowy Andes to us, and dared to demand our worship for their sublimity.

When our mortal nature is dazzled and wearied with too long gazing on the golden mount, where silence dwells and glory lingers longer than the day, we may descend to the Arcadian levels of the Llano at the " Heart of the Andes." See how the plain slides, smooth as water, carrying sunshine up to the stooping forests at the left-hand base of the central mountain. On the reaches of this savanna is space and flowery pasturage for flocks and herds. Llamas may feed there undisturbed by anacondas. No serpent hugs; no scorpion nips; never a mosquito hums over this fair realm. Perpetual spring reigns. If the Arcadians wish perpetual summer, with its pests and its pleasures, they have only to mount a mule and descend; the torrid zone is but a mile below. Life here may be a sweet idyl; and the great mountains at hand will never let its idyllic quiet degenerate into pastoral insipidity.

A sweep of this fair meadow-land, eddying along under steep banks behind the village, bears us unawares up steep acclivities, and we become mountaineers again, climbing the Cordillera.

The Dome was an emblem of permanent and infinite peace: — this central mass of struggling mountain, with a war of light and shade over all its tumultuous surface, represents vigor and toil and perplexity. The great shadow of the picture is opposed in sentiment, as well as in color and form, to the great light.

Begin with the craggy hillock at the centre of the background, behind the village tower. It seems a mere episode of the life of the great mountain above it; but observe how thoroughly, as in all Mr. Church's work, its story is told. Detail is suggested, and yet suppressed. The

hill is in shadow, but not consigned to utter blackness, and maltreated with coarse neglect. You
may perceive or divine every line of sinking surface, and every time-worn channel converging to
the gulf in its front. You may feel that it bears
up a multitudinous forest on its isolated crest,
where fires that sweep the mountain moors, or
"paramos," have not reached. Level with this
compact pyramid extends to the left a bench of
rocky plateau, where we can gird ourselves for
our sturdy task. Then, as we toil resolutely up,
we find that earth was not at play when this Titanic mass was reared. Here are mountain upon
mountain ; crag climbing on the shoulders of
crag ; plain and slope, and "huddling slant" and
precipice ; furrow, chasm, plunging hollow, que-
brada and abyss ; solitary knolls, groups of allied
hills, long sierras marked on their sheer flanks
with cleavage and rock-slides ; conical mounds,
walls of stern frontage ; myriad tokens of primeval convulsions ; proofs everywhere of change,
building, razing, upheaval, sinking, and deliberate
crumbling away, and how new ruin restores the
strong lines that old ruin weakened. Yet, with all
this complex action and episode, there is still one
steady movement upward of this bold earth-born
Hyperion higher toward the masterful heights,
with stronger step and larger leap as he learns
the power of sustained impulse, and mounts
nearer and nearer the region of final mysterious
battle in clouds and darkness, on the verge of

final triumph beyond the veil. Peace and light dwell upon the Dome. Here is a contrast of mystery and dim chaos; — yet no grim obscure; no shock of hurtling storms. The sun penetrates the veil, and the heights glow pallid-rosy. Over the edge, keen as a wave, of the topmost cliff, float showery mists of tender iridescence; then violet heights and rainbow-mists and wreaths of pale cloud fade together out of sight.

Over all this central mountain play of color rivals infinity of form. Evanescent blues, golden browns, pearly violets, tender purples, and purple greens mantle delicately over its giant shoulders. If the Dome was a miracle of light, this mountain is equally a miracle of light and shade. Gray forests clothe a narrow zone at its base. Then come the "paramos," the rocky moors covered with long yellow grass, where fires have frequent course and drive the trees down into gorges far beneath their proper level, — then the rocks, all stained and scarred with time, and enriched with lichens and mosses. Over all these many-colored surfaces, air, pale or roseate, floats and deepens in every hollow. Aerial liquidness, tremulous quivers of light, rest on seamed front and smooth cheek. Sunbeams rain gently down from the cloudy continent above. We know not where it is not sun, nor where the melting shadow fades. And all, whether sunlit slope, or profound retreating abyss, or sharp sierra, is seen through leagues of ether, a pellucid but visible medium. Forms become un-

w

defined, but never vague in this gray luminousness.
The enchantment of beautiful reality in all this
central mountain is heightened by the faint pencils
of light striking across the void.   And observe, as
an instance of the delicate perception of truth that
signalizes every portion of this picture, that these
evanescent beams converge.   Diverging rays are
familiar to every one who has seen sunsets.   Old
Sol in the almanacs is a personage of jolly phiz,
with spokes of light diverging from cheek and
crown.   But converging rays can only fall when
the sun is, as in this case, behind the point of view ;
and this disposition of light is a phenomenon com-
paratively rare.   A regard for such fine truths as
this arms the artist with a panoply, and makes his
work impregnable.

No substitution of trickery for tactics could possibly have drawn up this masterly array of mountain elements.   It is thorough knowledge and
faithful elaboration of detail that makes this central mass real, and not mythic ; a vast, varied
pyramid of rock, and not a serrated pancake of
blue mud set on edge.   Mr. Church proves that he
knows and feels grand forms, and the colors which
pertain to them as inseparably as the hues of a
diamond belong to the facets of a diamond, and
that he is able enough, and diligent enough, to express his knowledge and love.   This harmonious
contrast of sun and shadow, crag and glen, edu-
cates the eye forever to disdain those conventional
blotches of lazy generalization — vain pretenders

to the royal honors of mountains — which cumber so many landscape backgrounds, and demand as much of the student as if he should be required to construct Hamlet from a ghost, the Tuileries from a tile, or Paradise from a pippin.

A canopy of the lofty rain-clouds of this region overhangs the central mountain. We have already observed their shadows; let us now analyze their substance, and note their effect.

Western winds sweeping the Pacific catch dew from the thickets of palm-islands, and foam from breakers on the reefs that shelter blue lagoons, scoop handfuls from the deeps, where sunlight strikes like bended lightning, and tear away the stormy crests of surges. And as the winds hasten on in their hot journey, they play with their treasures of coolness, and find that vapor is a ductile thing, and may be woven into transparent fabrics of clouds, light, fragile, strong, elastic, and with all the qualities of dew and foam, sunny water, and the lurid might of angry sea. Such cloud-wreaths the warm ocean winds hold ready to fling upon every frigid slope of the Andes. No one of these aerial elements is wanting to the clouds over Mr. Church's majestic Cordillera. They have the shimmer of dew, and the bulk of the surge; they are light as a garland, yet solid to resist a gale. Flexible sunbeams can penetrate this texture, and twine themselves with every fibre, and yet bluff winds cannot shatter them. Brightness and darkness flow and fuse together among their rims and contours.

These are not woolly clouds, nor fleecy breadths
of woolliness ; not feathery clouds, nor brooding
feathered pinions.   They are not curls of animal
hair, nor plumes of fowls.   Only the morbid will
be reminded by them of flocks of sheep, or flights
of rocs.   They are clouds made of vapor, not of
flocculent pulp, or rags, or shoddy.   They are no
more like either syllabub or dumplings than Mr.
Church's air is like lymph, his water like yeast, or
his peaks like frosted plum-cake.   Epithets from
the kitchen or the factory are equally out of place.
These are veritable clouds of coherent, translucent
vapor ; — magical creations, because there is no
magic in them, but only profound, patient, able
handiwork guided by love.   They are beautiful
because they are actual clouds of heaven, and
show that the artist knew the infinite life of clouds
and the dramatic energy of their coming and
going, eventful with shadow and light, and sometimes with tears and dreary tragedies of storm, —
that he has seen what wreathed smiles they have
for sunshine, what mild rebuffs for boisterous winds,
— seen their coquetries of flying and waiting,
their coy advances, their wiles of hiding and peering forth with bright looks from under hoods of
gray.   And having thus studied the character and
laws, the use and the loveliness of these spirits
of the air, the artist, knowing that he cannot
better the models of Nature, has adopted them.
Painting of natural objects must be imitation or
mockery.   A great artist studies to master type

forms. When he has grasped the type, then he can construct individuals as he will, but any attempt to create new types results in inanity or caricature, in the deformity of feebleness, or the deformity of the grotesque.

Nothing in the picture is more masterly than these clouds upon the Cordillera. See how they climb and cling to the slopes, how they bridge the hollows, and fling themselves against the opponent cliffs, how they trail and linger, as if to choose their bivouac for the night-watches. They do not sag ponderous and lethargic, nor droop in sorry dejection, weeping out their hearts because their backs are broken. Nor do they fritter away their dignity in a fantastic dance. They are elate and springy with eagerness through all their brilliant phalanxes, and detach themselves with perfect individuality from the far-away sky and the dark mountain. They are naturally and rightly in their place, and give the needful horizontal, for change of line, after so much height, as well as the needful concealment and revelation of form.

But the Llano at the Heart of the Andes, the village, the Montaña, the cataract, and the inexhaustible charms of the rich foreground, invite us. Let us take at a leap the gulf on the mountain-side where a thread of cascade is faintly visible. We advance over the gradual slope behind the dark forest, and notice the forceful quiet of that breadth of gray woodland in shadow, in the middle distance, with its bold fronts of rock.

Let us here pause for a moment. What have we done? Where are we? Let us review our mountain work before we go among the groves and flowers of Arcady. We passed first up the misty glen to the left under the purple precipices, — a stern gorge and a terrible, though now it look so fair. We beheld the Dome, and approached it reverently. We climbed its three terraces. We studied its impressive mass. We saw where its foundations were laid deep and broad, — the triumphant peace of its golden curves against the sky, — and found exquisite light in its shadows. We noticed the magnificent rolling line of the Cordillera where it cuts against the sky and meets the snows, — observed its varied color and form, and marked what a cloudy world it upholds on Atlantean shoulders. We have, in short, studied the Andes, Cordillera and Nevado, the region of animated clouds above the one, and the realm of sinless sky above the other. This is what we have done; — what we have gained will appear when we come to review the whole picture.

The woods behind the village are next to be studied. Half-way down, a bench of warm rock breaks the slope abruptly. The same formation of precipice appears that reappears in the walls of the cataract. Below this the woods radiate over the descent toward the hamlet, and forward toward the water. In all this multitudinous forest of the Montaña, there is nothing of the gloom of the im-

penetrable vegetation of the fiery lowlands of the
tropics.   In this elevated valley vegetation assimi-
lates to that of the temperate zones; there is
never any nipping check of winter ; the tree can
develop its life without harsh discipline of frost,
and grow without need of frantic impulse after long
lethargy.   Hence we are at home, and yet strangers in these woods.   Our Northern comrades seem
to surround us, but they have suffered promotion.
They wear richer uniforms and more plentiful decorations.   Kindlier influences have been about.
Downright perpetual passionate sunshine has educated their finer spirit, and made gross wrappings
of protective bark, and all their organization for
enduring cold, needless.   It is a community which
has been well treated and not maltreated, wisely
nurtured and not harshly repressed.

The student will recognize the constituents of
these forests in the magnificent types of the foreground.   I desire at present merely to call his attention to the healthy cheerfulness of their color,
and the vigorous, but not rank, character of their
growth.   Down in the hot valleys, foliage sucks
dank from the sluggish air, and, growing fat and
pulpy, is not penetrated by sunlight, but only reflects a hard sheen.   Seen from above, lush greens
preponderate.   Few of the largest trees have
leaves of delicate texture like our maples.   But
the groves across the midlands of the Heart of the
Andes are gayer, as becomes their climate.   And
giving to them a higher degree of what they have,

Mr. Church has dashed his magical sunshine in among them everywhere, in every glade and cleft, making the whole scope one far glimmer of tremulous scintillating leafage and burning blossoms. It is, as we feel, a countless grove, with many masses of thicket and careless tangles of drapery, such as we see on the left-hand foreground, and vistas of ambrosial gloom, such as open down the ferny dell on the right.

By the skirts of this forest we come to the village. A city of citizens we should feel to be out of place here. Volcanoes may be suitable companions for the turbulent abodes of men, as men now are. A melodramatic little Vesuvius, threatening when it is not outraging, always discontented, and often an insurgent malecontent, grumbling and bellowing, "full of sound and fury," a demoniac and revengeful being, — this is a fit emblem of a modern capital. But the solemn peaks of snow must stand among the giant solitudes. And yet, that we may not be quite deserted of human sympathy, the Artist has placed here a quiet hamlet grouped about its humble sanctuary. This is memorial enough of humanity, — we need not stand here bewildered as if we were its first discoverers. We have no uneasy sense of loneliness and exile. Brother men have lived and loved in this paradise. We do not require a crowd of minor associations such as help to glorify tame scenes of every-day life. Petty histories and romances are wanted to kindle fervors for petty places. Sentimental art demands ruins, and strives to "make old baseness picturesque." But the magnificence of Nature here can be felt without aid from the past. Historic drapery is not needed. Absolute beauty can be loved at first sight. To think our noblest thoughts, we go away from relics to solitude, to God, and to the future.

There is poetic propriety, therefore, in this undisturbing village sanctified by its shrine of faith. Men have not forgotten their conception of God at the Heart of the Andes, — the heart of the heart of the world, where its pulses beat hottest and strongest. And the Artist sets up his own symbol of faith in the church and the foreground cross, and recognizes here that religion whose civilization alone makes such a picture as his possible. A pleasant hamlet is this, with its reed-thatched huts, — here where life is so easy and goes a-Maying all its days.

Divine repose was expressed by the Dome; manly energy by the Cordillera. And now we welcome a graceful feminine element. Water is the fair stranger we are now to greet. We have been all the while aware of her brilliant presence; and have not rarely wandered away from the rough hills to be refreshed by rainbow showers, and stirred with a sense of dancing motion. Now we may give ourselves fully to the river's bright influence. Forth from a sunlit spot it comes, as unexpected as if we had not seen its placid delay

16

above, where its pool attracted and fixed the village. It comes with snow memories in the foam of its rock-shattered flow. It curves with deep, clear fulness into an upper rocky basin. It gushes so firm and urgent against its walls that its reflected edges are seen to be heaped higher than the unchecked slide of its mid-current. One inch more in its angle of descent would send that whole smooth clearness flying into foam. But its strong speed does not spoil its mirror-like quietness. It moves steadily on to its beautiful duty, and then suddenly — "the wild cataract leaps in glory."

The river is transfigured before us. Motion flings itself out into light. Green water snows down in a glimmering belt of white. Every drop dashes away from every other drop. Each one has its own sunbeam. Diamond flashes join into jewelled wreaths. Pearl and opal blend their soft tremors. Sapphire and beryl mingle with the strong glow of amber. And the wreaths intertwine and float together, until the mid-whirl is a gemmy turbulence, a crush of foam and spray, and rays and rainbows.

There is no sharp line to mark where calm sliding water is instantly transmuted into wild falling water. The fall becomes a fall without any harsh edge of precipice. We cannot define where the shadowy gleam above bends fleeter over the first ledges ; nor where the bend first breaks with spray, and spray thickens, and the curve passes into a leap, and the leap into a resistless plunge, and all the bends, curves, leaps, and plunges fling themselves together in joyful abandonment, thrilled through and through with sensitive tremors of graceful daring.

As the cataract comes gushing forward rather than dropped in precipitous downfall, so it is not received on a flattened level of water below. Rocks break its plunge, and give it pause. And then this shape of beauty, disarrayed, but fairer thus, springs, not frantic or sullen, into a gloomy chasm, but sweeps, a mist of sunshine, down behind an iridescent veil, upon the white splendors of its own image. It eddies with lambent lights along the warm cliffs, and then glides down the steps and rapids of a new career — on to join the Amazon.

Serene sunshine fills the right of the gulf. On the left, where spray keeps the mosses of the cliff long and rich, is a flow of softened prismatic color, and the angle is filled .with opalescent reflected lights from the sunny cataract. This is one of the most enchanting effects in the picture.

The gleam of the Cataract recalls the snows of the Dome. The bending plunge of the one repeats the slow curves of the other. Across leagues of full distance, the light of the fall, secluded and subordinate, answers, like an echo, to the great dominant light. And observe also in the division of the cataract by its bold cliff, and in its parted cascade falling in dimness on the right, a reminiscence of the Cordillera, and the dependent misty light at its summit.   Such continuous effects sustain the dramatic unity of the picture, and show that one creative thought reigns everywhere. Observe again how the level of the basin below the cataract corresponds with the emphatic plateau below the mountains, — repose after power.   No discomposure or weariness is anywhere possible. We are nowhere beaten back and debilitated by stern, rude heights we cannot climb.   Slope and plateau and successive grades of ascent take us gently up from the lowest plane of blue water speeding toward ocean, to blue, illimitable space of sky.   Step by step the eye is educated to comprehend the vast scope of the scene, yet no step is abrupt.   There is always some spot where the precipice breaks off into ledges, and where steeps pass into declivities.

Before he comes to the complex beauty of the foreground, let the student make one more excursion over the large undulations and among the shady coverts of the central forest, — the Montaña of the Andes.   Glows of approaching evening lie among the long shadows and fall across the glades.   Not even where the dusky canopy of clouds shuts off sunshine can this become an austere woodland.   Trees of many-colored foliage make play of light even in the unillumined spots ; and sunshine, streaming low and level, betrays a wilderness of leafage and umbrage, stems and vines.

From these bright labyrinths we emerge again into open daylight. Here, above the basin, warm cliffs uphold a tablet where sunlight may blazon its last fond inscriptions. Other hieroglyphs are already there, — the story of the rock's own life told in crevice, ledge, and mossy cleft, and the myriad traces of Time, the destroyer and renewer. As air above, so water below has pencilled its legend. Lapping ripples have marked levels of drought and freshet along its base. And the cliffs, doing their part in this interchange of bland influences, send down their image to hang without heaviness in the shimmering water. The still water reflects, as perfectly as the arrowy, shattered water contained, light. How full of mild splendor is this pool of Nepenthe! Into its amphitheatre the river leaps exulting. A maze of woven sunbeams floats above her bold repetition of feats done in her youth among argent snows. She springs out upon her own image, which falls before her, a column of white lustre lengthening over the undulations, only to break in the swift silvery bends of the lower rapid. And above this wavering image Iris floats within her veil of mist, and her bright hues shine through it. The cataract sheds prismatic tints upon the unsunlit cliffs, and the cliffs that are in sunlight shed radiance upon the air. The void is flooded with a glow of reflected lights. All about, trees stoop over the brink and tassel the precipices with tendrils and pendent branches. Delicious spot, which he who will can

dream full of the music of falling water, as he
sees it brimming with effulgence.   It lies open
before us, a lucent shell lined with imprisoned rainbows, — a chalice of dissolved pearl, — a flushed
corolla, where the cataract rises like a white cone
of vestal leaves just opening, — a pool of newly
troubled water, where weary spirits may find heal-
ing and lightness of heart.

We come now to the right-hand foreground.
Three specific typical trees project over the basin,
— a trio of comrades sustaining each other in their
vanguard station, — unmistakable individuals, evidently not brothers.   I have no names for these
pioneers.   Probably no arborist, complacent with
offensive armor of Latin nomenclature, has penetrated these solitudes at the Heart of the Andes.
But no ungainly polysyllable could identify these
trees more completely than do their distinctive
qualities as here given.   Midmost stands the stalwart masculine tree, oak-like in its muscular rami-
fication, and upholding a compact crown of plentiful leafage.   Light flashes everywhere in among
its leaves, catches them as they turn and gilds
them, slants across them sheenily, pierces athwart
their masses into the dim hollows and fills them
with gleams, stands at openings of cavernous recesses in the dense umbrage and reveals their
mysterious obscurity.   Twigs and sprays bare of
foliage, and showing that the crumbling away
of soil beneath is telling upon the more delicate

members of the tree, strike forth and crinkle as they clutch sunlight. And yet there is no frivolous minuteness of detail in this masterly tree, leader of the trio, and its fellows; although every leaf and spray and twig seem to be there, alive and animate. The Artist has here, as everywhere, produced his effect by the peremptory facts of form and color, without weakening precision by attempts to convey ambiguous semblances. Hence his tree is a round salient mass, but not a cactus-like excrescence, and a maze of leafage without being a blur or a mop. In signal contrast to this sturdy, erect outstander is the tree with depending branches and delicate silvery-green foliage, — a tree of more elegance of figure and a mimosa-like sensitiveness of leaves, but vigorous and not at all shrinking from the forward and critical position which it holds. The third tree, the Lepidus of this triumvirate, keeps somewhat in the shady background, and leans rather toward the thicket, being of less notable guise and garb. His stiff, scanty leafage and channelled bark are entirely characteristic of the region. Each of these trees is not only a type in its form and foliage, but also, though less conspicuously, of the garden of smaller growth which, feeding on air, dwells on its trunk. Clustering luxuriance of boweriness belongs to the sheltered recesses, and does not inundate these foremost types. But each is a hanging garden, an upright parterre raising up to sunshine its peculiar little world of warm-blooded mosses, lichens, and tree-plants, sparkling over its trunk like an alighting of butterflies. The tropical sun loads his giants with his pigmies. Observe the rich contrast of the mound of vivid moss with the red trunk of the outermost tree. Each of these trees wears a splendid epiderm, but neither has had the leprosy, — an unpleasant malady which frequently attacks foregrounds. Mr. Church's trees are too freshly alive, and show that they digest air and water too healthily to suffer with any cutaneous disease. A somewhat formal personage the leader of the pioneer trio may be, but his stiff dignity is invaluable in this sybaritic covert, and to the picture, as giving determined perpendicular lines after so much level and slope. Behind this picturesque group, two companions of theirs come striding out of the dusky woodland, each a standard-bearer of a new, unknown clan, and wearing new insignia of rank.

Let us enter this delightsome pleasaunce whence they come. Sunshine streams in with us a little way, and leaves us for a spot it loves among the choirs of blossoms. So we wander on into ambrosial darkness. And over us the trailers stream with innumerable tendrils ; — our firmament is a gentle tempest of gold and green, — a canopy of showering clouds of verdure, — a rain of wreaths and garlands. A cascade of bowery intricacy shoots down inexhaustible, dashing into flowers at its foot, and pouring a slide of sparkling greenery among the ferns toward the pool. The cope of forest overhead flings itself down to mingle with the floral coppices, and lianas bind the bright shower to the bright spray below. Just where the bosk thickens, a tree fern stands like a plume, waving us inward. Lesser ferns carpet the vista, making a deeper, richer greensward than Northern climates know; but this one is the pride of its race. Its prim gracefulness gains the charm of " sweet neglect " by the droop of its ripened and withered fronds, and by the delicate creepers which climb upon the scales of its past leafage. No plant in the upland tropical woods is more elegant than the tree fern. It surpasses even the palm in refinement of foliage, and its plumes become the substitute for palms in the elevated zones where the latter would chill and wither. Behind this fair, bending Oread, under o'erarching darkness, extends the gloaming mystery of the Montaña.

This vista of forest conducts us inward to a region as doubtful and dim as the height of the Cordillera above, and contrasts with the open road on the left, guiding us up to the Dome. And when we have had enough of dreamy wandering deep in these bowers of Elysium, we may come forth and pluck flowers in the wondrous garden at the margin of the picture, — a maze of leaves and blossoms as intricate as the maze of vine-drapery above, or the maze of shower and rainbow at the mountain-top. The Artist has come with his hands full of tribute to Flora, and flung exuber-

16 *   x

ant beauty into this sunny, sheltered spot, where warm dewy airs, stealing up the river, bring summer higher than its wont.   Liberal as is the beauty here, there is no cramming, — no outlandish forcing of all possible and many impossible objects into an artificial clustering.   Here there is simplicity in complexity, — order in bewilderment.   Nor is this spot a glare of metallic lustres, and all aflame with hot splendors, or incarnadined with crimson hues.   Peaceful colors govern here as everywhere in this home of peace.   The feathery blue cymes of a plant which the Indians name "yatcièl" recall the quiet blues of the sky.   White spires mingle with the blues.   Below, the convolvulus strews its rosy-purple disks over mantling vines. A scarlet passion-flower, the " caruba," sparkles upon a garland of its own.   Reedy grasses start up erect.   And lowest, broad juicy leaves, gilded upon their edges with the all-pervading sunshine, grow full and succulent with moisture from the stream.

A perfect garden, — crowded with infinite delicacy and refinement of leaf and flower, — where there is no spot that is not blossom, or leafage, or dim recess where faded petals may lie, — where all seems so fair with these cloud-like creatures of white, these wreaths of azure bloom, and stars of scarlet, that this gentler beauty of earth almost wins us to forget the grander beauty we have known on the summits far away.   And as we turn away from the glade, with a boon of sweet flowers in our memory, the last foremost objects that linger with us are two brilliant white blossoms, dashed with the same light which flashes in the cataract, and burns sublimely in the far beacon, the giant dome of snow.

The sun, which loses no opportunity to pierce in unexpectedly anywhere among these scenes, beloved of sunshine, achieves a weird effect in the shadows upon the rock beneath the morning-glories, cast by the sprays and branches of a dead bush. And notice how these shadows have light in them, as shadows should, and are not dark like the unillumined hollows beneath the rocks and shrubbery. An admirably defined rock, part warm color, part purple shadow, part hidden by the caruba vines, leans against the bank, and aids in supporting it.

In the middle of the lower foreground a large-leaved tree, bristling with epiphytes, stands out in vigorous perspective. The water below is half seen through its branches, and gains by an effect of partial concealment and a passing away out of the picture behind a leafy screen.

The tawny slope of road in the left foreground leads us back to another tangle of forest. All the drooping, waving, tossing, prodigal luxuriance of the glade on the right is here repeated in half-distance, — another denser maze, wellnigh impenetrable, in which we may discern the tree fern, now familiar, and may feel that our previous studies

have taught us to know " dingle and bushy dell "
and " every bosky bourn of this wild wood from
side to side." A vista, or cleft, across its intricacy, rather suggested than patent, tells us where
the path leads towards the Llano and the Hamlet,
and the same vista opens to connect the nearest
glows and flashes of white light with the radiance
of the Dome. Forth from the forest the Road
dashes bright as another cataract, and yet a warm
surface of trampled earth. An infinite gemminess
of flowers scintillates along its course ; — there
seems no spot where the eye may not catch a
sparkle. The same brilliancy gilds the rocks
which support the road on the right, and over-
hang the abyss. Nothing in the picture is truer
or more marvellously salient in color and form
than the purple crag, with sunlight broken by
cross-shadows, lying upon its hither front. Nothing is more boldly characterized, and more full of
fresh and vigorous feeling, than the sweep of the
road, accurately and precisely defined in all its
structure, and bathed in mellow sunlight and mel-
lower shade.

Just at the top of the ascent stands a cross, —
a token of gratitude for labor past, and rest
achieved. Such crosses are usual among the
passes of the Andes, wherever a height has been
overcome. The natives pause and repose, and say
a thankful Ave, as the two figures in the picture
seem to be doing. Their presence is a cheerful
incident, and their bright pouchos throw in a dash

of gay tropical color. To us also the cross, promi-
nent against its dark background, has sweet sym-
bolical meaning, sanctifying the glories of the spot;
and, as in the old saintly legends flowers sprang
up under the feet of martyrs, so here a spontaneous garland has grown to wreathe this emblem
of sacrifice and love.

Observe next how exquisitely the sloping side
of the road toward the dim precipice on the left
clothes itself with a mossy verdure, and how the
moss thickens and streams down into the chasm,
meeting the slender line of sapphire water that
trickles from a crevice in the steep. Foremost of
all the picture the Artist has set up his trophy in
the broken shaft, — the stem of some ancient monarch of the forest. Upon this he has flung his
last brilliant spoils. The scarlet orchis stands out
like a plume from a tuft of other air-plants, a fall
of draping creepers hangs from above, strange rich
forms of plants cluster about its base, and, fastened
by a fillet of large leaves, each distinct upon its
own shadow, one burning white blossom gleams,
midway the column, like a jewel upon an argent
shield. Upon a branch just by, in bravery of
lustrous green plumage, sits the "royal bird of
the Incas," and below gay butterflies twinkle.
Through some cleft of forest, beyond the verge of
the picture, one trenchant sunbeam strikes, and,
falling upon this propylon shaft, seems to set upon
the whole great work the sun's final signet of
approval.

I have thus treated rapidly, and perhaps baldly, the signal facts of this picture. Its execution everywhere equals its conception. It is indeed many perfect pictures in one, — as a noble symphony bears in its choral swell a thousand hymns and harmonies. The lover of quiet beauty may here find solace, and he who adores supernal beauty has objects for loftiest worship. Yet so admirable is the dramatic construction of the work, that no scene is an episode, but each guides the mind on to the triumphal crowning spectacle, — every thought in the picture is an aspiration toward the grand dominant thought, the Dome of snow.

"The Heart of the Andes" is in itself an education in Art. No truer, worthier effort has ever been made to guide the world to feel, to comprehend, and to love the fairest and the sublimest scenes of Nature. It opens to us, in these ardent ages, a new earth more glorious than any we have known. What Beauty can do to exalt mankind is as yet only the dream of a few, but must some time become the reality of all. Toward this result Mr. Church offers here a masterpiece, the largess of his bountiful genius. Men are better and nobler when they are uplifted by such sublime visions, and the human sympathies stirred by such revelations of the divine cannot die ; — they are immortal echoes, and they

> " roll from soul to soul
> And grow forever and forever."

Cambridge : Stereotyped and Printed by Welch, Bigelow, & Co.

This book should be returned to the Library on or before the last date stamped below.

A fine of five cents a day is incurred by retaining it beyond the specified time.

Please return promptly.

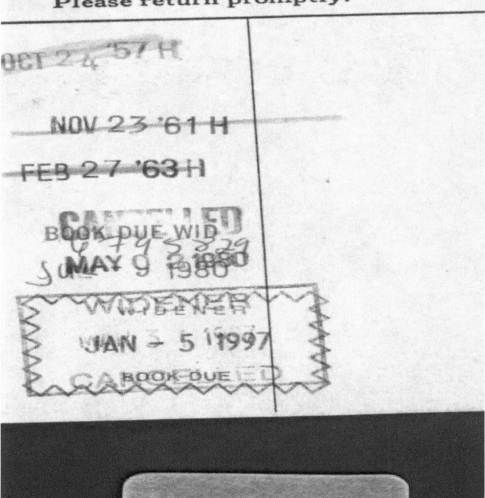

CPSIA information can be obtained
at www.ICGtesting.com
Printed in the USA
BVHW081807220819
556561BV00019B/4275/P